FACT OR FICTION?:
THE UNEXPLAINED

FACT OR FICTION?:
THE UNEXPLAINED

by
Nigel Blundell

SUNBURST BOOKS

This edition first published in 1995 by
Sunburst Books
Deacon House
65 Old Church Street
LONDON SW3 5BS

© Sunburst Books 1995

ISBN 1 85778 175 9

Printed and bound in Hong Kong

Every effort has been made to trace the ownership of all copyright material and to secure permission from
copyright holders. In the event of any question arising as to the use of any material we will be pleased to
make the necessary corrections in future printings.

Picture acknowledgements: Mary Evans Picture Library pp 30, 32; Associated Press p 95.

CONTENTS

Introduction

Man has explored every corner of the earth and plumbed the depths of the oceans. He has tamed the wildernesses and learned to forecast and sometimes tame the elements. Historians have neatly parcelled up our past, analysts have explained the complexities of the present, and scientists have forecast future events.

Homo sapiens has an answer for everything. Or so he would like to think!

Yet, as the sum of man's knowledge increases, a strange counter-balance seems to occur. For every question he answers, another is raised. For every mystery solved, a new one emerges. For every scientific breakthrough, there is a blank page.

Level the jungles and we find 'lost' cities from another age. Send scanners into the depths and we discover beasts from another millenium. Peer into the void of space and we find the invisible, impenetrable, timeless black holes.

This enigmatic universe keeps throwing up fresh mysteries to taunt our academic knowledge and scientific expertise.

Why, for instance, are birds more successful navigators than airline pilots? Why do some human beings have a limitless endurance for pain? How did man, as time's earliest builder, put in place such wonders as Stonehenge and the Great Pyramid that still survive to this very day?

Gathered together in *Fact Or Fiction: The Unexplained* are questions such as these which have tested man's knowledge and tantalised his imagination over the years. They continue to fascinate.

NOAH'S ARK

Did the Great Deluge ever happen? Did Noah's Ark ever exist? Was Noah, as described in the Book of Genesis, instructed by God to build the Ark and to fill it with animals to replenish the earth after the flood waters had subsided? Over the centuries, many people, from religious fanatics to professional archaeologists, claim to have solved the secret.

Accounts of the Flood and the Ark are not confined to the Bible. Research indicates that the deluge may actually have happened, and that at some time during human history the world was swamped with a flood, the like of which has never been seen since. Certainly eastern cultures – not just the Bible – have written records of the great deluge, and while the mystery remains as to whether these accounts are of legendary or real events, there is a body of evidence which substantiates the argument that at some time in human history a great flood did take place.

The first mention of a deluge engulfing the world comes in *The Epic of Gilgamesh*, a Babylonian work transcribed in the 7th century. It corresponds with the better-known Hebrew version recording Noah and his Ark, except that in this account the rains did not last 40 days and 40 nights, but 7. This, coupled with the Ark legend, and an Armenian text chronicling a similar event, has inspired archaeologists to try to find concrete evidence that a flood occurred.

In 1929 Sir Leonard Woolley, an eminent archaeologist, discovered at the ancient Sumerian city of Ur in Iraq some 3.6 metres (12 ft) of thick clay. He declared: 'So vast a mass of silt laid at one time could only be the result of a very great flood'. He dated the clay as having been deposited around 3500 BC.

Unfortunately, other eminent people decried his theory, pointing out the absence of evidence for a great flood at nearby sites and also the fact that Ur itself survived, indication that the flood was hardly the wholesale wiping-out of people and animals described in the Bible.

Other sites in Iraq have been visited over the years by archaeologists, particularly one at Kish. But again, the remains of the houses indicated that, although damaged by water, they were quite strong enough to withstand that particular deluge. These were, it is now generally assumed, local floods on a relatively small scale. Excavation of Mesopotamian sites proved nothing. But a prayer from 2200 BC, discovered earlier this century, records a chilling event: 'Waters pouring out – destroying cities like the flood wave'. This, say the believers, is one more piece of evidence that the deluge did take place.

As proof of Noah's existence, those who believe the Great Deluge did actually occur point out the strange findings on Mount Ararat, the place where the Ark is supposed to have come to rest after the waters subsided.

The mountain, soaring 5165 metres (17,000 ft) above a flat plain, situated 965 km (600 miles) east of the Turkish city of Ankara, has been scoured from base to summit in search of clues for the Ark. It is a bleak, snow-capped mountain at the top of which it would be difficult to breathe without oxygen. Nevertheless, priests of the 5th century record that they managed to climb it, scraped bitumen-coated wood from the remains of the Ark and brought it back.

More puzzling still are the timber fragments which have been found on Mount Ararat by successive Ark investigators. The timber is of a type that does not come from trees growing in the region. It has been identified as 4000-year-old wood, originating from the plains of Mesopotamia – where Noah is said to have lived.

The first pieces were retrieved by Victorian archaeologists, eager to reinforce Christian theories about the Ark. In 1969 the French industrialist Fernand Navarra, who had led an earlier expedition in 1955, returned to find further samples of wood. Thanks to advances in the science of carbon dating, he came up with an amazing result.

NOAH'S ARK

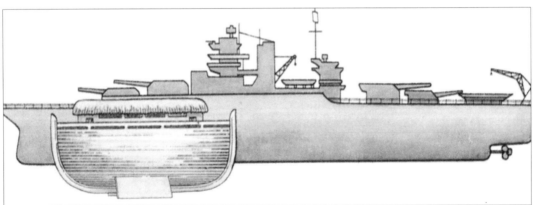

Noah and the Ark (top), as depicted in a medieval manuscript. The Ark (above) compared with a First World War battleship, both drawn to scale.

Carbon dating is a most accurate way of estimating the age of objects, whether they are natural or man-made. Everything contains natural radioactivity, and the radioactivity in the carbon contained in all organic material decays at a known rate. By measuring the levels of radioactivity in the carbon in anything from ash trees to zebra bones, a precise dating can be obtained.

Navarra determined that the wood on Mount Ararat was dated at 3500 BC!

Previous souvenir hunters included archaeologist Lord Bryce, who found a large chunk of wood – from the ship's hull, he surmised – in 1876. And a prominent Russian researcher 50 years before him mapped out the snub-nose peak of the mountain – flat enough, he thought, for a vessel to beach itself there once the flood waters had ebbed away.

What of the vessel itself? Could a ship large enough to take so many creatures 'two by two' have been constructed? Yes, say the Bible-believers. But the Biblical dimensions of the craft are truly enormous – it was said to be 300 cubits long, 50 broad and 30 high. This would put the Ark at 146 metres (480 ft) long, 22.8 metres (75 ft) broad and 13.7 (45 ft) metres high. A vessel, in fact, displacing 43,500 tonnes, with over 1,400,000 square metres (15,000,000 square ft) of deck space!

That, say 'Arkaeologists', would have provided ample room for the creatures Noah took on the voyage and would still have left plenty of room for himself and his family. Those who scoff at the notion of such a craft, and all the problems it would entail in terms of its construction and the sailing and navigation skills required to set forth in it, can only be reminded of the impressive knowledge of seafaring which ancient civilisations possessed – proved by artefacts such as the papyrus boats of Ancient Egyptians that were capable of mammoth voyages across the oceans.

There is one further theory of a Great Deluge: that the world was plunged beneath the waves, but long before any written records were kept.

Some scientists say that the submersion happened in the Stone Age, and may not have been so much a flood as a gradual upsurge in the level of the seas over years, perhaps caused by some colossal natural disaster, the nature of which is as yet unknown.

Was it distant memories of just such an upheaval that are responsible for the stories in the Bible and elsewhere?

It was not until 1994 that firm evidence arose that finally convinced the bulk of sceptics that an Ark actually existed. A team of scientists investigating the Turkish-Iranian border found a buried ship just 30 km (20 miles) from Mount Ararat.

It measured 180 metres (590 ft) long and 49 metres (160 ft) wide – almost exactly matching God's instructions to Noah in Genesis. Salih Bayraktutan, Head of Geology at Ataturk University, said: 'This is a man-made structure and, for sure, it's Noah's Ark'.

Since the remains of the giant craft were found at an altitude of 2100 metres (7000 ft), it also proves that the Deluge must have been one mighty flood.

STONEHENGE

Few relics of the ancient world are as mystifying as the great standing pillars of Stonehenge. These megaliths of ancient man defy belief: how did they get there, what is their purpose, where did the technology to erect them come from?

Across the centuries, the giant, brooding stones of this awe-inspiring ruin have stood as a challenge to humankind's knowledge of itself and its ancient world. Despite every theory they still keep their secrets. For they are made from rocks only found hundreds of miles from Stonehenge. How were the stones transported? How was this engineering miracle performed? And above all, why?

Stonehenge is but one cluster in a swathe of gigantic monumental rocks which stretches around Europe and the British Isles, from as far north as the Shetland Islands to Malta in the south. There are around nine hundred sites of standing stones in Britain alone. But Stonehenge, rising above the flat plateau of Salisbury Plain, is easily the most famous of them. Indeed, among all the great stone sites of Europe, Stonehenge remains unique because of the sophisticated way that the blocks appear to have been designed to fit one another and to form a carefully completed whole.

It is only relatively recently that archaeologists have been prepared to say that these great stones may have been constructed by advanced astronomers or mathematicians rather than barbarians and savages. Much astute detective work has resulted in extraordinary theories on the origin and history of the megaliths (the word is Greek for 'great stones') which should not be dismissed lightly.

Stonehenge was built in three distinct stages, spanning a period of over a thousand years. Each group of people who began the mammoth task did not quite finish it, leaving the legacy of completion to the succeeding generations.

The first builders were Neolithic, working on the site around 2700 BC. It was they who set up the encircling ditch and bank and the heel stone, which is aligned so that the first rays of light from the sun on midsummer's day strike both it and the central point of the two stone circles. These same people created the 56 shallow pits called the Aubrey Holes – named after the writer who discovered them – which form a ring just inside the bank, and which when excavated were found to contain bones and cremated objects.

Some eight hundred years on, the men and women who we call the Beaker People, because of their habit of burying ornate artefacts of pottery with their dead, moved in on the site. They, by means unknown, accomplished one of the truly great engineering feats of all time. In an age when tools were made of flint and bone and the wheel had not yet been invented, they hewed rock from the Prescelly Hills in South Wales and transported it the 480 km (300 miles) to the site we now know as Stonehenge. The 80 mammoth bluestones, each weighing more than 4 tonnes, were then assembled into a double circle inside the enclosure built earlier.

Around 1500 BC, the builders of the third Stonehenge again brought in massive boulders, this time from the Marlborough Downs, probably dragged to the site on primitive sledges by upwards of a thousand men. The individual boulders weighed more than 50 tonnes each, and were hewn from Sarsen rock, one of the hardest minerals. After the arduous journey, they were fashioned into the shapes which now stand like gaunt sentinels on the bleak, windswept plain.

Finally, a people who could not read or write or fashion a wheel devised a system to put the huge stone lintels on top of the upright stones. In addition, the builders of Stonehenge shared something with the prehistoric builders at other sites around Europe – all these monuments are constructed using the same unit of measurement, a unit archaeologists have come to call the megalithic yard: a distance of 0.83 metres. No one has yet been able to explain either how or why this common unit could have come to be used by so many distant peoples of the time.

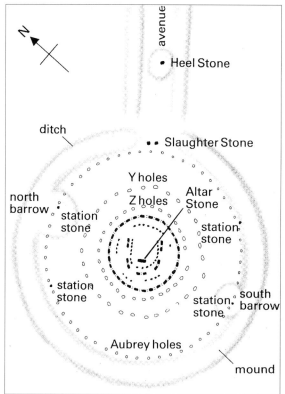

Twentieth-century Druids (top) celebrate midsummer at Stonehenge, even though there is no historical evidence to link the ancient druid cult with this site. The plan of Stonehenge (above) shows where the 56 Aubrey Holes were excavated.

STONEHENGE

Stonehenge and the mystery surrounding its origins continue to fascinate, drawing visitors to Salisbury Plain from every corner of the world.

Although the strange cult of the modern Druids, or Celtic Priests, now lays claim to Stonehenge, experts have concluded that it is far too old to have been constructed by their Celtic forerunners. So which cult and which men were behind the megalithic mystery?

Theories about the structure abound, but perhaps the one expounded by Oxford University professor Alexander Thom bears the most credence. In 1934, after a hard day's sailing, Professor Thom took his boat into Loch Roag on the Isle of Lewis, off Scotland's bleak west coast. Silhouetted against the rising full moon were the standing stones of Callanish, Scotland's Stonehenge.

The professor went ashore. Standing in the middle of the stone circle, he checked the position of the Pole Star and noted that it showed the structure was aligned north-south. Because this monument was prehistoric and was built in the days when the Pole Star's constellation had not reached its present position in the sky, Professor Thom deduced that the people who had built it must have had some other way of determining the alignment of the stones.

His discovery there launched him on a quest around 600 standing-stone sites both in Britain and Europe. It proved that although the stone circles may look rough and weathered today, worn down by both time and human activity, they were originally precise works of engineering skill. Of Stonehenge, he declared that it was a Stone Age observatory, where even small irregularities on the extremities of the site were created artificially, specifically to mark the significant moments when the sun and moon rose and when they set.

In 1963 Gerald Hawkins, Professor of Astronomy at Boston University, made another startling claim. He stated that Stonehenge was like a giant computer: a huge observatory capable of extremely complex calculations based on the position of the sun, moon and stars. When Hawkins fed all the data he had about the site into a computer, the startling result was that the stones could be used to predict the occurrence of eclipses. Why not accept such sophistication among the ancients, he argued to the critics, since the men who built it had proved by the feat itself that they were not primitive?

Hawkins' observatory theory gained ground, thanks to the work of C A Newham, who said the highly educated astronomer priests of the time could have stood in the centre of the great circle and determined the position of the sun or moon in its orbit by using the stones as a guide.

Professor Sir Fred Hoyle, one of Britain's most famous astronomers, supported the theory that Stonehenge was a giant observatory. Hoyle agreed that the megaliths could be used as markers to gauge the moon's activity as it passed through different stages of its cycle. He added that Stonehenge's construction 'demanded a level of intellectual attainment higher than the standard to be expected from a community of primitive farmers'.

If the academics are right, that Stonehenge and the other standing stone sites were designed for making astronomical observations, it is likely that there was an intellectual elite within the primitive Stone Age farmers we know inhabited the earth – an elite who carried out the complex calculations necessary to chart planetary movements in an age when there was no written word.

Other theories about Stonehenge exist – that the site was a beacon for aliens from outer space, a temple for human sacrifice, even that it was a place where infertile women went to be blessed by ancient gods. However, it is the observatory theory which best stands the test of time. Scientists now accept the once unbelievable proposition that a phenomenally intellectual race long ago learned to operate a gigantic stone 'computer'!

STONEHENGE

In 1909 historian and astronomer Sir Norman Lockyer charted the strangely geometrical pattern that existed between Stonehenge, a prehistoric hill-site nearby called Old Sarum, and another neolithic settlement called Grovelly Castle. The three sites are 9.6 km (6 miles) from each other so that, when joined on a map, a near-perfect equilateral triangle emerges. Was this town planning on a huge and precise scale, or just coincidence?

In 1976 Dr Euan Mackie of Glasgow's Hunterian Museum announced that he had found the site of the elite academy where the gifted priests of Stonehenge may have lived and studied their craft. He said that remains found at Durrington Walls, near Stonehenge, showed a race of people who ate a rich diet, who wore woven cloth and who enjoyed a status above that of their nearest neighbours.

THE GREAT PYRAMID

Of all the ancient world's Seven Wonders, only the Great Pyramid of Cheops survives. It stands as testimony to human genius, constructed 45 centuries ago to house the remains of a ruler judged by his people to be both mortal and divine. It covers an area of 5.25 hectares (525 acres), took 30 years to construct and is made from enough stone to build a wall all the way around Cairo, the nearest city. It is the Great Pyramid of Cheops.

The magnificent structure is the largest of three at Giza, outside Cairo. The colour of burnt ochre against a brilliant blue sky, it was built by an army of labourers, probably numbering in excess of twenty thousand for the Pharaoh Cheops, successor to Seneferu, who died around 2520 BC.

Little is known of the great Cheops, except that he started preparations for his afterlife while still a young man. It was his ambition to be interred in the greatest pyramid of all, surrounded by great treasures as well as the everyday implements necessary for survival in the afterlife.

Egyptian kings considered themselves living gods, destined to leave earth to travel with the other deities, particularly the Sun God, Ra, and to voyage with him in his 'boat of a million years' – by day through the skies, and by night through the dark and treacherous underworld.

The first pyramids were step-shaped in design, literally providing a walkway to the sky. It was in Cheops' reign (Cheops is the Greek name given to him, the Egyptian one being Khufu) that the golden age of pyramid building dawned and the greatest structures were made. These pyramids constitute feats of engineering that make modern-day architects and engineers gasp in awe at the astonishing accuracy of their construction.

The ancient Egyptians knew no metals other then copper and gold, so most tools for shaping and chipping stone were made from flint and wood. Wood was used, too, to hammer into faults in quarry stone. The wood was then soaked and, when it swelled, it split the stone into huge chunks, some weighing up to 15 tonnes. The stones were then hauled into place on wet rollers by teams of men.

The architects had to be certain of a flat surface for the site of the Great Pyramid. However, they had no means, such as modern-day spirit levels, of ascertaining where that might be. So in a long, laborious process, they dug canals, flooded an area and, knowing that where the water lay along the surface was flat land, chose their site. The land was then drained and construction could begin.

It is still staggering to think that mortals, even armed with that small knowledge, should have built a pyramid 147 metres (480 ft) high, covering a base 230 metres (750 ft) along each side and weighing in excess of 6,000,000 tonnes. The lengths of the longest and shortest sides differ by just 20 cm (8 in), and, incredibly, the pavement around the Great Pyramid is level to within 2.5 cm (1 in). Although these masters of civilisation chronicled so many things all those years ago, the Egyptians left no records to help us with this puzzle. When the first archaeologists studied the monumental structure, they found it was impossible to slide a needle between the great limestone, granite and sandstone blocks.

Mystics point out that the pyramid's walls run exactly from north to south and east to west, and believe that the ancient Egyptians used the star Alpha Draconis, nearest to the north celestial pole, to achieve this precise orientation.

The only entrance to the tomb is on the north side of the pyramid, and in case of the king's sudden death while work was still in progress, the pyramid was made with three tombs inside. The first was deep in the underlying rock, the second in the heart of the pyramid, and the final burial chamber 42 metres (140 ft) up. A great gallery, 47.5 metres (155 ft) long and 7.9 metres (26 ft) wide, was created to allow access to the burial chamber. However, the gallery itself could be reached only by walking bent double through narrow corridors.

THE GREAT PYRAMID

The pyramids at Giza: the central structure is the Great Pyramid of Cheops, constructed some 4500 years ago and the only one of the Seven Wonders of the World remaining in existence to this day.

Although the Great Pyramid is a work of technical brilliance, Egyptologists are still puzzled as to whether King Cheops was actually laid to rest in it. Certainly, it remained undisturbed for three thousand years until an Arab, Abdullah al Mamun, and his band of men discovered in AD 820 a passageway to the inside. Finding it blocked by huge granite boulders, they forced their way around into the King's Chamber – only to find his granite sarcophagus empty.

Did the priests ever inter him there? Or was the Great Pyramid, as many believe, constructed for more mysterious, secret reasons?

In 1864 Charles Piazzi Smyth, Astronomer Royal for Scotland, visited the site of the Great Pyramid and began work on a new theory. Ten years later he published a best selling work entitled *Our Inheritance in the Great Pyramid*. In the work Smyth concocted a fascinating, if not at times a little far-fetched, reason for the construction of the pyramid.

It was, he argued, a gigantic touchstone, a desert fortune-teller which, if all its measurements both inside and out were taken, had enormous religious and scientific value. The pyramid's measurements, when decoded, Smyth argued, foretold the history of man right up to the Second Coming of Christ. Smyth called his new theory 'pyramidology'.

One who was determined to debunk Smyth's theory of the Great Pyramid was the man destined to become the greatest Egyptologist of them all, the British archaeologist William Flinders Petrie. Petrie arrived at Giza in 1880 and began a methodical scientific survey, abandoning the preconceptions of the 'hogwash' (as he termed it) ideas of pyramidology.

In 1883 he published *Pyramids and Temples of Giza*, largely demolishing the myth that messages and mysteries were encoded in the great blocks of stone. Instead he took them for what they were – astonishing feats of engineering and design, replete with false passages and dead ends, boulders and sealed rooms to ward off tomb robbers. This was not, he declared, the creation of a great force, a mysterious and unknown being; it was simply the work of a gifted race which sought to ennoble its dead in man-made mountains for all eternity.

Even so, Petrie, who went on to study all the pyramids of Egypt and their origins, has not destroyed the belief of the many who say that, because of the way they are constructed, pyramids do exert a strange life-force – and that within them, strange things can happen.

Among these advocates is the Swiss author Erich von Däniken. He does not believe Smyth's theory that the pyramids were created by a divine force – rather, he advocates the theory that they were the work of creatures from another planet, arriving in spacecraft and erecting monuments before moving on.

Whichever theory you choose to subscribe to, everyone agrees on one thing: nothing like them has ever been built, nor has anything like them endured so long. And, save for the highly polished limestone-slab covering which would have been a metre thick, running from the apex to base of the pyramid on all four sides, the Great Pyramid of Cheops is the same as the one gazed upon by the great Pharaoh himself.

Some of the earliest Western eyes to gaze on the Cheops Pyramid did so when Napoleon, on one of his wars of conquest, went to battle with the Egyptians. Napoleon was spellbound by the magnificence of the pyramids, and together with his army brought out scholars and scientists to chronicle, decipher and plunder this cornucopia of ancient wonders.

The world owes the French scholars in Napoleon's ranks a great deal, for they unravelled the mysteries of hieroglyphics and the ancient Coptic scripts, and charted the great historical sites. But no one in 19th-century Europe could fathom why the pyramids had been built.

Napoleon instilled in his men the sense of awe they should feel when in the presence of such a structure. Before clashing with the forces of the Turkish emperor, outside the gates of Cairo in 1798, Napoleon exhorted his troops: 'Remember that from the top of these monuments, 40 centuries are looking down on you'.

An artist's impression of the Emperor Napoleon surveying in Egypt.

ATLANTIS

It is the essential stuff of legend. According to stories retold over the centuries, a people of great wealth, beauty and happiness inhabited an island called Atlantis. This paradise was blessed with lush vegetation, a cultured and civilised populace, a wealth of natural minerals including gold and silver, and food in abundance.

But did Atlantis really ever exist? If so, where was it – and what was the catastrophe that destroyed it?

Few great unanswered mysteries can have had as much energy, thought and words expended on them as that surrounding the legendary lost city. Some two thousand books (a conservative estimate) have been written about Atlantis, most of them hinging on the single most perplexing question of the whole story: where was it?

The source of legends about the great city of Atlantis was, of course, the first author ever to write about it: Plato. The great Greek philosopher wrote an account in 347 BC of a kingdom which vanished from the face of the earth centuries before the birth of Christ. He told how, as a young man, he listened to Socrates discussing philosophy with a group of students, including his friend Critias. Together the assembled group talked of Atlantis, a kingdom 'derived from historical tradition'.

It was described as a once-great nation, whose people became corrupt and whose leaders led it into decline. According to the Egyptian priests quoted by Critias, Atlantis was destroyed by a violent volcanic eruption, which was followed by a tidal wave that plunged the tragic island beneath the waves forever.

Since then, and thanks to Plato's account, Atlantis has become a holy grail for many adventurers, archaeologists, historians and others fascinated with legends. But not one of them has been able to find the submerged remains of the ancient utopia.

Plato puts the date for the destruction of Atlantis at some time around 9600 BC, the location being 'beyond the Pillars of Hercules' (or Straits of Gibraltar). He describes the magical land thus:

'At the centre of the island, near the sea, was a plain, said to be the most beautiful and fertile of all plains, and near the middle of this plain . . . a hill of no great size. In the centre was a shrine sacred to Poseidon and Cleito, surrounded by a golden wall through which entry was forbidden'.

He goes on to describe the magnificent hot and cold springs, the elaborate temples, and the luxurious accommodation afforded to visiting royalty. In all, he paints a splendid picture of a kingdom which enjoyed, before its decline and fall, the greatest benefits of civilisation.

Since Plato's day, Atlantis has been 'placed' in every sea and ocean – from the Sargasso to the Scilly Isles, from the Pacific to the centre of the Atlantic. Authors have envisaged a once-massive land bridge between Britain and America via Iceland and Greenland.

Perhaps the most credible possible site is that of Bimini, a small island in the Bahamas which, although its likelihood of being a place of great historical importance is small, has a gigantic question mark hanging over it as the result of a series of unexplained finds. In 1969 a fisherman known as Bonefish Sam brought archaeologist Dr J Manson Valentine to view curious rectangular stones lying in 8 metres (25 ft) of water, north of a spot called Paradise Point. Manson Valentine was ecstatic, believing the two parallel lines of stones, about 400 metres (1300 ft) long and 1.4 metres square (15 ft square), to be the remnants of a great harbour wall.

Hordes of archaeologists immediately descended on sleepy Bimini to investigate whether the stones were the work of Aztec, Toltec, Mayan or other civilisations.

No one has been able to prove their origins either way. However, two later expeditions to Bimini in 1975 and 1977 revealed a block of stone with a carved edge, something definitely crafted by man. To this date, its origin has not been established.

ATLANTIS

Was Atlantis wiped out by a volcanic blast as destructive as that of an H-bomb?

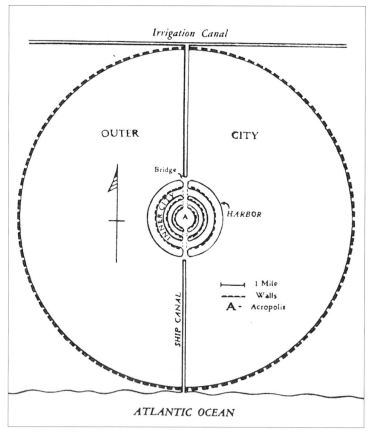

It is possible that Atlantis once contained a civilisation as flourishing as that of Athens (top). A map of Atlantis (above), drawn using Plato's description in Critias *as a reference.*

ATLANTIS

Although the Atlantis described by Plato has never been found, there are academics who subscribe to the notion that the philosopher mistook the location of Atlantis and that the catastrophe referred to was the mighty volcanic eruption which blasted the Minoan civilisation off the face of the earth.

Derek Ager, head of the Department of Geology at Bristol University, says: 'I have no doubt at all that there never was such a land mass beyond the Pillars of Hercules. The subject is just not worth discussing. On the other hand, I think it is quite possible, even probable, that the legend refers to the destruction of the Minoan civilisation by the volcanic process'.

So was the Atlantis described by Plato the Bronze Age Minoan culture which blossomed in the islands of the Aegean until around 1500 BC? There is a great deal of evidence that suggests it may have been.

The Minoans ruled from their magnificent city of Knossos, on the island of Crete. From here, the Minoan people dominated the Aegean Sea and the hundreds of islands in it. What became of this mighty civilisation in its dying days is now lost in time; or at least it was until 1967, when a Greek archaeologist, Spyridon Marinatos, began excavating on one of those isles, the southernmost of the Cyclades islands.

Marinatos' project was to delve into the history of the island of Kalliste, as it was called in ancient times, although it is now known as Santorini or Thera. There, buried beneath 30 metres (100 ft) of volcanic ash, he discovered the remains of a city whose people were civilised and refined. They enjoyed mains drainage and baths in their homes, unrivalled prosperity and command of the seas.

Then suddenly their golden civilisation was destroyed by volcanic blasts of such magnitude as to defy belief. Scientists believe the eruptions were four times greater than that which destroyed the Indonesian isle of Krakatoa in 1883, producing the loudest bang in recorded history. His find became known as the 'Pompeii of the Aegean' after the famous Roman town that was also destroyed by a volcano.

Archaeologists believe that when minor earthquakes and eruptions alerted the Minoans to the danger they were in, the population took to the sea in boats. They were probably no more than 240 km (150 miles) away, however, when the main eruptions occurred, raining down burning debris and choking ash on their vessels before tidal waves made matchsticks of the ones which escaped the firestorm.

The ash clouds which followed the eruptions are even believed by some historians to be the origin of the story of the Egyptian plagues described in the Old Testament. Certainly, the pall that hung over Kalliste would have been visible from as far away as Egypt.

So did the cultured Minoans become the fabled Atlanteans of Plato's story? For five hundred years they ruled supreme and then they vanished. Archaeology tells us that Kalliste may be the site of Atlantis – and that Plato may not merely have been reciting a legend.

TEOTIHUACAN

As Europe sank into a barbarous, dark age, there existed far across the oceans a civilisation that today we can only marvel at. Its principal city was Teotihuacan – and it was one of the most spectacular of the ancient world.

At a time when barbarian hordes were destroying the cities of Europe and the remnants of the mighty Roman empire had crumbled, this civilisation on the plains of Mexico achieved a level of culture and sophistication that puzzles and intrigues historians and archaeologists to this day. We know its inhabitants were literate, numerate and were deeply religious, but we have no idea who this race of cultured people was.

The builders of the city of Teotihuacan (a name given to it by those who populated it long after its founders had gone) displayed a skill almost as great as that deployed by the pyramid builders of ancient Egypt, and evolved a society as cultured as any of the ancient world. While the old European world burned under the torches of the Huns, Goths and Vandals, the educated citizens of this gracious city, with its pyramids and wide avenues, feasted on the finest produce, crafted beautiful pottery and stoneware and developed a system of counting and writing.

What is baffling about Teotihuacan, situated near the sprawling, modern capital Mexico City, is the lack of clues as to the identity of the race which created it – and why its people seemingly abandoned the city, like some landlocked Mary Celeste, and vanished from the face of the earth.

The ancient remains, which attract thousands of visitors each year, are part of a city which once stretched over 23 square km (9 square miles) and give the feeling that a race of people, numbering some 200,000, lived a good life in a well-ordered, well-structured society.

The city stands on a plateau 2250 metres (7500 ft) above sea level at a place where several important routes converge. The surrounding land is good for the cultivation of maize, tomatoes, beans, avocados and pumpkins. The city itself was laid out in precisely patterned streets, dominated by two pyramids, replete with ornately decorated temples and palaces.

When that other great Mexican civilisation, the Aztecs, stumbled upon the ruins of the city one thousand years after it reached its zenith, they bestowed upon it their own name, Teotihuacan, 'the place of those who have the road of the gods'. The Aztecs, like modern-day historians, were puzzled as to the origins of the people who built this great metropolis.

Archaeologists think that nine-tenths of Teotihuacan lies buried under the dust from the surrounding plains that has settled over the area through the years. It is generally thought to have been constructed in the 1st century AD, and during the eight hundred or so years of security and prosperity it enjoyed, its people engaged in regular building and restructuring work.

Archaeological exploration has unearthed several layers of the city. The Pyramid of the Sun is the dominating central feature of the city, standing beside the Avenue of the Dead, the main thoroughfare. Experts calculate that the pyramid would have taken three thousand men no less than thirty years to build.

Its axis is aligned east–west, reflecting the path of the sun across the sky. It is generally thought that the pyramid was built to represent the universe, with its four corners symbolising the points of the compass, with its apex representing the 'heart of life'. Each side of the pyramid measures 225 metres (750 ft) and is 70 metres (230 ft) high, with a total mass of some 2,500,000 tonnes of dried brick and rubble.

Its sister pyramid, smaller in size, is the Pyramid of the Moon, 43 metres (140 ft) high, standing at the northern end of the Avenue of the Dead. Directly in front of this pyramid is the Plaza of the Moon, which leads to the Citadel, the religious heart of the metropolis, where stands the Temple of Quetzalcoatl: the 'feathered serpent' god. The Avenue of the Dead contained the houses of the city's elite – the priests,

TEOTIHUACAN

This temple at Teotihuacan (top) was dedicated to the 'feathered serpent god' Quetzalcoatl. The mask (above) is an imaginative representation of Quetzalcoatl which may have been worn during ritualistic ceremonies.

A stunning photograph of the aptly named Pyramid of the Sun, which rises to a height of 70 metres at the centre of Teotihuacan.

minor functionaries and the leaders themselves – while the remainder of the population lived in the surrounding area.

At the height of its power, the city walls shone with brilliant frescoes of gods and men, emblazoned in beautiful, striking colours, while the temples were adorned with black basalt and elaborately stuccoed. Relics have been found which testify to the artistic genius of the populace, in such items as a tripod vase, pots, graceful eating bowls and numerous figures.

The inhabitants invented a system of writing (which has still to be properly decoded and understood) and a system of numeracy based on dots and bars. But just who were these people?

Research has shown that before Teotihuacan was built, Indians lived in and around the fertile plain in primitive wattle-and-daub huts, probably in clusters of no more than three hundred people. Some greater, more intelligent tribe or race harnessed the labour force already in existence in their primitive homes to construct the city with its road to the gods.

Various theories have been put forward as to who they were. A Frenchman, Desiré Charnay, who stumbled upon the site in 1880, believed it to be an ancient Toltec ruin. But it is generally held that the Toltec race arrived after Teotihuacan was in ruins, and its splendour decayed.

Mexican scholar Jimenez Moreno believes that Teotihuacan was ruled by a priestly autocracy because of the prominence of buildings of religious significance. He points to the celestial significance of the Pyramids of the Sun and Moon, and argues that the whole purpose of the city was the worship of the gods who had apparently blessed the surrounding region with agricultural and wildlife stocks in plenty.

The fact remains, though, that there is no real clue as to who this master race was. Certainly it was a religious race, as evidenced by the Temple of Quetzalcoatl, the god who represented the union of heaven and earth, land and water.

The French archaeological expert, Laurette Sejourne, argues that the whole city may have been built to Quetzalcoatl's glory, with the buildings around the temple reserved for priests. In those buildings they would have been initiated into the ancient rites before ascending the steps of the Pyramid of the Sun for a final ceremony that would mark them as fully-fledged servants of their deity.

It is safe to speculate that religion did indeed play a major part in the life of the people of Teotihuacan, shown not only by the name which the Aztecs were later to bestow on the city, but also by the countless religious artefacts that are slowly being unearthed from the site. But it was also more than just a giant place of worship; it was a busy, thriving city which positively hummed with activity.

There is a marvellous tableau showing market day in Teotihuacan which has been put on display in the Museum of Natural History in Mexico City. It vividly depicts thousands of peasants bartering meat, fowl, fish, vegetables and other goods just as in a modern-day street market.

The remains of vegetable and animal matter found in the cooking pots and refuse pits of ruined houses have indicated that the inhabitants enjoyed a healthy diet. The housing complexes were lavish or simple, depending on whether nobles, priests or commoners inhabited them. One palace, called Zacuala, covered an area of over 3300 square metres (36,000 square ft) and boasted its own private temple. Courtyard complexes which have recently been discovered showed that rainwater was carried away in an elaborate drainage system, which could be plugged if water supplies were getting low.

Remains have been found beneath the houses. It seems that the citizens treated their dead with great reverence. After the bodies of loved ones were cremated, the ashes were blessed by the high priests before being wrapped in linen shrouds and buried beneath the homes of their families. Apart from ashes, skeletons have been unearthed, buried with ritual offerings of pottery. Indeed, some of the most well preserved pottery of the highest artistic quality found at Teotihuacan has been discovered in the burial sites, denoting the importance of a dignified death ceremony which the inhabitants valued.

Professor René Millon, of the University of New York at Rochester, has devoted much of his life to the study of Teotihuacan. He thinks that by the year AD 150 there was a population of over fifty thousand – many of them the former hut dwellers who abandoned their primitive abodes for the safety and culture of the city. Professor Millon charts the growth of the city – at its height it was bigger than Caesar's Rome – until it reached its peak in the 5th and 6th centuries.

Teotihuacan fell into decline in about the middle of the 6th century, the inhabitants finally leaving the city around the 8th century. But why that decline occurred is as baffling a mystery as the foundation of the city itself.

There have been found none of the traces of pillage and bloodshed associated with cities that fall by the sword. Nor have there been indications that the citizens left in a blind panic, or were wiped out by plague or famine.

The theory has been put forward that the populace rebelled against the priest-rulers because of the ever-growing numbers of human sacrifices offered to the gods in harsh years. But there is little, if any, evidence that the people of Teotihuacan practised human sacrifice; and if they did, it was accepted practice in the majority of Central American cultures before the spread of Christianity. Some evidence of fires has been unearthed among the ruins. These may have been started deliberately, but it hardly seems likely that the people would have used this method to try to destroy a stone city. It is more likely that the race which followed and moved into the city put the artefacts of their predecessors to the torch.

Archaeologists continue to argue about the decline and fall of Teotihuacan. Did a marauding tribe sweep down from the north, driving civilian populations before them? Did the population rebel against the priesthood, corrupt in its power, or simply leave in a mass exodus? There are no answers to these questions, and the city of the gods stands as an enigma which will probably continue to defy explanation for centuries to come.

Controversy has in recent years surrounded the remains of Teotihuacan, situated near the sprawling modern capital, Mexico City. As work on the site continued to unearth beautiful artefacts crafted by an intelligent and skilful people, experts were flung into confusion over the discovery of ashes from a palace called Quetzalpaplotl, home of the priest elite. Carbon dating of the minute wood fragments provoked an argument which may lead to Teotihuacan's previously accepted dates of origin being re-examined, for the carbon-dating process has shown that the remains are much, much older than originally thought. It could even be that the 'city of the gods' flourished before the birth of Christ.

CAMELOT

He was called 'The Once And Future King' – and certainly the tales of his heroic exploits have survived the centuries to inspire and to intrigue. Legend has it that King Arthur battled to save his Celtic Britons from the invading Saxon armies. In a relatively barbarous age, he ruled his people with benevolence and justice for all. His Knights of the Round Table came to epitomise everything that is chivalrous in human endeavour. And his capital, Camelot, has become a byword for all that is gentle, noble, virtuous, righteous and learned.

So who was King Arthur? Did he, as the ancient tales tell us, have a wizard called Merlin, a queen named Guinevere, a sword Excalibur, a round table, an island of Avalon and a fabulous castle? If there was a Camelot, where was it located? Indeed, did its monarch and noblest of champions really exist – or is Arthur simply the most enduring and fascinating myth of English folklore?

The earliest reference to such a king is in the 7th-century epic Welsh poem *Gododdin*, which speaks of a 'mighty warrior' in the continuing battles against the Saxons. There is little historical doubt that about two hundred years before the poem was written there had indeed been a valiant leader in the southwest of England. The peasants of the time certainly needed one.

England had enjoyed four centuries of prosperity under the colonial rule of the Romans. There was a settled system of government and security under the protection of the legions. An admirable road system linked the entire country south of Hadrian's Wall, north of which the unconquered Scots remained at bay. Trade prospered with the rest of Roman-occupied Europe.

Soon after AD 400, however, the Romans finally pulled out, since attacks on their homeland required more and more centurions to defend Rome itself. This was the opportunity for the Angles, Jutes and Saxons, invaders from the Continent, to sail across the North Sea and around the English Channel to plunder the countryside. As the Celtic natives were forced ever westwards, they were desperately in need of a strong leader. It is likely that the man now known as King Arthur was a Romanised Briton who united the battle-weary peasants before turning the tide of war against the Anglo-Saxons.

He may even have been the military mastermind behind a little-known British general, Ambrosius Aurelianus, whose armies, pushed back to the Welsh borders by advancing Saxons, stood and fought at the Battle of Mount Badon in 518. Largely thanks to the tactical genius of one of his chieftains, known only as Arthur, the English army defeated the occupiers so convincingly that peace was restored in the region for half a century.

Early Welsh scribes called Arthur 'a king of wonders and marvels' and the Arthurian Legend took on a life of its own. In 1135 Geoffrey of Monmouth described Arthur in his *Historia* as the conqueror of western Europe. That is obviously far from the truth: Arthur's reign was over only a region of old England. In the 12th century another work *Roman de Bru*, elaborated on Arthur's prowess and imbued him with the virtuous qualities of chivalry and piety that have remained such an essential component of his legend ever since.

Knights were added to Arthur's court by the French poet Chrétien de Troyes. In his 13th-century romance Perceval, these valiant knights embark on a quest for the Holy Grail, the chalice from which Christ drank at the Last Supper. Sir Gawain and the Green Knight, published around 1370, was the next major work to reinforce the legend. Then came *Morte d'Arthur* by Sir Thomas Mallory, the most important and certainly the most detailed medieval account of the Arthurian Legend.

It is strange how the story of Camelot grew to reflect the aspirations of the peasantry of Britain, with a mixture of Christian beliefs and pagan wizardry. But how can one sift the fact from the fable – for fact there certainly is in the legend of this English warlord.

The round table, from where King Arthur's knights were sent in the quest for the Holy Grail.

CAMELOT

Supposedly, Arthur was the illegitimate son of Uther Pendragon, King of Britain, and his mistress Igraine. Upon Uther's death, Arthur inherited his throne simply by publicly declaring it was rightfully his. It was at this time, too, that Arthur pulled the legendary sword Excalibur from a block of stone. Engraved on the stone were the words: 'Whosoever pulls this sword from the stone and anvil is the rightful king of England'. Folklore has it that no one claiming the throne had achieved this before. Thus Arthur, who until this point had been brought up in secret and whose existence was not even known to most, became the rightful heir.

Merlin, the court wizard who was to become Arthur's mentor, bowed down before him and proclaimed him king. However, Arthur's success was not immediate. Contrary to what legend would have us believe, there were many years of fierce fighting before Arthur's right to the kingdom was accepted. Not everyone loved and revered him but he protected himself and his realm by instituting the glorious regime of his famous Round Table knights. And he married a beautiful bride, Guinevere (actually his second wife).

Arthur's principal enemies included his own treacherous sister, Morgan la Fay, and his nephew, Mordred. Morgan was a witch who plotted against her brother and once, while Arthur was away in battle, seized the throne. Arthur eventually killed Mordred, but not before he was fatally wounded himself. His body was buried on the holy isle of Avalon, where it was believed a miracle would one day take place and restore him to life. That burial place is still undiscovered and undisturbed.

So much for the legend. What of the facts that support the existence of such a man and his court?

We have heard how a warrior called Arthur did indeed live in England's West Country and Welsh Borders around the year AD 518 . But the legends that embellished his brief history might have remained no more than folklore but for research into the chronicles of Glastonbury Abbey, Somerset.

Writing in about 1120, William Malmesbury described Arthur's grave as having been discovered in the oldest part of the cemetery of the Abbey's Lady Chapel. The grave was marked by a cross inscribed (in Latin) with the words: 'Here lies the famous King Arthur with Guinevere, his second wife, buried in the Island of Avalon'.

This story conformed with the records of the Abbey. Some of the more important graves had been excavated in the 10th century as the level of the cemetery was raised. According to a Bishop Dunstan, the new surface level was protected by a wall. If the monks had gone to this trouble, it would have been logical to erect a fresh stone over the grave of Arthur and Guinevere. The abbey records also contain a report that in 1190 Abbot Henry of Sully exhumed the royal coffin from a pit about 5 metres (16 ft) deep and removed it to the Abbey's treasury.

Glastonbury received two other royal visitors in 1275 – this time live ones. King Edward I and his Queen Eleanor made a pilgrimage to consecrate the abbey's high altar. On this auspicious occasion, the abbot broke open the treasury's ancient coffin to reveal two caskets, each decorated with coats of arms. In one was the skeleton of a tall man, in the other was that of a slightly-built woman. They were rewrapped in shrouds and presumably returned to the vaults or reburied.

In 1960 archaeologists excavated the area within Glastonbury Abbey where Arthur's grave might have been. They discovered that a deep pit had once been dug out and refilled, with the indent of a headstone above it. But of the bones of King Arthur and his queen there was no sign.

Why should the Somerset town of Glastonbury, which is well inland, ever have been called the Isle of Avalon? In Arthurian times, the place was an isolated area of high ground surrounded by marshland, effectively turning it into an island. In Welsh, it is known as *Ynys Avalon*, meaning the 'Island of Apples'.

If Glastonbury was Avalon, where was Camelot? The conflict at which Arthur was reputedly killed was known as the Battle of Camlann and is believed to have taken place near Cadbury, Somerset, site of an ancient castle. Thousands of hours have gone into excavations there but archaeologists still have not found proof of the existence of Camelot, its knights or the most romantic king in British history.

Edyrn rides to King Arthur's court.

THE NEW WORLD

Christopher Columbus is credited with being the first European to set foot in America. But did he open up the New World to the Old? Or did the Chinese, Phoenician, Irish, Viking or Ancient Greek sailors get there first?

Undoubtedly, Columbus was the supreme voyager of his age. The brave, pioneering sailor is universally celebrated as the discoverer of America in 1492 when he sailed from Spain to the West Indies. But was he? Researchers suggest that many other races, equipped with vessels far more primitive than his, could have reached it before him. Thor Heyerdahl, the Norwegian ethnologist, showed that the ancient Egyptians could have reached America long before Columbus, when, in 1967, he crossed the Atlantic in a boat made of papyrus.

Indeed, scientists can prove that man has been settled in America for over twelve thousand years – a fact ascertained using the process of carbon dating, which accurately reads the amount of radioactivity in materials and is capable of pinpointing their date to within a hundred years. These first settlers were the descendants of Mongolian tribesmen who had reached the continent by crossing the land bridge across the Bering Straits from Siberia to Alaska. This much we know of the indigenous people, the first Americans. But who were the first people from other continents to reach America?

Could, for instance, the Chinese, masters of the seas long before European traders, have been the first outsiders to land in America? Sculptures found among the remains of ancient Central American nations have had such an uncanny resemblance to idols used in Buddhist religion that some theorists claim the Chinese arrived there in about 2000 BC.

One eminent academic, Professor Chu Shien-chi of Beijing University, believes a Buddhist priest named Hoei Shin voyaged across the Pacific Ocean and landed on the coastline of the Gulf of Mexico. He claims that documentary evidence in China shows that Hoei Shin named the site of his discovery Fusang, after a Chinese plant which he said was similar to flora growing there.

Another race which may have set foot in America before the time of Christ were the Phoenicians. In 600 BC the Ancient Greek historian Herodotus wrote of the Phoenicians when he told of sailors from Tyre and Sidon being hired by Pharaoh Necho of Egypt to sail around Africa and out across the Atlantic in oared galleys. If they did not reach the New World, they almost certainly reached the Azores, where a hoard of gold Carthaginian coins were discovered only in the 18th century.

But it was the discovery in South America of an inscribed stone which pro-Phoenician theorists hold up as proof of their claims. The stone was found in a Brazilian coffee plantation in 1872. Since then its script has been examined by many eminent academics. Some say it is counterfeit; others, like Cyrus Gordon, Professor of Ancient History from Brandeis University, Massachusetts, have declared it original. The translation reads:

'We are sons of Canaan from Sidon, the city of the King. Commerce has cast us in this distant shore, a land of mountains. We set (the word for human sacrifice) a youth for the exalted gods and goddesses in the 18th year of Hiram, our mighty King. We embarked from Ezion-Geber into the Red Sea and voyaged with ten ships. We were at sea together for two years around the land belonging to Ham (Africa). But we were separated by a storm and we were no longer with our companions. So we have come here, twelve men and three women on a new shore which I, the Admiral, control. But auspiciously may the exalted gods and goddesses favour us'.

Is this conclusive proof that they were there long before the birth of Christ? The Phoenicians may have been the greatest navigators of their age, but the scant historical evidence makes it difficult to substantiate claims that they were the first to reach America. The argument rages on to this day.

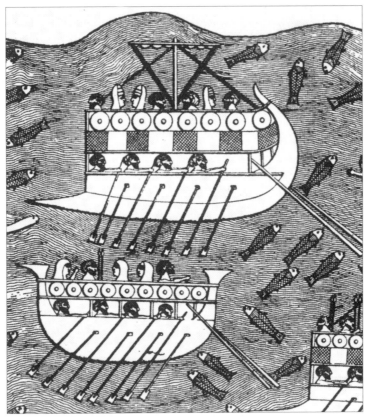

An artist's impression (top) of a possible historical event: Christopher Columbus holding the first mass in America. The Phoenicians (above) were the greatest navigators of the ancient world: is it possible that they reached the New World before the birth of Christ?

THE NEW WORLD

Genoa in the late 1400s (top). Although the city was Columbus' birthplace and a thriving seaport at the time, the explorer set out on his voyage from a Spanish port. Native North Americans (above) attacked Norse settlements in Vinland around AD *1000.*

Another claim for historical eminence is made for the ancient Celts. The evidence for such a claim lies on desolate Mystery Hill in North Salem, north of Boston, where lie a collection of ruins of a kind more usually associated with the great megalithic sites of Europe. There are the remains of 22 huts, passageways and cooking pits, and an eerie sacrificial table with a speaking tube through which voices can be projected – presumably for use during macabre ceremonies.

The huge blocks of granite comprising the passageways are held in place by their own weight, and many thousands of artefacts from different periods have been uncovered there. Stones bearing chiselled inscriptions in the ancient Celtic form of rune writing called Ogam have also been found.

The Celtic claim is, of course, often argued about and oft disputed. However, there is little dispute over the fact that Viking adventurers voyaged to North America in their longboats centuries before Columbus.

The discovery of eight houses, cooking pots, kitchen implements, boats and boat sheds at a site on the northern tip of Newfoundland offer, says Norwegian historian Dr Helge Ingstad, 'the first incontrovertible evidence that Europeans set foot in America centuries before Columbus' voyage of 1492'.

The Vikings travelled in short stages from Scandinavia, via Iceland and Greenland, establishing settlements en route. They were well supplied, developing a method of preserving their meats by trailing them in the salted water, and drinking water from cowhide pouches.

An ancient saga recounting the deeds of the great navigator Leif Ericsson recounts that he reached the New World in the year AD 1000 and called it Vinland. It was, he recorded, a land of beauty and contrasting climates. The great navigator was probably referring to the region now known as New England.

Evidence that the Norsemen trod further inland than even New England arose in 1898 when a farmer clearing land at Kensington, Minnesota, uncovered a large stone inscribed with the characters of a strange language. The Kensington Rune, as it became known, retold the story of a 30-strong party of Norwegians and Goths who went west from Vinland in 1362, ending with a massacre in which 10 of the party were killed.

The authenticity of the Kensington Rune has been disputed. So has that of another ruin which seemed to offer positive proof of the Vikings' first foothold on the continent. The Newport Tower, in Rhode Island, is a circular structure supported on eight columns and is reckoned to be old enough to have been constructed by the Vikings. Others, however, claim that the building is merely the remains of a church built by much later, Christian settlers.

Leif Ericsson's account of his adventures in the ancient Norse sagas are often fanciful, as is to be expected. But there is little dramatisation in their telling and, it seems, no boasting about their undoubted prowess. For the great Norse sailors testify in their sagas that it was not they but the Irish who were the first to reach America!

For further proof of this claim we must look to another ancient document: a 6th-century Latin manuscript, the Navigatio Sancti Brendani, which is often quoted as evidence for the Irish being the first Europeans to cross the Atlantic. The Navigatio, which has survived to the present day, tells how St Brendan, an experienced sailor from Kerry in the west of Ireland, and 14 monks set sail in AD 540 'to find the land promised to the saints'.

Their craft, an 11 metre (35 ft) ketch covered with the hides of oxen and waterproofed with butter, must have taken a northerly course. For the Navigatio talks of their encountering 'a floating tower of crystal' – probably an iceberg. St Brendan's expedition then passed through an area of dense mist – possibly the fog-shrouded Newfoundland Banks. Eventually they landed on a lushly vegetated island surrounded by clear waters and inhabited by pygmies. A final voyage took them on to a semi-tropical mainland.

The story is far from unbelievable. The island could have been one of the Bahamian chain. And the land they later found could have been Florida.

Apart from the Irish, Vikings and Phoenicians, there are many other contenders for the honour of being the first outsiders to discover America. But in every case, the evidence falls tantalisingly short of being conclusive proof.

Perhaps until that proof is obtained, Christopher Columbus, the Italian adventurer employed by a Spanish king, should be allowed to keep his place in the history books. The only tragedy is that, when he set foot in the New World, he did not realise where he had landed. When poor Columbus died on 20 May 1506, he still did not know that the land he had stumbled upon was in fact the vast continent of America.

EL DORADO

El Dorado! It's a name that has gone down in the varied languages of the world as a by-word for fabled wealth. It conjures up visions of idyllic landscapes and a flourishing culture. The legend has tantalised the inquisitive and tempted the greedy. And it has often been difficult to decide which has been the greater lure to mortal mankind: the search for El Dorado's lost civilisation or the search for its ancient treasure – gold.

The Old World first heard of El Dorado when the Spanish conquistadors, under the ruthless Francisco Pizarro, invaded the Incas in 1530, captured their capital city of Cuzco, and plundered their golden art treasures. After a terrible reign of looting and pillaging, in which the Spanish stripped the entire Inca empire of its age-old wealth, the conquistadors began to look even further afield for ever more valuable treasure chests.

The dream of a fresh fortune beyond the Inca empire was fuelled by extraordinary myths and legends. Sebastian de Belalcazar, who founded the Ecuador capital of Quito, heard the stories and coined the name El Dorado. But he failed to find the place. The Spanish believed that El Dorado was a secret Inca city surrounded by a land of treasure-filled temples waiting to be plundered.

Between 1535 and 1540 several expeditions led by different foreign powers sought the lost city supposedly lying to the north of known Inca territory. One was led by Georg Hohermuth, German governor of Venezuela, who, with four hundred men, searched for three years for the city. His expedition suffered starvation and sickness and returned empty-handed, leaving three hundred of his expedition dead in the jungle. Yet unbeknown to him, he had passed just 100 km (60 miles) from El Dorado!

The largest expedition ever assembled was led by the brutal Spaniard, Gonzalo Jimenez de Quesada, in 1536. Disease and battles with the Chibcha Indians of Colombia reduced his mercenary army from around nine hundred to two hundred. But Quesada succeeded in capturing villages, where the tortured inhabitants were forced to reveal their treasures of precious metals and gems.

Quesada was led by captive Indians to the town of Hunsa, described as the 'place of gold'. There they found a chieftain's house the walls of which were lined with massive sheets of beaten gold. The chief sat on a beautiful throne of gold and emeralds. His temples were stacked with gold plates and large hoards of emeralds and bags of gold dust. The Spaniards made a pact with the Indians – then slaughtered every one of them, even stealing the gold rings from the ears and noses of the corpses.

It was here in the blood-drenched streets of Indian jungle towns that the legend of El Dorado became not just a mystery but an enigma for all time – the natives told Quesada that El Dorado was not a place but a person.

El Dorado is Spanish for 'The Gilded One'. The Indians interpreted this as meaning the chieftain of the Muisca nation, who lived in the region in which now sits the Colombian capital of Bogotá. The remnants of Quesada's expedition were led to Lake Guatavita, 2800 metres (9000 ft) above sea level, where the chiefs of the Muiscas were once crowned in a unique ritual.

The chief's tribe would gather around the perfectly circular lake while the new chief, stripped naked and his body coated in gold dust, set sail for the centre. With the sun glinting on his body, the king would then make his offerings to the gods by dropping gold treasures into the deep waters of Lake Guatavita. His subjects would then follow his lead by hurling their golden offerings from the shore.

El Dorado, however, remained as elusive to the Spaniards as the sunset on the waters of Lake Guatavita. For the last Muisca chief to be enthroned on the lake had been deposed a few years earlier; and El Dorado's people had sought no new gold since they no longer needed it for the glittering but defunct coronation ceremonies.

EL DORADO

The cruelty meted out to native peoples by the Spanish Conquistadors during their quest for South American treasure is depicted graphically in this artist's impression.

Over the years, the Indians' greedy tormentors sent expedition after expedition to attempt to plumb the lake's depths. Members of Quesada's original team returned in 1545 to conscript the Muisca Indians into a human chain from the water's edge to the mountain top. Bucketful by bucketful, for three months they took water from the lake and passed it along the line to be tipped away. The level dropped by only 3 metres (9 ft) and several hundred gold artefacts recovered before the emptying of the lake was finally abandoned.

In 1585 another Spanish expedition recruited over eight thousand Indians to cut a deep channel to drain the lake. This time the level fell by 18 metres (60 ft) and many more golden objects were uncovered before landslides blocked the drainage channel.

The last serious attempt to drain the lake was undertaken by British fortune seekers at the beginning of the 20th century. They drilled a tunnel which lowered the water level, but again the drainage channels silted up.

The Colombian government has long since passed laws protecting the lake from treasure-hunters. However, it is a challenge to our belief to think that the poor Muisca Indians threw their precious treasures into the depths all those centuries ago.

THE MONEY PIT

A tiny island off the Canadian coast conceals one of the strangest mysteries on earth. For two centuries hopeful prospectors have sought buried treasure there in what is known as the Money Pit. Many have sunk their life savings in the venture; others have paid with their lives.

The Money Pit is located on Oak Island, in Mahone Bay, Nova Scotia. Its story began one day in 1795 when Daniel McGinnis, aged 16, gently paddled his canoe across the bay to one of the uninhabited islands. The one he alighted on was Oak Island.

He wandered from the beach to a small clearing where an old, gnarled oak stood, showing the signs of having been scarred by rope and tackle. On the ground in the clearing was a circular depression about 4.8 metres (16 ft) in diameter. Being a youngster brought up on the tales seafarers told about swashbuckling pirates, Daniel was immediately convinced that he had hit on a clearing where treasure had been buried, the oak bearing the scars of a makeshift crane that had been used to deposit the valuables deep inside the earth.

Daniel rowed back to the mainland to tell his friends, Anthony Vaughan, aged 13, and John Smith, 20. They went back to Oak Island next day armed with picks and shovels. They began to dig, realising that they were in a circular chamber of some kind that still bore pick marks on its smooth clay sides. At 1.2 metres (4 ft) they hit a floor of flagstones. They removed these on the first day and, over a period of a week, dug deeper and deeper, hitting a layer of close-packed logs at intervals of 3 metres (10 ft), 6 metres (20 ft) and 9 metres (30 ft) each one of which they removed.

The three friends, disillusioned but nonetheless intrigued by their findings, realised they could not continue with the tools at their disposal, and headed back for the mainland. They made a pledge to return.

It was to be nine years before John Smith returned with his friends, having persuaded a syndicate, backed by a well-off local man, Simeon Lynds, to finance a full-scale operation to search the pit. They were glad to see, on their return, that the shaft seemed to be as they had left it.

The excavation then began in earnest, with the help of a local labour force brought into the syndicate in return for a share of the treasure if and when it was discovered. More oak platforms were found as the shaft was sunk deeper: at 12 metres (39 ft), at 15.2 metres (50 ft), and at 18.2 metres (60 ft), the last of which was sealed with coconut fibre and putty. At 21.3 metres (70 ft) they hit plain oak, at 24.4 metres (80 ft) another platform of putty-sealed oak, and at 27.4 metres (90 ft) a stone of a kind not found in Nova Scotia, and bearing an inscription.

Smith, who by that time had bought Oak Island, fitted the stone in his fireplace. The significance, if any, of the illegible writing was lost on him and the other fortune hunters. After wedging the stone out, the trio discovered yet another protective layer of wood. They were convinced that under this lay the treasure chest that would make them rich. It was by now nightfall; since waterlogging was becoming more and more of a problem the deeper they got, they decided to abandon the quest until daylight.

The following day was a Sunday and, being religious men, they did not work on the shaft, returning on Monday morning instead – only to find it flooded to 10 metres (33 ft) from the top. They began bailing, and pressed an old pump into service. But no matter how much water they emptied out, the level in the shaft remained constant at 10 metres (33 ft) depth from the top.

They abandoned the workings for a year, returning to their respective farms until the following spring, when they hit upon the idea of burrowing a separate new shaft alongside the original to take out the water. When they got down to 33.5 metres (110 ft) they tunnelled across into the original shaft – and were lucky to escape with their lives. The walls gave in and the new shaft also flooded, again to within 10 metres (33 ft) of the top.

Smith and his partners, exasperated, gave up. They blamed their misfortune on nature and cursed their luck. The treasure remained out of their grasp.

It wasn't until 1849 that a second concerted bid was made to excavate the pit. A consortium of wealthy Nova Scotians calling itself the Truro Syndicate banded together to have another crack. Included in the Truro Syndicate was Anthony Vaughan, who had been one of the original searchers, and Dr David Lynds, a relative of Simeon Lynds.

They redug the original shaft, getting it down to a depth of 26.2 metres (86 ft). There was no problem with water. They called a halt on a Saturday night, attended church on Sunday, returned after the service – and found 18.2 metres (60 ft) of water in the shaft. They were back at square one.

After trying various pumping and bailing methods, the Truro Syndicate opted to employ a drill named a pod auger, which was driven by a horse and which could bring up materials and soil samples from below. Borings made by the drill, the latest of its kind and used in mining surveys of the day, produced clay, gravel, mud and sand.

To the east of the pit, at a depth of 32.3 metres (107 ft), they found fragments of oak, 56 cm (22 in) of metal, more oak, more metal, more oak and finally spruce, before striking the clay bed. A jarring motion as the drill went down induced the searchers to believe that it had brushed by two treasure chests, one on top of the other.

In 1850 a new shaft was sunk. After what looked like success, the water flooded back in again as the treasure-seekers tunnelled sideways into the original shaft of the Money Pit. It was only after this mishap that they set about solving the problem of the flooding. Samples taken from the drilling apparatus had shown them that the clay was impervious to water. One of the diggers tasted the moisture on his hand – and found it to be salt water.

The Money Pit was being flooded by the sea, and on a nearby beach the treasure-seekers discovered the amazing secret of the Money Pit. They saw that as the tide receded, the sand 'seemed almost to suck the water down, like the earth was thirsty', as one digger put it.

Whoever had dug the Money Pit had also constructed a drainage system under the beach, intended to flood the shaft if ever it was breached to a certain depth. Digging down, they found the same coconut fibre, and then kelp grass over a tunnel of stones, which led back in the direction of the pit.

The idea behind the tunnel was both simple and brilliant. The coconut fibre and kelp grass allowed water to run into the sluice which led to the pit, but kept the clogging sand out. The stone tunnel led straight back to the pit at a depth of around 30 metres (100 ft). As long as the shaft stayed full of earth, the pressure kept the water back. But as soon as the diggers reached it, the force of the water burst through, sealing the secret of the pit in a watery tomb. Poor Smith, all those years ago, had not been beaten by nature, but by an elaborate engineering system designed to keep people out of that great hole in the earth. Why?

At first the prospectors began construction of a dam, but that was smashed by an unusually high tide. Next they tried to block the tunnel, digging another shaft, the fifth to date, near to the site of the Money Pit. Water flooded in at 10.7 metres (35 ft) after they dislodged a boulder.

They thought they had intercepted the tunnel from the beach, but experience should have told them that they were not deep enough. Wood was driven in to stem the flow of water, a sixth shaft was sunk and, at 36 metres (118 ft), as a tunnel was again being dug sideways into the original shaft, the whole thing collapsed.

It was to be a further nine years before the syndicate, which had already poured $20,000 down the pit to no avail, tried again. More shafts were sunk, the pit still flooded, a man was scalded to death when a steam pump blew up – and still there was no sign of any treasure.

Soon the area around the Money Pit looked like a building site, as amateurs and experts alike sunk shaft after shaft in the quest for riches. It was all to no avail.

Over the years, several companies were formed to plumb the depths of the Money Pit. One used

THE MONEY PIT

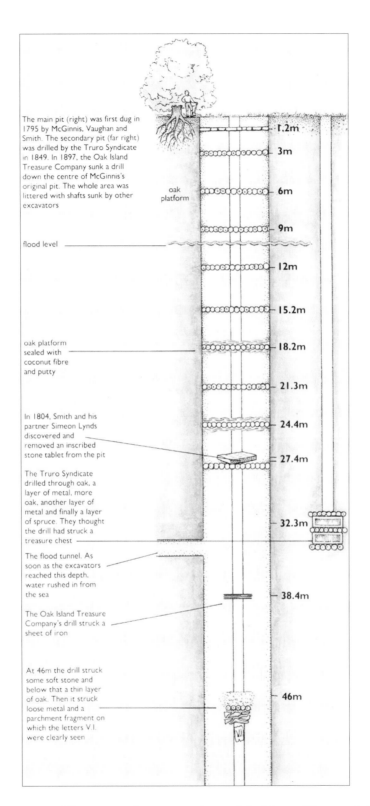

The main pit (right) was first dug in 1795 by McGinnis, Vaughan and Smith. The secondary pit (far right) was drilled by the Truro Syndicate in 1849. In 1897, the Oak Island Treasure Company sunk a drill down the centre of McGinnis's original pit. The whole area was littered with shafts sunk by other excavators

oak platform

— 1.2m

— 3m

— 6m

— 9m

flood level

— 12m

— 15.2m

oak platform sealed with coconut fibre and putty

— 18.2m

— 21.3m

In 1804, Smith and his partner Simeon Lynds discovered and removed an inscribed stone tablet from the pit

— 24.4m

— 27.4m

The Truro Syndicate drilled through oak, a layer of metal, more oak, another layer of metal and finally a layer of spruce. They thought the drill had struck a treasure chest

— 32.3m

The flood tunnel. As soon as the excavators reached this depth, water rushed in from the sea

The Oak Island Treasure Company's drill struck a sheet of iron

— 38.4m

At 46m the drill struck some soft stone and below that a thin layer of oak. Then it struck loose metal and a parchment fragment on which the letters V.I. were clearly seen

— 46m

The diagram illustrates what excavations of the Money Pit revealed.

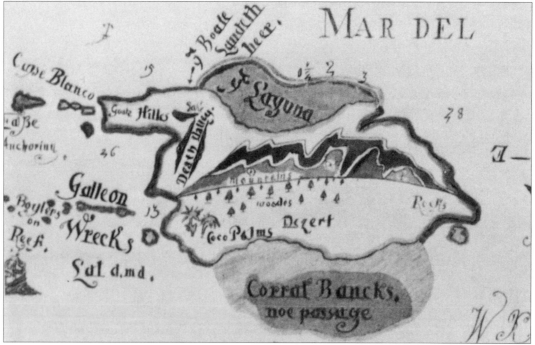

One theory about the digging on the Money Pit is that British troops may have secreted funds there during the American War of Independence (top). The map (above) is said to be of the island where Captain Kidd buried his treasure. Could it be Oak Island, site of the Money Pit?

dynamite to dam the tunnels connecting the pit with the sea in a vain bid to prevent the flooding. Another team struck metal, and a fragment brought to the surface on the bit contained a piece of parchment on which the letters 'V I' could be clearly made out. Another explorer published 'proof' that maps drafted by the infamous pirate Captain Kidd pointed to his treasure having been buried there.

In 1963 the pit claimed its worst casualties. On 17 August Robert Restall was overcome by the exhaust fumes of his pump, and both he, his son, John, and two other men who tried to rescue him died. In 1965 Robert Dunfield squandered $120,000, merely succeeding in making more huge holes. There have been several attempts since then, including one adventurer who swam up the deep flood tunnel to try to find the treasure.

Who built this amazing feat of engineering? One author who has studied the Money Pit thinks that it was the work of British Army engineers during the American War of Independence. Rupert Furneaux, who has written an authoritative account of the pit called *Money Pit: The Mystery of Oak Island*, claims that they buried money there in case of a reversal in the war's fortunes. But this does not answer the question of what happened to the money. Nor are there British Army records of such an enterprise.

The secret lies in the mud, along with the bodies, sweat and money which have been spent vainly trying to find the secret of the Money Pit.

An event occurred during John Smith's excavation of the Money Pit, no explanation for which has ever been found – but which could be a vital clue in the puzzle. The drilling foreman, a man named James Pitblado, was accused of taking something shiny from the drill as he scooped out the items brought up in the bit. The men, furious, demanded that he produce it, but he refused, pledging to reveal whatever it was to the directors of the syndicate the next time a full meeting was held. Pitblado later tried to buy the entire eastern end of Oak Island, hopeful that he could then launch his own drilling operations. Legend has it that Pitblado dragged out a jewel, but he vanished soon afterwards, and whether he had a gemstone or not remains a mystery.

CASPAR HAUSER

There was something about the boy that made him stand out from the throng. Aged about 16, he was shabbily dressed. He wore a cut-down frock coat with tattered breeches and split boots held together with horseshoe nails. He shuffled nervously, with faltering steps, across one of the grander squares of the German city of Nuremberg on a Whit Monday holiday of 26 May 1828.

Perhaps it was the boots that made George Weichmann, a cobbler, pay particular attention to the boy. Or perhaps it was a paternal streak in the gentle cobbler. Whatever the reason, he approached the youth – and heard him whimpering softly to himself, apparently oblivious to his surroundings.

The boy's response to Weichmann's questions of concern were unintelligible; it was as if he did not understand a word. Instead he thrust at him an envelope bearing the legend: 'The Captain of the 4th Squadron, 6th Cavalry Regiment'.

Weichmann took the sealed envelope and led the strange youth to the captain's residence nearby. The captain was not at home but his servant invited the shoemaker and his new companion to wait for his master's return.

Meanwhile the servant offered them food. The strange youngster turned up his nose at fine beer, and food that included the famous little sausages of the town when they were produced for him – but wolfed down plain brown bread and water.

He managed to grunt a few words to the shoemaker when he asked who he was and where he came from. He replied: 'I want to be a soldier, like father . . . horse . . . home . . . father'. And he pointed to his feet, encased in the shabby boots, and cried, as in pain.

The captain arrived presently, provoking great interest in the young man, who was obviously excited by his uniform. Weichmann handed the captain the envelope, which turned out to contain not one but two letters.

The first purported to be written by a labourer into whose charge the unfortunate boy had been delivered in 1812. He said that he could no longer look after him, as he had 10 other children and could not support Caspar as well. He also said that the boy, since being deposited with him (it did not make clear why or how) had spent the whole time locked up in his house, with no contact with the outside world.

The letter was dated 1828 and ended: 'If his parents had lived he might have been well educated; for if you show him anything he can do it right off'.

The second letter was dated 16 years earlier, in 1812, and claimed to be from the boy's natural mother. 'Take care of my child', read the scrawl. 'He has been baptised. His father was a soldier in the 6th Cavalry.'

This was too much for the captain, who turned the boy over to the city authorities, who in turn gave him over to the police as a waif. They locked him in a cell, where a jailer made the curious observation:

'He can and does sit for hours without moving a limb. He does not pace the floor nor does he try to sleep. He sits rigidly without growing in the least uncomfortable. Also, he prefers darkness to light and can move about in it like a cat'.

He was given a piece of paper upon which he scratched just three words. One was Reiter, German for cavalryman. The other two words were 'Caspar Hauser'.

Among his meagre possessions were found a black silk neckerchief and a white handkerchief with the initials 'C H' worked in red in one of the corners. He was immediately named Caspar Hauser, although there was not one single tangible clue as to his identity or to where he originated from.

One kind jailer took Caspar into his own private apartment and observed the boy unseen. He thought him a creature of childlike actions, but believed there lay behind his apparent imbecility a stronger, more intelligent force. Caspar could sulk like a baby, but when amused or interested his face positively beamed with an engaging smile. He walked like a child, too, overbalancing and unsteady as though he had had little practice of this most elementary of human skills. It was as if he had had very little contact with people or with the outside world.

His attentive jailer provided Caspar with a toy wooden horse which the boy loved, and within six weeks he had learned a string of new words, showing an impressive eagerness to learn and an innate, natural intelligence. He set about introducing his protégé to the outside world.

In the 19th century the gracious German city of Nuremberg was the epitome of a provincial centre slowly coming to terms with the great changes brought about by the industrial revolution. The second city of Bavaria, after Munich, it enjoyed the distinction of being replete with fine buildings and many art treasures. It was known as the treasure house of Germany.

But it was not Nuremberg's churches, or its paintings or sculptures, which rocketed it to European fame in 1828. It was the arrival of the jailer's protégé. Such a curiosity – as he emerged into a world intrigued by fables and the extraordinary – made Caspar the talk of Nuremberg. Within six weeks, the shabbily-clad waif from nowhere was the talk of all Germany.

Caspar's fame impelled the Burgomeister of Nuremberg to don his official robes to visit him. His purpose was to elicit the secrets of Caspar's past; and, while he was not much enlightened, he was certainly not at all disappointed by the tale Caspar Hauser had to tell.

 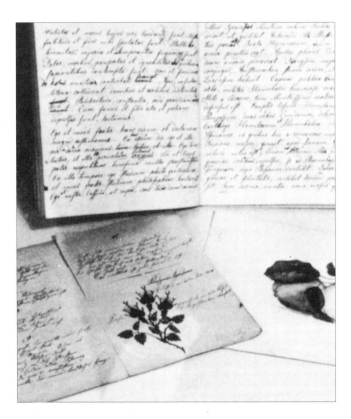

Caspar Hauser playing with a wooden horse, and his protector and tutor, Professor Daumer (left). The drawings and writings (right) made by Caspar were quite accomplished.

An artist's impression of Caspar Hauser as he would have appeared to the cobbler, George Weichmann.

CASPAR HAUSER

Caspar said he had lived all his life in a tiny cell 1.8 metres (6 ft) long, 1.4 metres (4½ ft) wide and 1.7 metres (5½ ft) high. The windows were permanently shuttered, he had to sleep on a straw mattress, and his feet were kept bare. His only nourishment was bread and water, and he said that the water often tasted bitter. When it did, he recalled falling asleep immediately after drinking it. When he woke up, he would find a clean shirt in his cell, next to the two wooden horses and wooden dogs that were left for him to play with.

A mysterious man was behind all this. Caspar said he never saw his face, but before he was turned out and sent to Nuremberg, the man, wearing a mask, showed Caspar how to trace the letters of the words Caspar Hauser.

Finally, Caspar recalled how he was taught to stand and walk. He said he had been given the letters and then set about his journey to Nuremberg, an odyssey about which he could remember nothing except the pain in his feet.

The Nuremberg council published this account in a much edited text, and the document on the 'Child of Nuremberg' took Caspar's story to the far corners of Europe and beyond. He became, in 20th-century parlance, a celebrity.

An appeal was sent out from the city fathers for information about Caspar. Rumours flourished – not least that he had been shut away because he was the illegitimate son of royalty.

Occultists said he came from the Devil, while fortune tellers and mystics blamed Caspar's arrival on beings from another world. And there were those, too, who denounced him as a charlatan and a con man. Whatever the reality, the authorities entrusted to trace his origins were stumped.

While these searches continued, Caspar was placed into the care of George Daumer, a professor noted for his work in education and philosophy. Daumer was impressed by Caspar. Caspar had a finely attuned, almost animal sense of smell. He could see well in the dark, identify trees by sniffing the air, and soon learned to write and draw extremely well.

What seemed to baffle him were elementary physical phenomena of the age. He would even try to pinch the flames of burning candles, recoiling in pain when the fire burned him.

Like John Merrick, the Elephant Man, who drew crowds of visitors eager to gawp at something so utterly different from the norm, Caspar Hauser became a sideshow figure, receiving at his apartment in Professor Daumer's home the elite of German drawing room society.

Caspar seemed to revel in the attention showered upon him. The visits of educated men and women fuelled their interests and suspicions, which soon fell on the Duke of Baden who was believed to have cruelly imprisoned Caspar because he was his bastard son. Needless to say, such charges have never been proved.

In October 1829, some three months after Professor Daumer had set himself the task of writing a full and detailed biography of Caspar, there was a startling development.

On 7 October Caspar was discovered unconscious, with a stab wound in his head, in the cellar of the professor's home. He said, when he came round, that he had been attacked by a man wearing a black mask. The news was electric, fuelling rumours once again that someone, somewhere, probably highly placed, had loosed an assassin on the unfortunate Caspar to silence him in case he revealed details of his past. The cynics, naturally, said the wound was self-inflicted.

Nevertheless, Caspar was moved from the custody of the benevolent Professor Daumer and given into the care of the city. He was placed at a secret address, under police guard, and for two years enjoyed the benefits of being looked after out of the public purse – a situation of which even the citizens of Nuremberg soon tired.

The story could have ended here, with Caspar being put back upon the highways, had it not been for the arrival in May 1831 of the eccentric Englishman Lord Stanhope, who came to Nuremberg and virtually adopted Caspar. He persuaded the city authorities to allow him to become his guardian, and he promised to look into the boy's past.

Sadly, Stanhope treated Caspar more like a fairground attraction than an enigma to be deciphered; he touted him around the minor courts of Europe, and the relationship between the two of them was less than harmonious.

In 1833 he took him to Ansbach, near Nuremberg, to lodge in the care of Pastor Meyer, a suspicious, mean-minded man who employed a bodyguard named Hickel to watch over Caspar. Hickel was a thug but restrained from harming Caspar because of the enormous public and royal interest in him.

Both Stanhope and Meyer, however, seemed to lose interest in the boy. Stanhope left him in the permanent care of Meyer in 1833. And Meyer himself virtually abandoned him some months later after he failed to acquit himself well in the Latin and religious studies he had been set.

On 11 December 1833 Caspar Hauser was savagely attacked by an unknown assailant as he walked in a local park. He staggered back to Meyer's house, bleeding profusely. In his great pain he managed to communicate that he had been stabbed by a man who had asked him his name. Upon hearing it he had plunged a knife into his ribs.

Meyer refused to believe Caspar – but three days later Caspar Hauser died, denying that he had killed himself and maintaining that he was not an impostor.

Before Caspar's assassin had run off, he had dropped a black wallet which the police later found. In it was a note, written in mirror writing, which said:

'Hauser will be able to tell you how I look, whence I came from and who I am. To spare him the task, I will tell you myself. I am from . . . on the Bavarian border . . . on the river . . . My name is MLO'.

And that, in effect, was the last scrap of evidence about Caspar Hauser. He was buried in a quiet country churchyard. His gravestone reads: 'Here lies Caspar Hauser, enigma. His birth was unknown, his death mysterious.'

Ever since the arrival in Nuremberg of Caspar Hauser (if, indeed, that was his true name) there has been unending exploration into his past. Was he an impostor, a royal prince, an alien being, a true waif? Researchers have come to the same dead end. Caspar Hauser is as mysterious today as he was when he hobbled into the square in Nuremberg on those painful feet.

THE YETI

In 1832 the British explorer B H Hodgson travelled deep into the Himalayas to record the lifestyle of the Nepalese. In one letter home he told how the tribespeople lived in fear of a mysterious, tall, erect creature covered in thick black hair. In one incident reported to Hodgson, porters had fled in terror from this animal. They called it the 'Rakshas' – Sanskrit for demon.

Hodgson himself was scathing of the eye-witness accounts. He believed the porters had probably seen a stray orangutan. But as the years passed by, evidence of an unknown creature living in one of the world's last great wildernesses was mounting.

Though he hadn't realised it, Hodgson had been first to tell the Western World of the possible existence of the Yeti.

It was 50 years before the tale was revived in the West, courtesy of Major L Waddell of the Indian Army Medical Corps. He told of seeing large footprints which, it was claimed, belonged to 'one of the hairy men who live in the eternal snows'. Waddell however was also sceptical, believing the Yeti were in fact snow bears.

In his book *Among the Himalayas* he reported: 'The belief in these creatures is universal among Tibetans. None, however, of the Tibetans I have interrogated on the subject could ever give me an authentic case. On the most superficial investigation it always resolved into something that somebody had heard tell of'.

Then in 1914 a British forestry official, J R P Gent, told of discovering bizarre footprints near a remote lodge in Sikkim. He noted: 'The peculiar feature is that its tracks are about 45 to 60 cm (18 to 24 in) long and the toes point in the opposite direction to that in which the animal is moving. I take it that he walks on his knees and shins instead of on the souls of his feet'.

Gent's observations were largely ignored at home. There was, after all, a war on and men with a taste for adventure were rushing to sign up for king and country. But during the 1920s his account was given a much wider circulation. One newspaper referred to the unknown creature as the 'Abominable Snowman'. This phrase gripped the public's imagination and soon there were dozens of mountaineering expeditions heading for the Himalayas. Many climbers claimed to have seen the Snowman. None produced any hard evidence.

But some of the sightings simply could not be put down to over-active imaginations.

The photographer N A Tombazi saw a Yeti in the spring of 1925 when he was climbing the Zemu glacier. It was about 300 metres (1000 ft) away in a low valley and at first the sunlight glaring off the snow made it almost impossible for him to describe. Slowly, as his eyes adjusted to the intense light, the image became clearer. His account later appeared in the book *Bigfoot* by author John Napier.

As a Fellow of the British Royal Geographical Society, Tombazi is deservedly regarded as one of the most reliable witnesses in the whole Yeti mystery. A seasoned traveller, he was certainly well aware of the tricks which light could sometimes play. He also knew the importance of accurate observation.

Tombazi told how one of the Sherpas spotted the creature and drew his attention to it. This is how he described the next few moments:

'Unquestionably the figure in outline was exactly like a human being, walking upright and stopping occasionally to uproot or pull at some dwarf rhododendron bushes. It showed up dark against the snow and, as far as I could make out, wore no clothes. Within the next minute or so it had moved into some thick scrub and was lost to view. Such a fleeting glimpse, unfortunately, did not allow me to set the tele-photo camera, or even to fix the object carefully with my binoculars.

'But a couple of hours later, during the descent, I purposely made a detour so as to pass the place where the man or beast had been seen. I examined the footprints, which were clearly visible on the surface of the snow. They were similar in shape to those of a man. The prints were undoubtedly biped, having no characteristics whatever of any imagined quadruped. From inquiries I made a few days later at Yokson

Is this the face of the Yeti? Reports of sightings emphasise its hairy, ape-like appearance.

Relics that are said to be a Yeti scalp and hand.

on my return journey, I gather that no man had gone in that direction since the beginning of the year'.

Tombazi's account was given added weight by the 1936 expedition of Ronald Kaulback, who also reported seeing giant footprints. The following year the first photograph of the mysterious tracks were published, though this actually proved very little. The Abominable Snowman remained as he had always been – both reclusive and elusive. On 8 November 1951 another highly-regarded witness emerged in the form of the respected mountaineer and naturalist Eric Shipton. He and his British colleague Michael Ward, together with their Sherpa, Sen Tensing, came across some perfect tracks some 5500 metres (18,000 ft) up the Men-lung glacier in the Gauri Sankar mountain range.

Shipton judged that the 33 by 20 cm (13 by 8 in) print was made by a flat-footed beast up to 2.4 metres (8 ft) tall. He produced photographs of a second trail, which was later dismissed by critics as goat hoof-prints which had expanded in the heat of the sun. This theory was itself ridiculed by many eminent scientists. Besides, Shipton was an acknowledged world expert on animal tracks and not a man to reach conclusions lightly.

Throughout the 1950s the hunt went on. Everest conqueror Sir Edmund Hillary was deeply sceptical of the Yeti's existence, yet sufficiently intrigued to mount his own expedition in 1960. He returned with a scalp claimed to have been hacked from a Yeti. Zoologists identified it as antelope hair yet it was still a valuable specimen. The hair contained a type of parasite unknown to scientists. Right up to the present day reports have continued to filter in. Careful analysis shows certain common threads which will undoubtedly prove invaluable for future expeditions.

The Yeti appears to live at heights of between 3600 and 6000 metres (12,000 and 20,000 ft), preferring dense forests close to the seasonal snow line. Nepalese villagers believe they live mainly in caves, venturing out mainly in darkness but occasionally driven by hunger to hunt for food in the daytime. Some witnesses claim the creature is 3.6 metres (12 ft) high and extremely agile; others put it considerably smaller and talk of it lolloping along swinging its arms.

The head is apparently conical with facial characteristics somewhere between humans and apes. The fur is thick and red and covers every part of the body except the face. The creature's diet is rumoured to be mainly rodents and lichen and they apparently show the curiously human trait of disembowelling meat before beginning their meal.

It is all fascinating stuff. But what about the oh-so-elusive hard evidence? Critical observers still question why, in an age of ever-expanding technology, scientists have not been able to come up with some more concrete proof – a body or bones, for example. The answer has been succinctly summed up by Richard Greenwell of the American based International Society of Cryptozoology. He observed: 'You would need 10 thousand people to actually catch a Wildman because the area is so vast and densely forested. You could pass a yard from one and not know it was there'.

For the time being, at least, the mystery remains unsolved.

THE YETI

To the surprise of sceptics, recent hard evidence of the Yeti's existence has now been presented – though not from the Yeti's traditional stamping ground. The specimens which set anthropologists into fits of excitement came from across the Himalayas in China.

For decades China had sealed its borders to the West and it was not until the late 1980s that a more open view began to prevail in Beijing. This new mood set off a rush of scientific expeditions from the West, including one financed jointly by six countries, including the United States and Britain. The aim was to find evidence of the Wildman of China, a creature apparently similar to the Yeti and its North American equivalent, Bigfoot.

The party led by Gene Poirier, professor of Anthropology at Ohio State University, collected a number of hair samples. These had been found by farmers working some of the most remote regions of central China. Shanghai's Fudan University had already declared that the samples were not from any known man or ape.

At Ohio and at Birmingham University in England, researchers used special electron microscopes to establish that the hairs contained 54 times as much zinc and iron as human hairs, and 8 times as much as animal hairs. Professor Poirier, an avowed sceptic of Yeti-type creatures declared: 'We have established that the animal does not fall into any known category. This is the first evidence of the existence of a new higher primate'.

BLACK HOLES

Black holes are one of the great mysteries of space. They are the powerhouses of the universe: forces of unimaginably concentrated energy. Their gravitational pull is so strong that even light cannot escape from them. If manned spacecraft were sent to distant planets, black holes would be among the greatest hazards faced on the journey.

Black holes, the collective name given to stars which have collapsed in on themselves, are as mysterious as they are fascinating. What little is known of the phenomena is largely due to theories painstakingly worked out by scientists and astronomers through recent years. As one eminent observer of the universe put it: 'Black holes are as pervasive in theory as they are evasive in observation'.

It was in the last century that experts began to piece together the puzzle of black holes. In life, a star contains almost inconceivable amounts of energy, so dense in matter that if it collapsed in on itself, the gravitational pull would be so strong that nothing, not even light, would escape from it. It would become invisible, the extraordinary gravitational pull allowing nothing whatever to escape from its clutches. Even light which passed near the black hole – from stars, planets, passing meteorites – would be sucked in and vanish forever.

The laws of nature as we know them on planet Earth would no longer apply in such an alien environment. The largest battleship ever built could be plunged into a black hole and it would stretch like a piece of elastic – before disintegrating into a billion particles of matter. The matter itself would also disintegrate in time, leaving only the image of the battleship for all eternity on the outer fringes of the hole where the last dying particles of light linger.

If this scientific theory is hard to follow, consider the gravity of the Earth: were a man to fall from a skyscraper, he would plummet to his death, drawn irresistibly downwards by the Earth's gravitational pull. But it takes the whole gravitational pull of the entire planet to make even a feather fall downwards; so, relatively, gravity is a weak force.

However, if the Earth were condensed in size to something with the circumference of a tennis ball, it would be so dense that no light would be able to escape from it. The density would, say experts, be upwards of three thousand times that of known matter. And a tonne of it would be small enough to fit into a matchbox!

The stars nearest in structure to black holes are white dwarfs. They were discovered in the 19th century by the German-born astronomer Friedrich Bessel, who was studying the star Sirius, brightest in the galaxy. In 1844, using the most sophisticated telescope available to him, he noticed that Sirius' movement was wavy rather than in a straight line – as if some unseen force had a gravitational pull on it.

It was only 20 years later that an American astronomer spotted small diffusions of bright light while testing a new telescope. The white light indicated an intensely hot star which, by the rule applied then, suggested a huge mass. Yet the nature of the diffused light implied that, although it contained massive amounts of energy, it was small; only its mass was gigantic. This was the energy source which scientists christened a 'white dwarf'.

Scientists believe that a star turns into a white dwarf in four stages. First, hydrogen in the star's core is fused into helium; and, after several billion years, all the hydrogen is used up. Second, the star's core contracts, its exterior expands and the star becomes a red giant. Third, the outer layers of the red giant are gradually expelled until, finally, all that remains is the super-dense mass of the white dwarf.

The black hole is one stage advanced from the white dwarf, where no light can be seen and the gravitational force is millions of times greater than anything we know. According to Einstein's famous theory of relativity, a black hole would appear infinite inside, and there would be no escape for anything.

BLACK HOLES

The Andromeda galaxy (top) is similar in size and mass to the Milky Way, which contains our own solar system – and probably innumerable black holes. Albert Einstein (above), the most famous physicist of all time, recognised the existence of black holes.

A black hole would swallow the largest space craft in a millisecond.

BLACK HOLES

Because there are so many stars in the universe capable of collapsing in on themselves and turning into black holes, scientists estimate up to 90 per cent of space travel could be exceptionally hazardous for manned craft.

Because of their very nature, no one has ever seen a black hole, although a great deal of research is going on to find them. At present scientists can only point to where some may be by applying Bessel's logic and studying those stars which seem to be affected by the gravitational force of an invisible body.

A further problem in studying black holes is that even if astronomers knew when a star was going to collapse in on itself, the event would occur so quickly that they would not have time to witness it. Professor John Taylor, a British mathematician, says in his book *Black Holes: The End of the Universe?* that a star ten times the size of our sun would fade from view in four-millionths of a second, while one that was a million times heavier than the sun would vanish in one-quarter of a second.

As black holes are sources of such immense energy, some scientists are investigating ways of harnessing that energy – a task which sounds, on the face of it, quite impossible. Cambridge genius Stephen Hawking argues that the extraordinary gravitational pull near the entrance to a black hole would be strong enough to split atoms into particles and anti-particles, which on Earth would mean that atoms would destroy themselves in much the same way as in a gigantic nuclear blast.

But because the laws of nature and science do not apply to black holes, one of the pair – particle and antiparticle – would escape back into the hole, and the process would be continued.

Albert Einstein went one stage further down the doomsday road. Since the universe is littered with black holes, he and many scientists have argued that eventually all galaxies risk collapsing in on themselves, turning the universe into one giant black hole. This would occur, according to Einstein, because of the 'big bang' theory – which surmises that the universe was formed by a gigantic explosion and is constantly expanding. If that is so, what is to stop it from flying apart?

Einstein said there must be enough mass in the universe to hold it together. This mass could be in the form of black holes, acting as the counter-weights to the big bang and drawing the stars and planets back towards them. Taken to its logical conclusion, the black holes would eventually consume everything – and our universe would simply disappear!

Theorists argue that soon it might be possible to create a black hole in a laboratory, bringing to life the theories of Einstein, and giving mathematicians and astronomers perspectives on space never before realised. Professor Taylor, however, is one sceptic of such an experiment. According to his prediction, if a black hole weighing just 16 tonnes were somehow artificially constructed in a laboratory, it would immediately sink to the centre of the Earth and destroy it, much as a black hole would destroy the unwary space traveller who strayed into it. Perhaps that is one experiment best left untried.

BIGFOOT

The first frontiersmen who braved the wilderness in the northwest of the United States were also the first white men to hear the amazing stories of wild, hairy beasts of the woods. Throughout the forests and mountains that covered the uncharted terrain, from California in the south to Alaska in the north, lurked an awesome creature that struck fear into even the bravest settler. According to the Indians whose domain this once was, these man-like beasts of no known species were about 2.5 metres (8 ft) tall, with broad chest and shoulders but virtually no neck. They were covered in auburn hair and walked with a stoop. It was known by the Indians as Sasquatch – later named by the white man as Bigfoot.

The reason for the beast's new name became clear to the world in the 19th century when explorer David Thomas discovered evidence of the strange animal, in the shape of footprints, at least 35 cm (14 in) long, near Jasper, Alberta.

In 1851 the first recorded newspaper report of such creature was published in Arkansas, far from where most Bigfoot sightings have since been made. The creature, which was seen chasing a herd of cattle, was described as 'an animal bearing the unmistakable likeness of humanity, thought to be a survivor of the earthquake which devastated the area in 1811'. The report went on: 'He was of a gigantic stature, the body being covered with hair and the head with long locks that fairly enveloped the neck and shoulders. The wild man, after looking at them deliberately for a short time, turned and ran away with great speed, leaping 3 to 4 metres (12 to 14 ft) at a time. His footprints measured 32cm (13 in) each'.

In 1884, *The Colonist*, the principal newspaper for British Columbia, gave an account of the capture of a Sasquatch. This creature, nicknamed Jacko by the local settlers, was spotted by the crew of a train travelling along the Fraser River from the town of Lytton to Yale. They pursued it, captured it by knocking it unconscious with a rock and, having locked it in the guard's van, took it into Yale.

There it was examined and was described as being 'gorilla-like, with coarse black hair' except for its hands and feet. It was presumed to be a young Sasquatch, as it was only 1.4 metres (4½ ft) tall and weighed 60 kg (127 lb). Its diet was berries and milk. The poor creature was exhibited in the Yale area before being sold to Barnum and Bailey's Circus. But Sasquatch Junior is said to have died in his crate while on the long rail journey to his new circus home.

The Bigfoot stories gained ultimate credibility, however, in 1903 when no less a person than President Theodore Roosevelt retold the story of two trappers in the Salmon River district of Idaho who were attacked by a mysterious creature.

In 1918 the *Seattle Times* reported a dramatic attack by 'mountain devils' on a prospector on Mount St Helen, Washington. In the same state, a lumber camp worker came face-to-face with a large 'ape-like' beast.

Of all encounters with Bigfoot, the most dramatic was reported in 1924 by Albert Ostman, also a lumberman, from Langley, British Columbia. Ostman was camping opposite Vancouver Island when he was abducted by a giant Bigfoot. Ostman said the beast, about 2.5 metres (8 ft) tall, picked him up, still in his sleeping bag, and carried him 'like a sack of potatoes' for 3 hours. As dawn broke, he realised that they had reached the creature's lair.

Ostman now surveyed his captors. He was being held by four Bigfoot: male and female adults and a pair of male and female children. Dumped in their lair, the lumberman still had his rifle with him but was reluctant to use it since the ape-like family had done him no harm. He also still had a few cans of food and other provisions that were buried in his sleeping bag. Some of these he ate while the Bigfoot family dined on spruce tips, sweet grass and roots. The woodsman was allowed the freedom of the valley in which he was held, although always followed by at least two of the creatures.

BIGFOOT

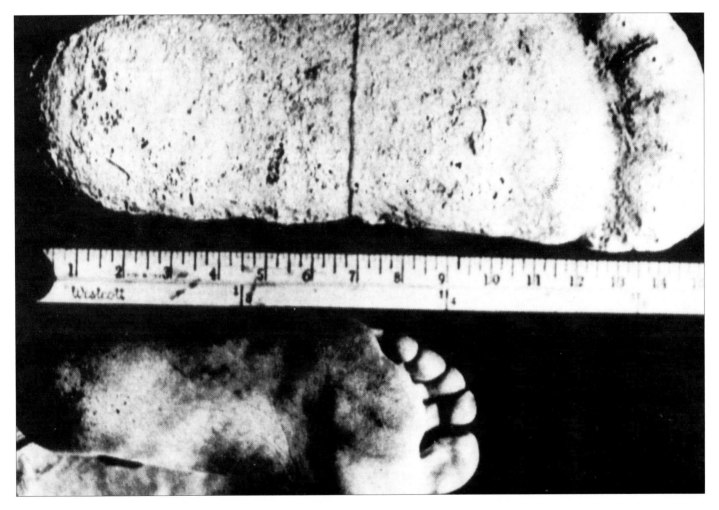

A creature reported to be Bigfoot, also known as Sasquatch, fleeing through timberland. A man's footprint, compared to a giant footprint (above) claimed to belong to Bigfoot.

Eventually, fearing that he had been kidnapped as a possible husband for one of the children, he determined to escape. He fed the largest Bigfoot some snuff and, while the creature rushed to bury his face in a stream, Ostman fled. He had been held captive for an entire week but, fearing ridicule, did not immediately tell his story. And when he did, it seemed incredible – except for the many later pieces of evidence which backed his descriptions of the beastly Bigfoot.

Another encounter the same year was reported from the area now known as Ape Canyon, on the Oregon-Washington border. When prospectors there shot and killed one of a group of Bigfoot, the survivors attacked their camp, causing considerable damage but no serious injury. Reporters who later visited the site told of seeing hundreds of giant footprints. The man who had fired the first shot, Fred Beck, gave a full version of the attack to Dr John Napier, author of the fascinating book *Bigfoot*.

Napier tells his story:

'At night the apes counter-attacked, opening the assault by knocking a heavy strip of wood out from between two logs of the miners' cabin. After that there were assorted poundings on the walls, door and roof but the building was designed to withstand heavy mountain snows and the apes failed to break in. The miners fired shots through the walls and roof without driving them away. The noise went on from shortly after dark until nearly dawn. Mr Beck could not say that there were more than two creatures outside. There were that many because there had been one on the roof and one pounding the wall simultaneously. However many there were, it was enough for the miners, who packed up and abandoned their mine the next day'.

In 1933 two men observed a Bigfoot leisurely munching berries in a clearing at Pitt Lake, northern British Columbia. They described it as having 'a human-like face on a fur-clad body'. In the same province, the Chapman family, of Ruby Creek, fled their lonely farmhouse when a Bigfoot attacked it. But it lost interest and meandered away after overturning a barrel of salted fish.

In 1955 occurred one of the clearest-ever sightings of a Bigfoot. It was made at Mica Mountain, British Columbia, by William Roe from his vantage point behind a thick bush. Suddenly, out of the undergrowth appeared a female Bigfoot, about 1.8 metres (6 ft) tall and weighing around 135 kg (300 lb).

The giant creature approached Roe, unaware that she was being watched. When she got to within 6 metres (20 ft) of him she squatted down in front of the bush in which Roe was hiding, enabling him to make a thorough study of the beast. He was later able to describe in detail her enormous body, the shape of her head, what kind of face and hair she had and the way she walked. His report of the event continued:

'Finally, the wild thing must have got my scent, for it looked directly at me through a small opening in the bush. Still in a crouched position, it backed up three or four short steps then straightened up to its full height and started to walk rapidly back the way it had come. For a moment it watched me over its shoulders as it went, not exactly afraid, but as though it wanted no contact with anything strange'.

Roe admitted that he had thought of shooting the creature as proof of its existence. He even got as far as raising his rifle and aiming – but he could not fire.

Further south, in Humboldt county, northern California, truck driver Jerry Crew found clear 'Bigfoot' tracks in the mud and took a plaster cast of one. The photograph prompted fresh interest in the mystery.

At nearby Bluff Creek, in 1958, a road construction worker encountered a Bigfoot which, he said, he could only get rid of by offering a candy bar. Later, construction site workers awoke one morning to find 40 cm (16 in) footprints in the snow around their cabins at Bluff Creek. The distance between the prints meant that a creature or creatures had been prowling around during the night, taking strides of up to 1.5 metres (5 ft). They also discovered that a huge fuel drum had been moved from one end of the camp to the other. A search party set out to hunt the beasts and picked one of them up in their truck headlights before losing it in dense woodland. In 1963 one of the creatures returned to Bluff Creek and attacked another construction site. A newspaper report at the time credited the beast with sufficient strength to overturn a truck.

BIGFOOT

The famed explorer and aptly named oilman, Tom Slick, whose passion had been hunting the Abominable Snowman of Nepal, now launched himself into the search for Bigfoot. But in 1963 he crashed in his private plane, leaving the findings of his expeditions unrevealed.

The big breakthrough in the hunt for Bigfoot came on 20 October 1967. Roger Patterson, a former rodeo cowboy and rancher, was tracking the forests around Bluff Creek with an Indian friend, Bob Gimlin, when they emerged from woodland into a clearing – and came face to face with a Bigfoot. Patterson took his movie camera from its case and aimed it at the beast as it ambled along the bank of the creek. He shot an amazing 9 metres (29 ft) of colour film as it loped across his field of vision. Patterson and Gimlin also took casts of footprints left by the creature.

The film was shown worldwide and most experts believed it to be genuine, although some disputed Patterson's belief that the creature was female. One copy was given to Bigfoot investigator Dr Napier, who was more sceptical. He wrote:

'The upper part of the body bears some resemblance to an ape and the lower half is typically human. It is almost impossible to conceive that such structural hybrids could exist in nature. One half of it must be artificial'.

Other pieces of evidence were shown to Dr Napier over the years, principally the so-called 'Minnesota Iceman', a hairy gorilla-like humanoid at first said to have been found preserved in a massive block of ice in the Bering Straits. Later versions of its discovery had it being shot by hunters along the snowline of a northwestern mountain. Dr Napier judged this specimen – as many others – to be 'transparently dubious'. This leading expert on Bigfoot does have the final, convincing word on the mystery, however. He wrote:

'The North American Bigfoot or Sasquatch has a lot going for it. Too many claim to have seen it, or at least to have seen footprints, to dismiss its reality out of hand. To suggest that hundreds of people at worst are lying or at best deluding themselves is neither proper nor realistic'.

This is Albert Fletcher's account of his encounter with a Bigfoot:

'In the fall of 1917, when I was 17 years old, I was working for a lumber camp on the Cowlitz River. One moonlit evening, I was walking down a logging road en route to a dance when I had the uneasy feeling that something was following close behind me. I kept looking over my shoulder but could not see anything. When I came to a bend in the road I ducked behind a tree and waited to see what it was. Almost immediately a very large man-like creature about 6½ or 7 ft (about 2 metres) tall came into view.

'It was walking on its hind legs, was covered with dark hair, had a bearded face and a large chest and, so far as I could see, was not wearing clothes of any kind. Startled, I let out a yell of alarm and the creature instantly turned and ran off into the woods, still on its hind legs. I told some of my co-workers about it and some of them laughed but others said they too had seen it. No one had an explanation for it and no name was given to it, but all agreed that it was a large, ape-like something and that it also resembled a very large man'.

THE MARY CELESTE

She emerged as no more than a speck on the horizon. The crew of the *Dei Gratia* looked out to sea from time to time as she grew closer and her shape clearer. She was a two-masted, square-rigged brigantine, just like the *Dei Gratia* – but something was wrong about her.

The *Dei Gratia* gained steadily on the strange ship throughout a long, hot day until the two vessels were parallel. By afternoon, the fascinated crew of the *Dei Gratia* took turns to examine the mysterious vessel as she wove her way erratically through the swell of the Atlantic. The deck of the *Dei Gratia* was by now crowded. The deck of the other vessel was entirely deserted.

Through his spyglass, Captain David Morehouse examined the brigantine from bow to stern. The ship was lurching through the water in an ungainly fashion and Morehouse found it difficult to keep his eye focused on the strange scene. He saw that she had only two of her sails set, the others being still furled or ripped to tatters. There was not a soul in sight. No one was at the wheel. There was no sign of life what-soever. Morehouse aimed his spyglass at the bow and focused on the ship's nameplate. It read: *Mary Celeste*.

The *Mary Celeste*, built at Spencer Island, Nova Scotia, was launched in 1861 as the Amazon and imme-diately hit a series of mishaps. Her first skipper fell ill and died on the eve of her maiden voyage. His replacement ran her into a fishing boat on her maiden voyage and the brig had to return to port for repairs. In dock, a fire broke out.

On her first Atlantic crossing, the jinx seemed to have been lifted. But as the Amazon entered the Straits of Dover, she collided with another brig, which sank. Again patched up, the Amazon returned to Nova Scotia where she promptly ran aground on a sandbank.

This time the owners had run out of patience. The ship was sold several times and ended up with a New York consortium who renamed her the *Mary Celeste*. The name itself was reputedly a mistake. The signwriter was supposed to have painted the word 'Marie' to match the spelling with the French 'Celeste'! (Ironically, 'Marie' is the name by which most people today incorrectly refer to her.)

And so it came to be that the *Mary Celeste* set sail from New York's Staten Island on 7 November 1872 under the captaincy of Benjamin Spooner Briggs. This proud, puritan, teetotal, Massachusetts mariner had hired an experienced crew of mate, second mate, cook and four seamen. Also aboard were Captain Briggs' wife Sarah and one of their children, two-year-old Sophia, leaving an elder son at home. The cargo was 1700 barrels of denatured alcohol bound for Genoa, Italy.

Eight days later, on 15 November, the *Dei Gratia* also left New York, bound for Gibraltar with a cargo of petroleum – and at 3 pm on 5 December the two ships met about 640 km (400 miles) west of Lisbon, Portugal.

Having hailed the *Mary Celeste* without result, Captain Morehouse ordered the ship's boat launched, and first mate Oliver Deveau, second mate John Wright and crewman John Johnson rowed across to the mystery brig. While Johnson remained in the boat, the other two men hauled themselves over the rails and for an hour searched the boat for any sign of life. There was none.

The rigging, seemingly battered by a storm, flapped in the wind. The jib, fore topmast staysail and fore lower topsail were all set; but the foresail and the upper foresail had been blown away and other sails were either still furled or in shreds. The binnacle had been knocked over, the compass lying smashed on the deck. The wheel spun freely. The cargo hatches were still securely battened, although water slopped in and out of an open galley door.

Below decks, the scene was even more eerie. In the galley preparations seemed to have been made for a meal, although nothing had been served. (Later stories that a meal had been set and the plates were still

MARY CELESTE

The Mary Celeste, *popularly, but wrongly, known to many as the* Marie Celeste.

Mrs Spooner Briggs (top left) and her husband (top right), captain of the ill-fated ship. The abandoned Mary Celeste *was sited by the crew of the* Dei Gratia *(above) in the Atlantic, 640 km west of Lisbon.*

warm are fiction.) In the crew's quarters, clothes lay on bunks and washing hung from lines. In the mate's cabin was a chart showing the position of the *Mary Celeste* up to 24 November.

In the captain's cabin, a melodeon belonging to Mrs Briggs still had a sheet of music in it. A sewing machine lay on a table. Daughter Sophia's spinning materials were undisturbed. On another table lay the log of Captain Benjamin Spooner Briggs. It read:

'Monday, 25th. At five o'clock made island of St Mary's bearing ESE. At eight o'clock, Eastern Point bore SSW six miles (10 km) distant'.

As fascinating as these discoveries were, more telling were the items that were missing from the ship: the sextant, chronometer, navigation book, cargo documentation – and the ship's small boat. A length of railing had been broken off where the boat had been lowered over the side.

When the crewmen of the *Dei Gratia* returned from their inspection, they and Captain Morehouse debated what could have caused the abandonment of the brigantine. The crew had obviously launched the small yawl and fled the safety of their ship. But why?

Had the *Mary Celeste* been abandoned in a storm? If so, why was there so little storm damage aboard? Crew crockery and the captain's fine bone china was unbroken. A bottle of cough medicine stood uncorked and unspilt on a table.

Had there been a mutiny? Why then would the mutineers abandon the ship along with the captain? In any case, there had been no sign of a struggle. Had the crew gone on a drunken rampage? True, as it was discovered later, nine of the alcohol casks in the hold were empty. But, as Deveau stated, the cargo hatches were perfectly battened down. And Captain Briggs was a strictly teetotal puritan who would not have countenanced drink being consumed on his ship. In any case, the cargo was denatured alcohol, which would have given the crew acute pains before they could have drunk enough to become intoxicated.

Had the ship been taking in water? A sounding rod was found on deck and there was 1 metre (3 ft) of water in the hold. But that was no more than any old wooden brig would have taken in over such a voyage and could easily have been pumped out.

All these speculations were to remain unanswered. An even greater mystery, however, was how the ship had managed to keep on course without a crew for 10 days and 800 km (500 miles). When the *Dei Gratia* had come alongside the *Mary Celeste*, the former had her sails set on a port tack while the latter was on a starboard tack. There was no way that the *Mary Celeste* could have travelled the entire course she had with her sails set that way. Someone had been on board after the last log entry of 25 November.

With these questions unanswered, Captain Morehouse put three of his men aboard the *Mary Celeste* and sailed with her to Gibraltar, where he claimed her as salvage reward. There he had to argue with the colony's bumbling Attorney General, Frederick Solly Flood, who at first accused the captain of being a conspirator with the missing Briggs in a plot to abandon the Mary Celeste in order to extort salvage money from her owners. His next ludicrous suggestion was that Captain Morehouse himself had slaughtered the crew.

Eventually Captain Morehouse and his men were granted the inadequate sum of £1700 – a fraction of the ship's worth – and the *Mary Celeste*, under a new crew, was allowed to continue her voyage to Genoa to offload her cargo before returning to the United States.

Over the next 11 years the *Mary Celeste* changed hands no fewer than 17 times. She was considered a jinxed ship, and none of her new owners would keep her for long. She sailed up and down America's eastern seaboard, losing crew and cargo alike, and suffering mishaps from collisions to shipboard fires.

In 1884 her final owners over-insured her and sent her to Haiti where, in the calmest of seas and with the clearest visibility, she ran aground. The conspirators were brought to court but the poor *Mary Celeste* rotted away forgotten on a coral reef.

The *Mary Celeste* was not the first ship to be found abandoned in the Atlantic Ocean. On 28 February 1855 the cargo ship *Marathon* encountered the barquentine *James B. Chester* about 1000 km (600 miles) southwest of the Azores. A boarding party discovered that drawers throughout the ship had evidently been rifled and that the ship's compass and log were missing. The cargo was intact but of the crew there was no sign.

THE SIBERIAN FIREBALL

Siberia is unquestionably one of the last great unexplored places on earth. Like the great oceans, it holds mysteries still unfathomable to scientists. Its vastness alone makes it unique in its ability to keep secrets; and, since it also has a climate that can be the most atrocious in the world, it is no wonder that stories abound of what lurks in the unexplored wastes. There are dozens of reported sightings of woolly mammoths and sabre-toothed tigers – creatures that have been extinct for thousands of years. And there are the reports of mysterious footprints in the constantly frozen ground which testify to a race of giants – Russia's own Yeti monsters.

These are often dismissed high-handedly by the cynics who believe the snow-swept tundra is a fertile breeding ground for the over-active imagination. However, what no-one can yet explain away is the Siberian Fireball, which, in 1908, devastated an area the size of modern-day Leningrad.

In the white-hot explosion, more powerful by far than the atomic bombs dropped on Japan at the end of the Second World War, all life was incinerated. Trees were downed like so many matchsticks and nomadic tribesmen over 70 km (45 miles) from the centre of the blast were lifted into the air and their tents blown away. It was the greatest cosmic disaster ever recorded.

An area some 65 km (40 miles) wide was devastated. In seconds, the great sparsely-inhabited Tunguska River valley looked like a no man's land. Had it happened in say, Moscow, London or New York, it would undoubtedly have been the greatest disaster in history.

It was just after 7 am on 30 June 1908 that the fireball struck. Farmer Sergei Semenov was one of the few witnesses whose recollections of the disaster were recorded. He was lucky, being some 80 km (50 miles) from the blast centre; everything within a radius only slightly closer was incinerated. This is part of his account:

'There appeared a great flash. There was so much heat, my shirt was almost burnt off my back. I saw a huge ball of fire that covered an enormous part of the sky. Afterwards it became very dark. It shook the whole house and moved it from its foundations'.

When investigators from the great Russian academies made the long and arduous journey into the wasteland, they were astonished by what they saw. Originally they had thought that peasants were exaggerating the effects of what they believed must have been a minor comet, or a particularly savage storm. Nothing prepared them for the herds of reindeer literally roasted where they stood grazing. Nor for the vast tracts of pine forests flattened like wheat in a field after rain. But what had caused it?

Because of the political turmoil surrounding the Russian Revolution of 1917, it was not until 1930 that a serious scientific study to probe possible causes was launched. Mineralogist Professor Leonid Kulik, of the Soviet Academy of Science, journeyed through the wastes of the tundra with a small team.

'The results of even a cursory examination exceeded all the tales of the eye-witnesses and my wildest expectations,' said the professor. He not only took mineral samples and chronicled the devastation, but also recorded the words of the peasants who witnessed it. People spoke of the 'terrible vibrations', and of the River Kan, foaming and broiling like a tormented sea, with waves actually lapping on to the banks.

In the town of Kirensk, survivors told of a pillar of fire – like the now all-too-familiar mushroom cloud of a nuclear explosion – rising above the devastation. One said how he found a friend, who had gone on a fishing expedition, burned to death on a riverbank, still clutching the charred remains of a rod. For two years Kulik investigated the area and eventually decided that a mega-meteorite must have hit the Earth.

Since Kulik's day, however, other scientists have poured scorn on the meteorite explanation. There was, for instance, no massive crater and little evidence of the meteorite dust which is normally left behind in copious amounts. Something else must have caused the disaster.

Tribes people (top) of the Tunguska River Valley, blighted by the Siberian fireball. Of the trees left standing after the disaster, there were only charred remains (above).

THE SIBERIAN FIREBALL

The theories range from the probable to the bizarre. One is that a spaceship visiting Earth blew up and its nuclear reactor exploded, triggering the devastation. That aside, there is evidence which suggests that the blast could well have been nuclear – in an age before man had mastered the splitting of the atom. For instance, the Earth's magnetic field was disturbed after the blast, just as it is after nuclear bomb tests. There were weird floral mutations after the Nagasaki and Hiroshima explosions.

Also, nuclear blasts leave a 'trademark' of trinites, tiny green globules of melted dust. These were found after the Russian blast, and metallurgists confirmed that the trinites did not come from the Tunguska River valley. It could indeed have been some form of nuclear explosion. One test carried out as far away as the United States on tree rings – to gauge the level of radioactivity at the time of the blast – showed an increase of 1 per cent.

The horrific results of the fireball could still be seen some 22 years after the fireball devastated the land.

Other theories include :

• The Black Hole Theory. Little is known of these space phenomena, investigated elsewhere in this book. They are thought to be stars which have collapsed in on themselves – their gravitational pull is so strong that no light escapes, so there is just a 'black hole', hence their name. A black hole is a ball of massive energy which could have hit the Tunguska region, causing the nuclear explosion but leaving no crater.

According to American physicist and eminent authority on black holes, John Carlson: 'A massive atom-sized black hole entering the earth's atmosphere at a typical collision velocity for an interplanetary body would create an atmospheric shock wave with enough force to level hundreds of square kilometres of Siberian forest, ionise air, produce flash-burning and seismic effects. No major crater or meteoritic residue would result'.

• The Comet Theory. Comets are giant balls of frozen gases and space debris. If a comet strayed from its space orbit and into the earth's atmosphere, it could have exploded, say scientists.

A 1977 paper written by two British university professors, A A Jackson and M P Ryan, on comets and the possibility that a comet caused the Siberian disaster says that its energy would have been too low for a full-scale nuclear explosion but that it could have created a blast of almost the size of an atom bomb. No comets were detected in the skies at the time of the explosion, but the academics say this could be due to the comet only becoming visible to the naked eye at dawn, which may have made it indistinguishable from the sun.

• The Anti-matter Theory. This suggest that positrons – sub-atomic particles – of anti-matter swirling in the vastness of space came into contact with atoms of ordinary matter on earth, triggering a massive blast. The two main proponents of this theory are Clyde Cowan and Hall Crennell of the Catholic University in Washington. Many academics believe their theory.

• The Meteorite Theory – with a difference. Some scientists say that the cause of the blast could have been a giant meteorite which exploded before hitting the ground. The effect would have been like that of a giant shrapnel shell, showering the tundra with white-hot heaps of rock, causing a furnace-hot blast capable of uprooting the vast areas of trees, but leaving no crater.

Despite the advance of technology, mankind is no closer to solving the riddle of this disaster than it was the day it happened.

THE ROMANOVS AND ANASTASIA

Fed by poverty and hunger, the revolutionary movement grew inexorably throughout Russia. Calls for democracy were as loud as the cries for food. It was the turn of the century and time was running out for the last Tsar, Nicholas II.

Nicholas was a well-meaning but weak character. By the time he came to the throne of the Romanov dynasty, in 1894, his country was already on the way to revolution. Handsome but introverted – and, sadly, not very bright – he was unable to face up to the reality of ruling a country so vast and complex as the one he had just inherited.

His young wife, however, was the domineering and impetuous Tsarina Alexandra Feodorovna who further sowed the seeds of discontent by seeming aloof and distanced from her subjects.

Indecisive as ever, whenever a crisis arose the Tsar would take his family to their country palace at Tsarskoe Selo, near St Petersburg. All he achieved was to increase the alienation and isolation of the Romanov dynasty as the revolutionary subversives became more powerful.

When he went to war with Japan in 1904 – an adventure that was characterised by bungling and corruption and ended in humiliation – the revolutionary underground erupted onto the streets. In January 1905 a group of metalworkers marched to the Winter Palace. Their intent was peaceful and their leader, the priest Georgi Gapon, wrote to the Tsar asking him to receive a petition and address the crowd. Nicholas followed his usual procedure and fled with his family to Selo.

Meanwhile, the soldiers left to guard the palace panicked when they saw the crowd and fired volley after volley into the defenceless ranks of men, women and children, killing about five hundred and injuring thousands more. It was the beginning of the 1905 revolution.

The situation was calmed only by the outbreak of the First World War, when patriotic fervour united sworn enemies. However, when the Tsar took personal command of his armies, he left the government in the hands of the Tsarina – or rather in the hands of Rasputin, the demonic monk who had a hypnotic hold over her. Now enraged nobles, as well as militants among the masses, were plotting the downfall of the Romanovs.

Rasputin was their first victim in 1916. He was butchered, not by the proletariat, but by aristocrats. Nicholas returned home in 1917 but the situation still deteriorated. Severe winter conditions caused food shortages. Lenin returned from exile, preaching violent revolution. On 8 March Nicholas again sought refuge in Selo – and the Russian Revolution started in earnest.

For a week, violent demonstrations raged across the country. Strikes became riots, police stations and law courts were looted and burned and the army mutinied. On 15 March Nicholas accepted the inevitable end of the Romanov dynasty and abdicated in favour of the Grand Duke Michael Alexandrovitch.

The royal family was placed in 'protective custody', being moved from palace to palace until, in 1918, they ended up in Ekaterinburg (now Sverdlovsk) in the Ural Mountains, near Czechoslovakia. Here they were in the hands of secret police under the command of Jakov Yurovsky. These were not guards – they were executioners. On 13 July, as the loyal White Army beat back the Red Army and closed in on Ekaterinburg, the order went out to kill the entire royal family. Three days later the Tsar and his family were woken at midnight, and herded with their servants into a dingy cellar. What happened next will probably always remain a mystery.

Piecing together soldiers' accounts, it seems that Yurovsky informed the group that they were to be shot. As the Tsar rose to protest, Yurovsky fired a bullet into his head. A fusillade cut down the Tsarina and three of her daughters, along with two servants and the family doctor. More soldiers entered carrying rifles with fixed bayonets and accounted for any other adults still standing. The family's pet dog had

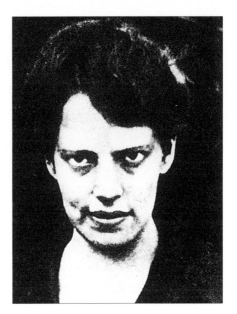

The woman (top) who claimed to be Anastasia, photographed in Berlin in 1922, four years after the Romanovs were put to death. A photograph of the Grand Duchess Anastasia (above).

its skull smashed in by a rifle butt. The Tsar's son, Alexis, had been wounded, and when he stirred was brutally kicked by soldiers. Yurovsky administered the final blow, placing his pistol to the boy's ear and firing two shots.

The bodies were bundled into lorries and driven into a forest. Yurovsky is believed to have chosen a derelict mine shaft for their disposal but is thought to have become lost in the woods. Other soldiers had bought drums of petrol and sulphuric acid, and the corpses were mutilated and buried. They did not stay there long, however, because word soon spread about their whereabouts, and the White Army was closing in. A day or so later, they were removed to a secret resting place deep in the forest.

And that is the point at which a mystery began which lasted for most of this century. Two mysteries, in fact – one was the location of the bodies and the proof of the nature of their deaths which forensic examination could provide, and the other was the possibility that there had been a survivor.

According to legend, one of the Tsar's daughters, Anastasia, escaped the carnage. Over the years, a number of women have claimed to be the princess and hence the heir to the Romanov fortune. Official Soviet records show that Anastasia was killed on that fatal night in 1918, and that no one escaped. However, an American, Anna Anderson, could not be budged in her lifelong claim to be the princess.

If Anderson were indeed Anastasia, the picture she painted of the horror that overwhelmed her family was very different from the official version. Every member of the group in the dungeon was violently raped before death, with the exception of Prince Alexis, who was saved by the Tsar volunteering to submit to the ordeal for a second time.

Anderson, who would have been aged 17 at the time, said: 'They used us all except for my brother Alexis. The Tsar gave himself again to save his son'.

According to Anna Anderson, she was saved from the slaughter by being shielded behind her elder sister Tatiana, who took a direct hit. The impact knocked her backwards against Anastasia and, as they fell to the floor, the younger sister passed out. After the carnage, she was presumed dead and bundled with the other bodies into the back of a lorry.

She claimed that, as she bumped along on her journey to the woodland burial site, she regained consciousness and was saved by a local peasant, Alexander Tschaikovsky, who had been press-ganged into helping dispose of the bodies. Alexander, whom in one version of events she later married, concealed her in a cart and drove her west to Romania. From there she made her way to Berlin, where she contacted surviving relatives, principally the Tsar's sister, Grand Duchess Olga. At first the duchess accepted the girl's claims – but when she began inquiring about the Romanov family's fortune, supposedly salted away by the Tsar before his arrest, the aunt disowned her.

'Anastasia' moved to the United States, changed her name to Anna Anderson and was subsequently married, to John Manahan. They settled near Charlottesville, Virginia, but Anna continued to campaign for her right to be recognised as the last Romanov.

In 1979 Anna was operated on for a bowel blockage and the small section removed was kept by the Martha Jefferson Hospital in Charlottesville as part of a routine procedure to guard against subsequent legal action. Writer James Blair Lovell learned of the existence of the sample while researching his book *Anastasia, The Lost Princess*. Anna died in the United States in 1984 at the age of 82 but Lovell continued his attempts to prove her case.

Then came a breakthrough. The revolutionary technique of DNA 'fingerprinting' created a worldwide breakthrough in forensic science. Author Lovell fought to have the Virginian hospital authorities release the section of Anna's bowel so that it could be tested for DNA links with descendants of the surviving Romanovs. He met fierce legal obstructions – but before he could reach his goal, a fresh discovery was made.

In 1991 bones were discovered by accident in a forest near Ekaterinburg. Eventually nine skeletons were unearthed. Russian and British scientists made tests on them for two years and took blood samples from Romanov descendants, including Prince Philip, husband of Britain's Queen Elizabeth II. In July

1993 the British scientific team announced: 'We are more than 98.5 per cent certain that the remains are those of the Romanovs'.

One of the greatest mysteries of the 20th century, the fate of the Russian Tsar, had been solved – but another one, the fate of Anastasia, had not.

Blood samples from Prince Philip, who was closely related to the Tsarina, proved beyond doubt that she and three of her children had been slaughtered at Ekaterinburg. Links with blood samples from other royal descendants established that all the other skeletons were victims of the massacre. But the bones of two of the Tsar's children were missing – and tests could not distinguish between the sisters. Further DNA testing was still required to determine if there was any truth in Anna Anderson Manahan's claims.

It was not until 1994 that samples from Anna's bowel were released and brought to Britain where the Home Office Forensic Science Service compared them with DNA samples of the Romanov family's remains. There was no doubt. Anna Anderson was a fraud.

Tsarina Anastasia, born 1901, murdered 1918, was finally pronounced dead on 1 October 1994.

Rasputin (centre), the monk who held the Tsarina in his power, pictured here with other members of the court.

NESSIE

They call her a monster – but no one ever thinks of her as such. Of all the mysterious creatures that waft through the skies, creep across the earth or lurk in the depths, Nessie scares no one! She is everyone's favourite, this lady of the lake, this gentle giant of Loch Ness.

Locals around the Invernesshire lake have known for centuries about their mysterious neighbour, which they have always referred to in Gaelic as a 'water horse' rather than a monster. As children, they were warned not to swim in Loch Ness because of the 'kelpie'. But it was only in the 1930s, when a new road was being cut into the rocky north shore of the lake, that outsiders began to take notice of Nessie.

A gang of workman engaged on blasting operations in the summer of 1933 were startled to see Nessie, with 'an enormous head and broad body', speeding up the centre of the lake in the wake of a fishing boat. Another three witnesses spoke of 'several humps' rising and falling across the perfectly calm lake in an undulating motion 'rather like the movement of a caterpillar'.

The most detailed sighting of 1933, however, and the one that really gave birth to the worldwide legend of the Loch Ness monster, was recounted by Mrs John Mackay. She was being driven by her husband along the new road which, now that trees and undergrowth had been cut down, gave a perfect view of the vast lake. 'I couldn't believe what we were seeing', she said. 'I had never seen such an enormous thing. It was just an enormous black body, going up and down. You could not put a name to it. It could have been an elephant or a whale'.

That same year, Mr E G Boulenger, director of the aquarium at London Zoo, said that reports of Nessie were 'a striking example of mass hallucination'. He claimed that once Nessie was seen by a few people, she would be reported by many more.

He was correct – but only in that sightings came thick and fast in the following years. Over three thousand claims have been taken seriously by experts since Boulenger's dismissive words – from that of a ship's captain and crew to that of a vicar's tea party guests and even to that of a saint!

For the first sightings of Nessie predate the 1933 publicity by over a thousand years. In AD 565 St Columba was travelling through Scotland's Great Glen converting the Picts and Scots to Christianity. He came to Loch Ness, where he found local people recovering the body of a neighbour who had been savaged by a monster while out swimming. One of the saint's followers swam out into the loch to retrieve a boat when he, too, was confronted by the beast. According to the then Abbot of Ionna, who wrote St Columba's biography, 'A strange beast rose from the water something like a frog, only it was not a frog'. St Columba ordered the monster: 'Go no further, nor touch that man'. Meekly, the predator turned on its tail and fled.

That was the beginning of the legend of the Loch Ness monster, a legend kept alive over the centuries through Scottish folklore which tells of kelpies (malignant water sprites) disguising themselves as horses in order to lure and kill human victims. In Gaelic, the monster was known as 'Niseag'.

The Victorians' favourite novelist, Sir Walter Scott, was obviously familiar with the stories. He wrote in his journal in 1827: 'Clan Ronald told us that a set of his kinsmen, believing that the fabulous water cow inhabited a small lake near his house, resolved to drag the monster into day. With this in view, they bivouacked by the side of the lake in which they placed, by way of nightbait, two small anchors such as belong to boats, each baited with the carcass of a dog slain for the purpose. They expected the water cow would gorge on the bait and were prepared to drag her ashore the next morning'. Happily, Nessie did not take the bait!

Many have believed that Nessie and her breed can live on land as well as water. Margaret Cameron told of her youthful experience during the First World War when she heard 'crackling' in the trees and

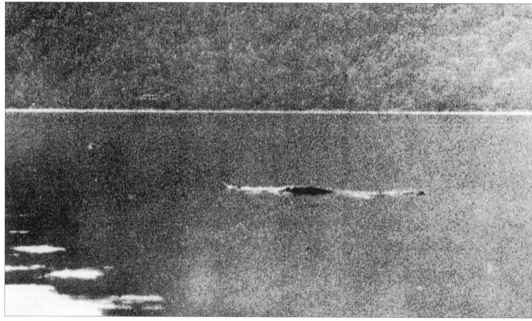

A photograph taken on Loch Ness (top); could these humps possibly belong to Nessie? The second photograph (above) was also reported to be a photograph of the monster.

saw a creature slither down into the water. She said that it had a shiny skin the colour of an elephant and two short round feet at the front. 'It had a huge body', she said, 'and its movement was similar to that of a caterpillar'.

Farmer Jock Forbes and his companion had a similar experience in 1919. The pony pulling their trap suddenly reared up at the sight of a beast in their path. 'It came out of the trees, moved slowly across the road and then went down the bank', he said. 'I heard a splash as, presumably, it went into the water'. Jock estimated that the beast was as long as the road was wide.

In 1923 chauffeur Alfred Cruickshank described his sighting of a monster he encountered on a country road: 'It had a large humped body standing about 6 ft (2 metres) high with its belly trailing on the ground. Its belly was about 12 ft (3.5 metres) long to which was attached a long thick tale about 12 ft (3.5 metres) in length. It was moving slowly, sort of waddling on two legs'.

Tourist George Spicer, from London, described the monster in 1933 as a 'loathsome sight' – a huge snail with a long neck and carrying what looked like a dead lamb in its mouth. He said: 'It did not move in the usual reptilian fashion but with a sort of arched walk. The body shot across the road in jerks. The body was about 5 ft (1.5 metres) in height and filled the road. Its colour could be called elephant grey'.

More usual are sightings of the Loch Ness monster in her own watery environment. In 1938 a tug captain and his mate noticed a 'huge, black animal with seven humps' emerge from the depths of Loch Ness and swim alongside their vessel before accelerating away 'at terrific speed', leaving large waves.

Forestry worker Lachlan Stuart, who lives on the lochside, told in 1951 how he had got up early to milk his cow when he saw humps speeding along the middle of the lake. He immediately thought that it was Nessie, 'which has been seen several times in this vicinity this week'. He said that the monster swung towards him and swam within 3 metres (10 ft) of the shore. He was so frightened, he said, that he retreated into trees before Nessie turned with a great splashing and vanished.

In 1960 the Rev W L Dobb had just finished a lakeside picnic with his family and guests when their attention was diverted by mysterious waves moving across the loch. Then a large hump broke the surface; a second hump followed, rising and falling as they moved down the loch.

In 1974 truck driver Andy Call and his mate Henry Wilson saw foaming water as they drove along the side of the loch. A creature surfaced. Call later said: 'It was black, 50 to 60 ft (15 to 18 metres) long, with a horse-like head. We watched it for 15 minutes before it submerged for a third and final time'.

Lorry driver Hugh Chisholm had told his wife Mhairi that he had seen Nessie but she did not believe him. However, in 1978, both of them were driving along the loch and spotted the monster. 'It was really huge', they said, 'with the head and one hump clearly visible. When it vanished under the water it left large waves behind'.

Two of the strongest pieces of evidence to support the existence of Nessie were put to stringent scientific analysis. They were two cine films, far more difficult to fake than still photographs, and were submitted to the Joint Air Reconnaissance Intelligence Centre by David James of the Loch Ness Investigation Bureau. The first, shot by Tim Dinsdale, shows a hump moving slowly away from the camera then speeding sideways across the field of vision before submerging. Analysts said the object was about 1.5 metres (5 ft) wide and moved at around 16 km (10 miles) per hour. And, they added, it was 'probably animate'.

The second film was taken by Mr Richard Raynor in 1967. It clearly shows an animal speeding through the water, then submerging when a boat enters its vision. Raynor was prepared to accept that it was an otter – but the reconnaissance experts said that it could have been more than 2 metres (7 ft) long, far too long for such a creature!

In recent years, Loch Ness Monster hunting has become a minor industry, with hides, lookout points, visitor centres and museums. Underwater cameras, echo sounders and even minature submarines have plumbed the depths but have failed to find conclusive proof of Nessie's existence.

However, one of the world's most respected naturalists, Sir Peter Scott, who helped launch the Loch Ness Phenomena Investigation Bureau in 1962, was sufficiently impressed with research to announce:

There are probably between 20 and 50 of them down there. I believe they are related to the plesiosaurs'.

Since the plesiosaur is long extinct, Scott's theory means that Nessie and her ancestors must have been cut off from the sea when the loch was formed at the end of the last ice age. That makes Nessie and her ancestors over 70 million years old!

Loch Ness, a slash across the map of Scotland, is the result of a giant tear in the Earth's surface, gouged out around 10 thousand years ago by the last of the ice age glaciers. The lake is 300 metres (1000 ft) deep, 40 km (24 miles) long, with water blackened by the peaty rivers that flow into it. So cold is it that bodies of drowned men never return to the surface.

The loch itself presents problems in investigating the Nessie legend because of its situation. It can play tricks on the eyes. It is a large mass of water sometimes completely calm in a way that the sea rarely is and its high shoreline casts deep shadows and reflections. Sceptics of the legend say that sightings can usually be put down to the wake of passing vessels, ripples caused by wind changes or simply logs floating in the water.

The sheer volume of eyewitness evidence, however, has made many scientists sit up and take serious notice. They recognise that it is not possible for all the witnesses to be either drunks, liars or just plain mistaken.

If Nessie exists, why then have no bodies or bones been found on the loch's shoreline over the centuries? Scientists say that the water pressure in the great depths would slow down decomposition and allow time for eels to dispose of the remains.

THE MOVING STONES OF DEATH VALLEY

American Indians five centuries ago first noticed the phenomenon of the moving stones in America's Sierra Nevada mountains. There, across a plain of cracked mud dotted with rocks and boulders, many of them weighing up to 320 kg (700 lb), were tracks which made it look as if the stones had been dragged across the ground by humans or beasts.

Indian sentinels would stand guard in the freezing night air for a sight of the unknown people responsible for hauling the rocks. They saw no one – but by the morning many of the rocks would have moved. It was no wonder that the primitive Indians attributed a mystical status to the moving stones.

Now, centuries later, the riddle of the moving stones across the plain known as the Racetrack Playa still arouses fierce debate. Are the scientific explanations offered up the key to the puzzle, or is there something at work that humans have failed to fathom and which will continue to baffle them?

Racetrack Playa is part of the Death Valley National Monument. It is 2 km (1¼ miles) wide and 5 km (3 miles) long and is situated 1200 metres (4000 ft) above sea level. From various vantage points around the plain, the visitor can clearly see the hundreds of rocks which litter the ground. And there is not a visitor to the area who does not harbour hopes of being the first human actually to witness the rocks moving across the dried-up lake bed, which was formed during the last ice age.

Earlier this century a band of students from Yale University camped out in the region to try to unravel the mystery of the stones. They failed. However, one of their number, a geologist named Mary Felton, put forward a theory that the stones were blown along on a sheet of water when the wind was high. Sceptics immediately poured scorn on her assumption, arguing that while this might be plausible for some of the smaller rocks, how could it be true of the gigantic boulders which had also left the same snake-like trails in their wakes.

Experts and amateurs alike could see from the trails that the rocks had not rolled along. The furrows were consistent with them having been pushed, leaving behind them a tell-tale groove the same size as the stones themselves.

In 1955 geologist George Stanley wrote in the Bulletin of the Geological Society of America that wind and ice were the two main factors in the movement of the rocks. He alleged that ice, which often forms at night in the region, forms a thin sheet over the whole of the plain. When the wind blew at the same time, a skating rink effect was created, propelling the rocks over it. Again, this was not a satisfactory answer to the question of how the huge boulders moved. And besides, argued the academics, the ice formed was so thin as to be virtually worthless as a vehicle for the strange stones.

During the 1960s Racetrack Playa began to rival the other great American natural wonders, like the Yellowstone National Park Geyser and the Niagara Falls, as a huge tourist attraction. Newspapers ran competitions offering big prize money to any reader who could capture the phenomenon on camera. Naturally, there were no winners.

Then, in 1969, the second serious study of the stones was embarked upon, by Dr Robert Sharp of the geology department of the California Institute of Technology. His was to be a study over seven years, incorporating all factors, such as wind, water, ice, air, temperature, size of stones and the structure of the soil on the lake bed itself. Sharp realised that only by plodding, methodical examination could he hope to yield up the secret of the moving stones.

He selected 25 rocks weighing from under 1 kg (2.2 lb) to a huge monster dubbed 'Big Daddy', weighing 450 kg (1000 lb). He used metal stakes to mark the positions of the rocks and, to make sure no one tampered with them and upset the experiment, he ensured a strict regime of careful monitoring by park officials. He later marked 5 more boulders, making 30 stones in all. Repeatedly making the arduous journey to reach the Playa, and suffering the sharp changes of temperature, Sharp doggedly stuck with this extensive study until, more than seven years later, he had built up an amazing dossier on the movement of the stones. 28 of the 30 stones had moved. The furthest distance travelled was 262 metres (850 ft). This occurred over a number of months and years, rather than in one spectacular journey. The longest single journey was by a stone he nicknamed Nancy, which weighed in at less than 500 g (1 lb) and which, according to his measurement, meandered an incredible 200 metres (600 ft) in one go!

Sharp's study reached three conclusions:

1. Small heaps of the racetrack bed were pushed up in front of the stones as they travelled along. This indicated that the stones moved when it was wet, because they would be unable to create such a residue from the hard, caked surface in dry weather.

2. Most of the movements happened in the winters of 1968-9, 1972-3, and 1973-4; all winters which had inordinately high rainfalls and high winds.

3. He calculated that, with precisely 0.6 cm (1/4 in) of water lying on the surface of the Playa, the whole of the topmost soil became delicately balanced. Any more water and the rocks would sink into the surface of the valley; any less and they would not be propelled by the wind.

Sharp wrote in the Bulletin of the Geological Society of America for 1976 that conditions could be created in which the stones might indeed move. He said: 'The secret is to catch the play of the wind and the water at precisely the right moment'.

He added that the rocks were sent on their strange journeys around the lake bed by a powerful gust of wind, and that the momentum was maintained on the thin film of water by gentler breezes. He said that the surrounding mountains directed the wind around their numerous peaks and crevasses so that it hit the plain at speed, enabling the rocks to get that initial impetus to set them on their journeys.

Not every one, however, was convinced by the hypothesis propounded by Dr Sharp. Centuries before, the Indians had recorded movements of the stones even when the skies were clear and the lake bed was dry. Other scientists were sceptical that the wind speeds could be anything like sufficient to launch a static stone into motion and to keep it moving.

Two years after Dr Sharp's article, there was a severe frost on a December night.

The moon was high and clear in the cloudless sky after a week of rain and the temperature was low even for that freezing part of the globe. By morning, several of the stones had moved.

If that night's phenomenon was not the work of nature, as seemed to be the case, whose work was it?

THE POWER TO ENDURE PAIN

The chanting reached fever pitch in the tiny Pentecostal church as the fire-and-brimstone preacher exhorted his flock to purge their souls and make their peace with the Lord. The church authorities in Montana, United States, were used to the melodramatic gospel services practised by the impoverished backwoods scommunities of the Free Pentecostal Holiness Church. These people lived in scattered humble smallholdings in the shadows of the Allegheny Mountains and the gospel services were a celebration of their devotion to God and the expression of their hopes for a better way of life.

In the mid-1970s, however, their religious fervour reached new heights when revivalist meetings took disturbing – some would even say unchristian – turns. They became forums for fervent, primitive emotions and spectacles of bizarre rituals. At these services, the farmers displayed their ability to overcome intense pain through faith.

In an attempt to demonstrate how God's power protected them, the men took to burning their feet with spirit lamps, drinking deadly strychnine, and handling venomous snakes that spat at them and bit them – apparently without suffering any ill effects. The events were reported by journalists and photographers who were invited to witness the power of faith. They came away astonished at the phenomenon: a belief so strong that it gave the faithful the power to overcome pain.

This group of Pentecostalists in the United States were the 20th-century exponents of an art which mankind has practised for centuries, and which still defies belief. Even now there is no logical explanation. How can a person can walk on white-hot coals, plunge a red-hot iron bar into their mouth, or insert a spear through their cheek?

Every year in the Kataragama temple in Sri Lanka a religious festival is held which involves acts of extreme self-mutilation and, one would imagine, unbearable physical pain. The festival is held in honour of friendly spirits, and over a 10-day period members of the sect subject themselves to the most grotesque punishments. Without causing lasting harm to themselves – and seemingly without pain – they systematically walk over hot coals, have their tongues nailed to planks of wood, spear their faces from cheek to cheek with long knives, and walk in clogs studded with sharp nails that point upwards into the soles of their feet.

The most extreme ritual consists of securing hooks through the muscles of the participant's back, thighs and buttocks. They are then suspended from a frame and left to hang for several hours. Their triumph over their ordeal is viewed by the crowds as a symbolic gift from the Gods which bestows great blessings upon them.

When Western doctors have examined the devotees who subject themselves to this torture, they have found no signs of lasting physical harm, even though all the evidence might suggest that the shock alone would be enough to kill a person.

In Fiji today, the fire-walking tradition is as strong as it was in the days of the great Polynesian chieftains. Not only do the practitioners walk over hot coals but they perform the most staggering feats. Rocks are heated until they glow red and white, and are then left all day in a pit fuelled with dried logs. At nightfall the fire-walkers, dressed in traditional Polynesian costume, are ready to make their incredible crossing of the coals. The contact of their bare flesh on these white hot boulders should cause instant pain and horrible, mutilating burns. Yet Western scientists who have studied the ritual testify that they have carefully examined the feet of the participants the day after – and found them quite normal. How is it that some strangely gifted people can conquer intense pain?

In 1935 the first experiment was conducted, at London University, to try to determine whether pain or injury could be nullified by someone who believed deep within that they could overcome it. A young

Mind over matter: an Indian fakir (top) lies on a bed of nails; in Thailand, a man (above) walks over hot coals.

Indian, who had participated in fire-walking ceremonies in his homeland, calmly walked across a bed of glowing embers that had been heated to a temperature of 250°C (475°F). He was in a calm mental state and had not worked himself into any religious fervour or hypnotic trance. His feet were examined before the experiment took place to ensure that nothing had been attached to the soles of his feet to protect them.

The scientists who examined him afterwards concluded that he was neither burned nor at all traumatised by his experience. He had defied medical and scientific knowledge.

In 1952 an American doctor, Harry Wright, witnessed a fire-walking ceremony on the Fijian island of Biti Levu. As far he could determine, the fire-walkers experienced no pain, either physical or mental, when they walked barefoot across white-hot coals. Afterwards Dr Wright asked them if they would take part in an impromptu experiment. The doctor examined the soles of their feet and then prodded them with needles and burned them with a lighted cigarette. The men who minutes earlier had walked over heated coals winced in pain, and their feet bore burn marks from the doctor's tests.

What can explain this? Mind over pain is one thing but mind over physical damage is another. The men had walked over a carpet of fire unharmed, yet their skin had blistered at the touch of a tiny, glowing cigarette end.

Practitioners of the art of yoga say they know the key to the inner soul which allows the accepted mental and physical order of the body to be altered. To illustrate their point, they draw attention to the famous fakir (magician) of Lahore whose amazing feat is unexplained to this day.

In 1838 the magician, who had deep mystical beliefs, was buried alive in a padlocked box at the bottom of a pit, 3 metres (9 ft) deep. The pit was then filled with earth and was guarded over by British soldiers around the clock. Thirty days later the padlocked box was exhumed and the witnesses prepared themselves to see a corpse. But the magician emerged unharmed!

He had survived without food, water or air and had borne the insufferable weight of the earth on top of him. Yet he emerged unscathed and was able to stand unaided and walk away. His own explanation for his ability to put his body into a state of suspended animation was his innate faith in Islam, in himself and in the power of his soul.

One hundred years after this, an Egyptian called Rahman Bey performed a similar miracle in England. He was buried in a pit filled with earth in Carshalton, Surrey. The experiment was observed by scientists and doctors. He too emerged unharmed.

There is still no satisfactory explanation for the miraculous ability some people have to endure unimaginable pain. Dr Robert Felton, of the University of Colorado, who made a long study of the phenomenon, said:

'The ability to fight pain is something inherent in individuals at different times and at different places. But don't ask me to explain what the magic "Ingredient X" is . . . Science has not yet travelled far enough to explain these powers'.

American Dr Robert Felton, who studied power over pain, said: 'Imagine a power that could inure its soldiers against feeling pain. If a state could have produced such a race of warriors any time in our history, they could have threatened the armies of the world – and would probably have overwhelmed them all'.

CROP CIRCLES

During the mid-1980s, reports of a weird phenomenon across rural England began to filter into the newspapers. Soon dozens of photographs appeared showing perfect circles of flattened crops clearly defined against the up-standing cereal around them.

There was no sign of any footprints, no damage outside the circle and, apparently, no motive. It was for all the world as though some alien spacecraft had hovered above the flattened area, left its mark and then zipped back into hyper-space. This was how the UFO lobby explained the whole curious affair.

There were plenty of other theories though. Whirlwinds, hedgehogs, rabbits, the Devil, fairies, ancient earth power lines – all were volunteered as explanations. And then there were the hoaxes.

It was always obvious to investigators that there were a lot of hoaxers around, and scientists conceded that distinguishing fact from fantasy was nigh on impossible. Parties of hoaxers with names such as 'Merlin & Co', the 'Bill Bailey Gang', the 'Wessex Sceptics' and 'Spiderman and Catwoman' ran rife in cornfields to the irritation of farmers. The average bill for crop damage was put at £60.

Farmers themselves were not entirely innocent. A surreptitious night's work and a phone call to the papers the next day often produced a queue of sightseers anxious for a close-up glimpse of one of the strange circles. There were stories of landowners charging a £2 admission fee plus £1 for parking.

The fact that a few country folk managed to trick scientists and car-loads of gullible townies is one thing. To conclude from this that all crop circles are hoaxes is quite another. It is tantamount to saying that because art experts are often fooled by forgers, all old masters are fakes.

The plain fact is that there is nothing new about crop circles. They have manifested themselves in England for at least four thousand years. And while the modern-day farmer is mostly able to shrug off crop damage, his Bronze Age counterpart, struggling to survive, may have taken a dim view. Any circle prankster living around 2000 BC could probably expect to get an axe through his head.

A study of the circles' history shows that in many cases the theories behind their creation have a strikingly familiar ring. Professor Plot, of Oxford University's Faculty of Science, and a fellow of the Royal Society, published a book called *The Natural History of Staffordshire* in 1686. In it he told of his desire to identify a 'higher principle' which might explain crop circles other than the then-fashionable claims of rutting deer, over-active moles, urinating cattle and the fairies. One pamphlet published eight years earlier told of a field 'neatly mowed by the devil, or some infernal spirit'.

Plot did not dismiss these ideas but his own conclusion was that equally bizarre ball lightning was to blame. 'They must needs be the effects of lightning, exploded from the clouds most times in a circular manner,' he said. Today, the reality of ball lightning is only just gaining acceptance among mainstream scientists.

It is far from clear why there has been a three hundred-year gap in the study of crop circles. Perhaps it is because genuine cases are extremely rare. But for the labours of today's hoaxers the phenomena might never have been brought to the attention of a wider audience.

A study by Colin Andrews, carried out at a cost of £50,000 in 1983, concentrated on southern England. His 12-strong team concluded that the circles were somehow linked to disturbances in the earth's magnetic field, which in turn stemmed from the hole in the ozone layer of the atmosphere. Sensors had picked up violent fluctuations in the force field around areas where a plethora of circles had appeared.

Mr Andrews, an electrical expert with his local council, reported: 'One of the circles that appeared recently in Hampshire amazed us even more than the others because the flattened crops grew back in dartboard formation. There were seven concentric rings of crops with a series of perfect spokes going out from the centre'.

CROP CIRCLES

A spate of crop, or corn, circles appeared in the fields of southern England in the 1980s and early 1990s.

The Andrews team even claimed that the molecular structure of the crops might have been damaged. Later, they returned to the fray asserting that circles were being created by 'some form of higher intelligence'. Andrews went on: 'They are caused by some sort of high energy, but we don't know what. The shapes are becoming more and more complex and I believe that what we are heading for is circles in the form of snowflakes or flowers. The shapes we have seen recently are just the start of what is to come'.

Throughout the 1980s reports of crop circles became even more widespread. Although southern England was still very much the epicentre, examples were found in Australia, North America and Japan. Scientists from these countries were soon clamouring for the chance to spend a summer in Britain to conduct in-depth scientific studies.

Amid all the outlandish theories, the most straightforward explanation continued to come from consultant meteorologist Dr Terence Meaden, head of the Tornado and Storm Research Organisation. He reckoned unusual air vortices were a factor behind many circles. Such vortices occurred when a gust of wind on one side of a hill struck still air behind it.

'Some bone-headed people are trying to turn this whole thing into something spiritual or as a phenomenon from outer space', he said. 'Basically, the circles are formed by a spiralling ball of air which comes down to the ground'.

Strong support for the Meaden theory came from a couple out walking along the edge of a corn field in the Hampshire countryside. It was a still August day in 1991, yet suddenly Gary and Vivienne Tomlinson, of Guildford, Surrey, saw the crops around them begin to move. They were caught in the middle of a forming circle.

Vivienne takes up the story: 'There was a tremendous noise. We looked up to see if it was caused by a helicopter but there was nothing. We felt a strong wind pushing us from the side and above. It was forcing down on our heads, yet incredibly my husband's hair was standing on end. Then the whirling air seemed to branch into two and zig-zag off into the distance. We could still see it like a light mist or fog, shimmering as it moved'.

'As it disappeared, we were left standing in a corn circle with the corn flattened all around us. Everything became very still again and we were left with a tingly feeling. It all happened so quickly that it seemed to be over in a split second'.

Dr Meaden later interviewed the couple and was impressed by their power of recall. 'The story these people told is so detailed they cannot have made it up', he said. 'They had no knowledge of corn circles yet they described a scientific process that could easily cause them. This really is a magnificent eye witness account – much better than any we have had previously'.

When the mystery is finally solved it will be hard to judge who is the more embarrassed – the 'experts' fooled by a few amateurs carrying planks and string, or the hoaxers, who arrogantly believed it was all down to them.

CROP CIRCLES

Viewed from a plane, these marks have an unearthly quality. Could they possibly be of significance to creatures from other planets?

In the summer of 1991, with the corn circle debate raging across the country, two elderly British artists dropped a bombshell on the 'cerealogists'. Dave Chorley and Doug Bower claimed responsibility for all the main circles of the previous 13 years. Their motive was to see how many so-called experts and New Age followers they could embarrass and fool. They were also intrigued to know how long the hoax would last.

Chorley and Bower claimed to have fooled the two leading British investigators, Colin Andrews and Pat Delgado, a team of Japanese scientists, farming groups and several government departments. They insisted that only poles, boards and ropes were necessary to construct a perfect circle.

The hoaxers told how they met in the late 1960s with a common interest in art and UFOs. A few years later, inspired by a famous 'flying saucer circle' in northeast Australia, they made their first attempt in Strawberry Field, near Cheesefoot Head, Winchester. These early circles attracted no media attention and the pair were soon on the brink of giving up. However their 1981 efforts at Cheesefoot Head were widely reported and their enthusiasm was rekindled.

Whatever their claims, Chorley and Bower's pranks do not explain the existence of the crop circle phenomenon over many centuries, not just in the recent spate.

BIRD MIGRATION

Humans can navigate to the stars, across continents and great oceans. With pinpoint accuracy, astronauts can land in deserts and make prearranged rendezvoux upon the seas. But all these feats are managed only with the aid of a dazzling array of electronic gadgetry, compasses and high-tech wizardry.

How then is it that creatures with no access to any kind of technology can guide themselves across vast areas of territory, crossing oceans and mountains in an annual migration without so much as a signpost to guide them? The miracle of migration by birds of different species is just as awe-inspiring today as it was when first noted by our ancestors. And the answer to the mystery remains as elusive as ever.

Birds which leave winter shores for warmer climates follow specific routes across the skies, sometimes in narrow, well-defined air tunnels, sometimes on broad fronts often hundreds of kilometres across. The physical effort alone – quite apart from the navigational skill – is staggering.

The small American golden plover, which winters in the Pacific, flies directly from the Aleutian Islands near Alaska to Hawaii in 35 hours non-stop across 3200 km (2000 miles) in an effort requiring 250 thousand wing-beats. And Nova Scotian and Newfoundland populations of Arctic tern, which seek out the ice-packs in winter away from their breeding grounds, fly an astonishing 16,000 km (10,000 miles), first crossing the Atlantic, then following the coastlines of western Europe and Africa to the Antarctic, a feat that makes them the record holders in migration distance.

Birds accomplish these astonishing feats of endurance with an economy of energy unknown in mammals. Fish-eating birds often replenish themselves en route by diving into shallows for food or eating the food rubbish dumped by ships at sea.

Birds all over the planet migrate; and for different reasons. The bird populations of northern and eastern Europe tend to migrate much more than those in western Europe. Tits, goldfinches and blackbirds tend to migrate from northern Europe to north Africa to spend the winter. Insect-eating birds like wagtails and warblers flock to the tropics in winter, chiefly to the east and west coasts of Africa where there are rich pickings of insect life to be had for winter sustenance.

The white stork population that lives west of the Weser River in Germany flies to Africa to enjoy the winter warmth afforded there. Meanwhile, ducks that shed their feathers annually (effectively grounding them) fly to predator-free territory to escape the threat of death during the time they are immobilised.

The puzzle that has baffled humans for centuries is: how do all these different creatures manage to complete these amazing feats?

It has long been known that birds possess an uncanny compass sense; an innate ability to fly in a single constant direction regardless of their point of departure. One theory is that their navigational expertise derives from magnetic forces in the earth which trigger stimuli in their brains. But while many believe this hypothesis, it remains just that. There is no positive proof.

Experiments have demonstrated that the sun may be the orientation point for birds flying by day. Birds can correct their flight patterns by gauging the sun's movement while they are airborne. Similarly, birds which have been subjected to light deprivation over long periods and then released, show classic signs of disorientation and are unable to function normally.

The British ornithologist G V T Matthews offers the following explanation of bird migration. He suggests that birds have an innate ability to 'read' the sun and stars. In the northern hemisphere, for instance, the highest point reached by the sun lies in the south, and that highest point comes at noon: two facts which give the traveller reference points in both time and space.

Matthews argues that, in their local environment, birds soon become adept at 'reading' the position of the sun at any given moment. Going one step further, he says that a migrating bird, able to translate time

An American bald eagle: in the late 1980s, one of these magnificent birds crossed from America to Ireland – incredibly, flying a distance of 4800 km.

and distance into latitude and longitude, would also be able to set a course across large distances – and still return to its old nest after completing the return journey, aided by its unique guidance system. The same applies, he suggests, to those birds which prefer night flights, in this case using the star systems as navigational aids.

In support of this theory, an amazing experiment took place in a planetarium at the University of Frieburg, Germany. It proved that garden warblers, set free while an artificial autumn sky was projected onto the dome of the building, instinctively tried to head south-west – the direction they would have taken had they been let loose into the wild at that time of year.

However, those who claim that this is conclusive proof of how birds manage their long-haul flights still cannot explain how the creatures steer themselves when out at sea, under cloud, in snowstorms, in thick fog, hail or rain.

For instance, late in 1987, an American bald eagle made what can only be termed an amazing journey. The unlucky bird took off for some destination that remained secret to it alone – and ended up in Ireland, 4800 km (3000 miles) away.

The eagle was completely exhausted by the time it reached the coastline of the Emerald Isle. Ornithologists nevertheless concluded that, marvellous though its feat was, it was no accident of nature that that bird landed where it did. It was lost, they concur, in foul weather. But somehow, instinctively or otherwise, it winged its way halfway across the northern hemisphere, relying not on luck but on skill.

Another example of bird genius is well illustrated by the story of a Manx shearwater. Ornithologists captured one on the island of Skokholm, off the south coast of Wales, crated it up with plenty of food and water, and flew it from Heathrow to the United States. It was deprived of light, sound and smell for five days before being released from a cliff top in Boston, Massachusetts. Placed on a continent it had never seen before, the bird made it back to its nesting place on Skokholm just 12 days later. How can a bird plot a course to a place it knows when it has never made the journey before?

Whole flocks of great shearwaters make the annual migration from Greenland, Newfoundland and locations in northern Europe to lay their eggs in their traditional nesting place on the tiny island of Tristan da Cunha, in the southern Atlantic, over 3200 km (2000 miles) from the nearest mainland. They make the journey with unfailing accuracy and at the same time every year.

The origins of migration itself as a behaviour pattern are thought to stretch back to the last ice age, which ended around 10,000 bc. As the ice retreated, a few birds would have left the hostile terrain for better feeding grounds. Eventually predators would have driven most winged creatures to migrate – except for hardy ones like the Arctic owl, itself a predator.

Today birds migrate for winter warmth, feeding, breeding or to replenish their feathers, as in the case of moulting ducks. Whatever the reason, bird-brained they are not. The fact is that they possess an intelligence in navigation which mere humans can only hope to emulate – and only after centuries of research and millions of pounds of expenditure.

Ornithologist William Keeton, a biology professor, stated that the homing instinct of birds is a mystery that may never be solved. He wrote:

'Homing requires more than a compass. If you were taken hundreds of miles away into unfamiliar territory, given only a magnetic compass and told to start walking home, you would not be able to get there. Even though you could determine where north was, you would not know where you were with respect to home, hence such compass information would be nearly useless'.

GLORIA RAMIREZ

The death of 31-year-old Gloria Ramirez is unique in the annals of medical history. Never before have doctors trying to save a life been knocked unconscious by the fumes seeping from their patient.

Exactly how the woman from Riverside, Los Angeles, became a walking gas chamber is likely to remain a mystery. So is the fact that while some nurses attending to her passed out, others carried on their work unaffected. The case adds up to an account far stranger than the weirdest plot of any 1950s Sci-Fi B-movie.

On Saturday evening, 19 February 1994, Ramirez was brought in to Riverside General Hospital complaining of chest pains and breathing problems. She also confirmed to nurses that she was suffering from cervical cancer, as a consequence of which she was taking pain killers and an anti-nausea drug.

As the staff prepared her for a series of tests Ramirez collapsed from an acute cardiac arrest. Exactly 36 minutes after being admitted she was now the subject of a full-blown emergency. Death would follow within the hour.

Nurse Susan Kane was first to succumb to the gas emanating from Ramirez. She had been taking a blood sample when she noticed a smell like ammonia coming from her patient. The blood in her syringe also seemed to have been contaminated with tiny yellow or white flecks.

Kane collapsed. Dr Julie Gorchynski immediately took her place but then passed out as well. Seconds later the respiratory therapist Maureen Welsh keeled over followed by nurse Sally Balderas and one of her colleagues. The emergency room was by now beginning to look like a bomb had hit it. Yet strangely, the only member of medical staff who seemed totally unaffected was Dr Humberto Ochoa, who didn't even notice the fumes.

For a week Dr Gorchynski remained in intensive care at Loma Linda University Medical Center, Los Angeles, as scientists tried to understand what had happened to her body. She was suffering breathing problems and muscle spasms, conditions which lingered for months afterwards. In April she had to undergo major surgery to save her knees. The bones were somehow being starved of oxygen.

The other medic badly affected, nurse Balderas, suffered intense headaches, sleep deprivation, stomach ache and vomiting. Both she and Dr Gorchynski were diagnosed as sleep apnoea victims, a condition in which breathing stops temporarily.

Balderas told doctors that Ramirez 'had this film on her body, like you see on the ground at a gas station'. Tests indicated that the victims had suffered organophosphate poisoning. There were the same white and yellow crystals present in their bodies as had been reported in Ramirez's blood sample. But this conclusion produced more questions than answers. For a start, Ramirez had not taken organophosphates as far as anyone could tell. Her family emphasised that whatever pain she had been in from cancer, she would never have committed suicide. She would never have abandoned her two children.

The senior medical coordinator for California's Department of Food and Agriculture, Peter Kurtz, said: 'I know of no organophosphate in use today that would cause the kinds of things reported in that hospital'.

The post-mortem on Gloria Ramirez took place on 24 February under the most extraordinary conditions. Pathologists wore anti-chemical warfare suits and gas masks, breathing apparatus and two-way radios. A mini TV camera, air samplers and sensors were poked into the body bag before it was lifted out of its air-tight aluminium coffin and all medical staff were prohibited from working longer than a 30 minute shift inside the morgue. It was almost as though they were dealing with an alien from outer space.

The medical cause of death – cardiac arrest caused by kidney failure, in turn caused by cancer – shed little light on the mystery. Unable to comprehend the bizarre events, the local Coroner's Office resorted

GLORIA RAMIREZ

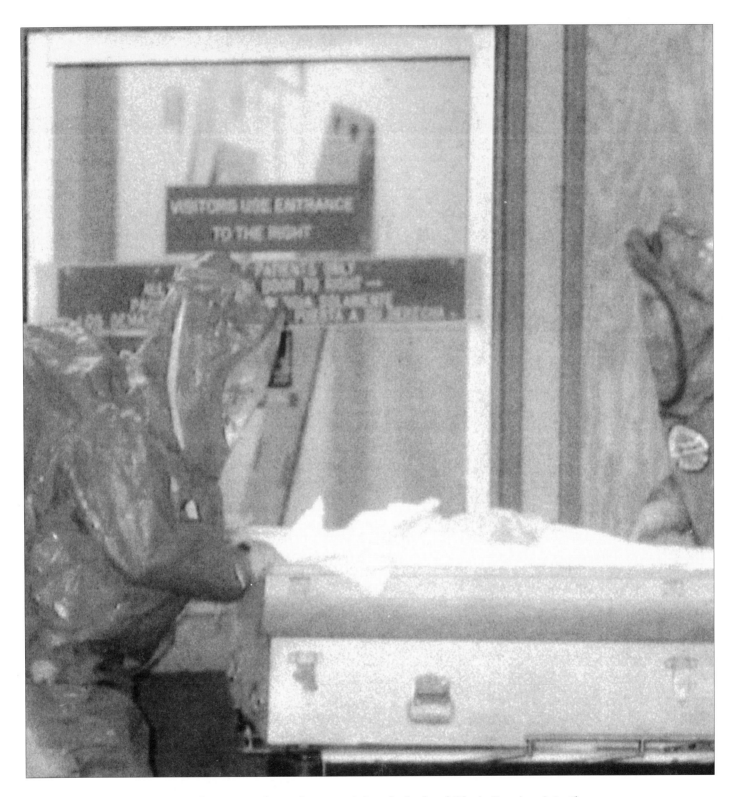

Hazardous material workers move the casket containing the body of Gloria Ramirez into the emergency room.

to the hopelessly unscientific and inadequate explanation that the fumes emanating from Ramirez's body were nothing more than the 'smell of death'.

Just about the only believable theory so far submitted has come from Californian police sources. They allege that Ramirez was a some time drug user who got her kicks from Phencyclidine (PCP), also known as angel dust. This anaesthetic compound is manufactured in illegal laboratories across the state of California. Ramirez was known to frequent one of them.

Had she experimented by rubbing one of the chemicals used in PCP manufacture onto her body, perhaps by first dissolving it in a medicine called DMSO? DMSO, which has the characteristic of smelling differently depending on the user's body tissue, draws substances into the bloodstream through the skin.

This could explain the film on her skin and the strong smell of ammonia. But it is a theory supported by few hard facts. The mystery of Gloria Ramirez looks likely to endure for many years yet.

FORMULA 1
THE PURSUIT OF SPEED

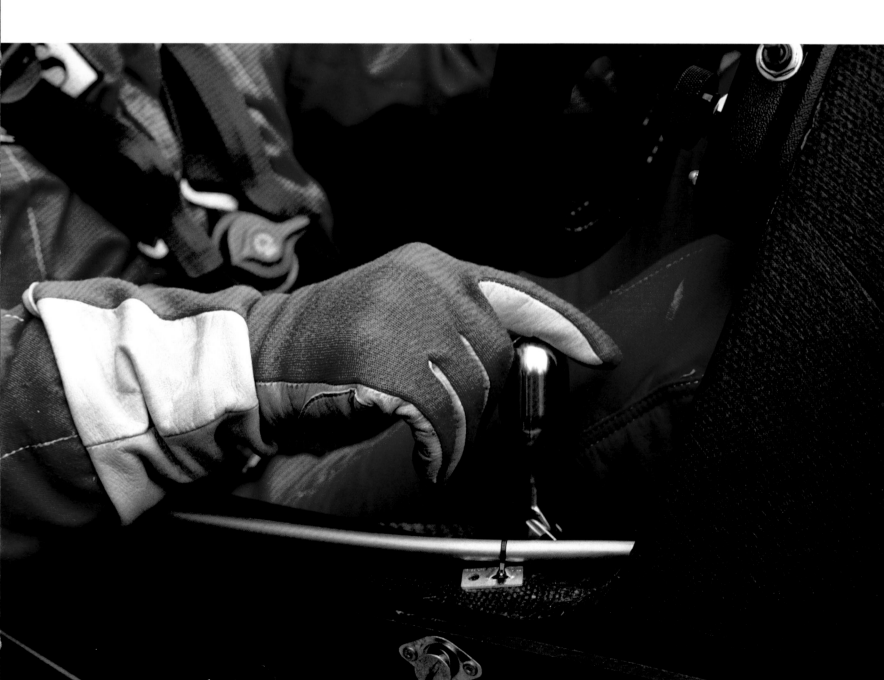

FORMULA 1
THE PURSUIT OF SPEED

photography by **Paul-Henri** & **Bernard Cahier**
words by **Maurice Hamilton**

Aurum
Press

Quarto is the authority on a wide range of topics.

Quarto educates, entertains and enriches the lives of
our readers —enthusiasts and lovers of hands-on living.

www.QuartoKnows.com

First published in Great Britain
2016 by Aurum Press Ltd
74—77 White Lion Street
Islington
London N1 9PF

A catalogue record for this book is available from the British Library.

ISBN 978 1 78131 583 5
Ebook ISBN 978 1 78131 649 8

10 9 8 7 6 5 4 3 2 1
2020 2019 2018 2017 2016

Designed by Ashley Western
Printed in China

The pictures in this book are the work of a father and son photographic dynasty, and *The Pursuit of Speed* is the result of a project I had been wanting to do for quite a long time. A book that would blend and showcase the work that my late father and I have completed during the past sixty-four years in the extraordinary world of Formula One Grand Prix Racing (F1), a body of work that comprises what is known as The Cahier Archive.

So when I was contacted by Lucy Warburton from Aurum Press, telling me she had a book idea on the inside world of F1, I thought to myself that this could be a great opportunity. But selecting the relevant pictures from a collection of well over half-a-million photographs was no easy task. The tremendous evolution of both men and machines, from the glorious days of true camaraderie and endless tragedy to today's world of high-tech show, had to be blended into a coherent, harmonious and beautiful book. That was indeed a challenge, and the result is here, for your viewing pleasure. I hope you will enjoy reading the work as much as we have relished putting it together. Motor racing at the highest level is all about addiction to speed; it is the dance of life and death on the very edge of sanity. Intense emotions, unlimited courage, outrageous dexterity, powerful rivalries: all are blended in *The Pursuit of Speed*, and the result is a sort of visual symphony of this unique spectacle. My dad would be very proud.

CONTENTS

It's seldom in any business, sport or the world of entertainment, that sons become as successful as their fathers; but Paul-Henri Cahier has achieved this feat.

When I entered Formula One Grand Prix racing, Bernard Cahier was already one of the most globally recognised journalists and photographers in motorsport. As I write this foreword, Paul-Henri enjoys the same impressive presence and respect as an F1 photographer.

Bernard Cahier became more than a journalist and a photographer, even though he was hardly ever to be seen without a camera around his neck. He wrote for many of the top motorsport magazines in the world and beyond that, he had commercial relationships with companies such as Goodyear, in which he served at the highest level, including as President and Chairmen. Bernard's presence in the sport is further noted by his advisory role on the ground-breaking film on Formula One, *Grand Prix* by John Frankenheimer. Bernard even featured in the film from time to time.

It was Bernard's close relationship to many of the top drivers that stood him apart and produced such resonating photographs. One of whom was Baron de Graffenried, known to his friends as *Toulo*. It is amazing how serendipitous life can be. When I was driving F1 cars, Bernard took me to Toulo's lovely chalet in Villars for lunch. To my absolute amazement, the great Juan Manuel Fangio was at the same table; what a great thrill for a young Grand Prix driver. Even more incredible, that same chalet today belongs to Paul Stewart, my eldest son.

A very important element of the Cahier family partnership was Joan, the wonderful wife of Bernard and mother of Paul-Henri. What a great combination they were and what a wonderful reality that Paul-Henri is today carrying on so successfully the same high skills that he has inherited from his father and mother.

In today's world of photography, Paul-Henri isn't as lucky as his father. I see Paul-Henri at almost every Grand Prix and he is absolutely laden down by huge cameras, extraordinary lenses and the backpack of support equipment required by today's incredibly high standard of photography and definition – rather different to the early days of his art. The combination of two great photographers compiling a book that ranges so widely and demonstrates the immense change that Formula One and motorsport in general has undergone – transforming the look, the speed, the colour and the personality of the sport – is so well revealed in this excellent collection of wonderful photographs.

Formula One: The Pursuit of Speed gives an insight into the world of F1 which few might get to enjoy if it wasn't for the talents of people like Paul-Henri Cahier, Maurice Hamilton and, of course, Bernard Cahier. Bernard was one of the true pioneers of the photographic journey and his and Paul-Henri's work are the reason that we are able to celebrate the world of Formula One.

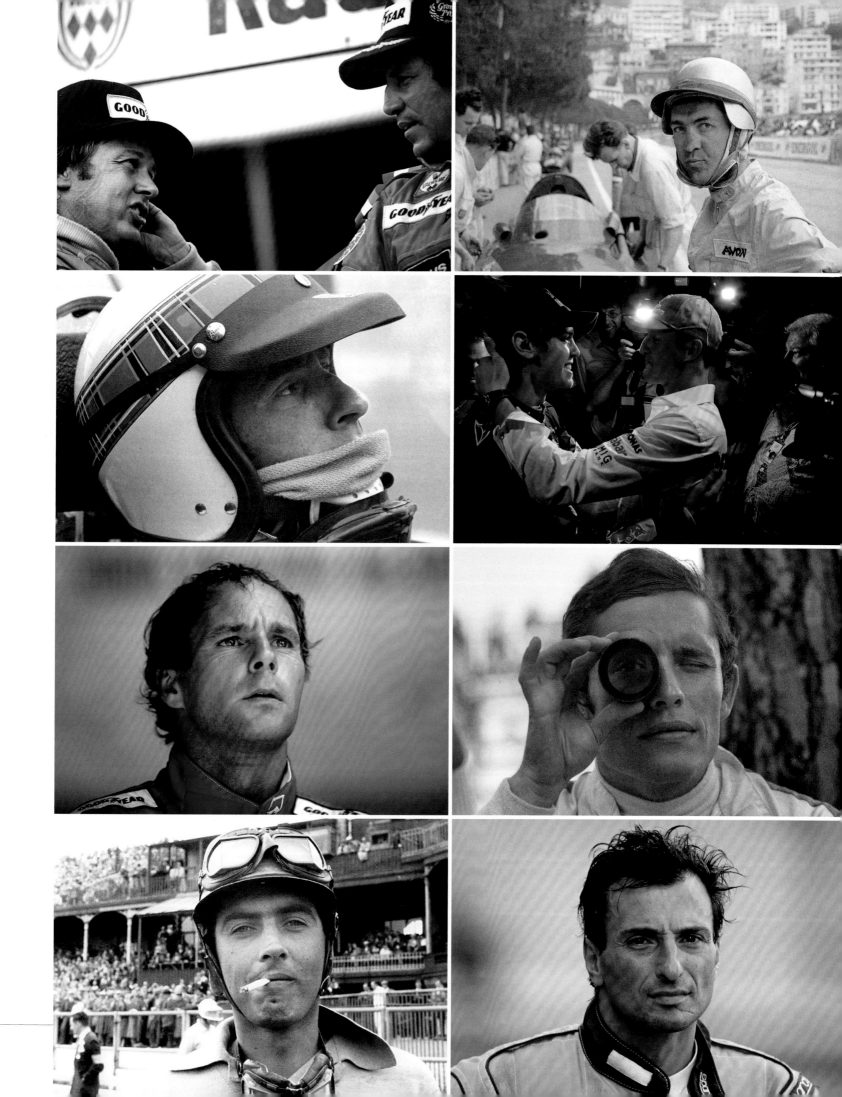

INTRODUCTION

Sixty-four years is a long time by any standard. In Formula One, the progress and change have been immense. To have this evolution recorded is one thing; to enjoy the benefit of images exquisitely captured on camera is quite another.

That is precisely what we've got between the pages of this book, thanks to the precision, imagination and brilliance of the late Bernard Cahier and his son, Paul-Henri. Between them, father and son have reflected the growth and transformation of a sport that has been glamorous and spectacular throughout.

During this time, and despite enormous evolution, F1's fundamental framework has remained unchanged. The drivers are heroes, no matter what they drive; the rivalries and friendships continue exactly as they were in the 1950s, even if today's enmities are mercilessly exposed by social media.

These central themes are caught perfectly thanks to both photographers enjoying the privilege of being allowed behind the scenes and having the patience to recognise and catch the intimate and tense moments when up close. The subsequent images are unique and priceless.

In the same way that a racing driver's attire defines each era, the size, shape and sophistication of his car marks huge advances in technology across the decades. The teams may have expanded to match this progress but, like the drivers, at heart they remain exactly as they were.

Famous names such as Ferrari, McLaren and Williams continue to be motivated by a massively competitive urge that has not changed regardless of the high-tech trappings. The absolute focus is on finishing first. Second place is no more an option in 2016 than it was in 1956.

The canvas for this thrilling competition has been provided by more than seventy different race tracks since the World Championship began in 1950. And, once again, while the backdrops may have altered in keeping with the necessary demands for safety, the challenge provided by the slow corners and fast curves places the same call for that intoxicating mix of accuracy and daring by the men in their machines.

In the 1950s and 60s, street circuits were more prevalent than today. The images in this book highlight the raw and fairly basic demands placed on drivers by kerbs, lampposts and walls waiting to penalise the smallest error. More recent photographs bring home the understandable need for reducing these hazards while, at the same time, highlighting the sometimes extreme dangers endured decades before. This book brings a striking comparison between these vastly different eras, and only adds to the sense of respect for drivers and their exceptional skills.

When the cars are at rest and crash helmets are removed, there is the opportunity for photographers to capture the more candid moments. The authors have done this with an exquisite stealth that creates the relaxed impression of subjects not being aware of the camera's presence.

At the time of taking each photograph, the focus is literally and naturally on people. But looking at the images with hindsight, a study of the surroundings presents a penetrating portrait of how F1 and its trappings have changed, almost beyond recognition.

From the mechanic in oily overalls with a cigarette and a spanner, to the technicians in crisp uniforms tapping keyboards; from perspiring drivers with grease-stained faces in polo shirts, to today's sponsor-bedecked heroes with shining faces in flameproof overalls; from a kettle and teapot in the back of a shabby truck, to Michelin-inspired cuisine delicately served in air-conditioned business and social enclaves; from team management identified by smart suits and collars and ties, to serious-looking men and women wearing headsets and electronic credentials; all of these arresting comparisons of progress are graphically displayed across the following pages.

If a picture is worth a thousand words, then this book is the photographic equivalent of a major literary work on motor racing at its highest and most dramatic level.

RIVALRIES
THE LEGENDS OF F1

Rivalries exist in motor racing, just as they do in any sport. One competitor wants to beat another. The major difference is that racing drivers are doing it wheel-to-wheel, at anything up to 200mph.

The associated danger is obvious and significant, particularly when defining parameters. A feud will find its limit when physical contact could lead to injury – or worse.

But that does not lessen the impact of searing ambition, as one driver desperately wishes to prove himself faster than another. Sometimes that rival may be in the same team, thereby bringing a further intriguing dimension to a contest that already has a sense of gladiatorial conflict. When Grand Prix drivers don their flameproof overalls and crash helmets bearing personal colours, they are preparing for battle on an asphalt playing field, often with unyielding edges.

The key point – amply illustrated on the following pages – is that the strength and depth of competitiveness has intensified over the decades. Paradoxically, a massive improvement in safety has brought an accompanying increase in potentially threatening enmity. Banging wheels in 2016 leads to outrage and, at worst, a puncture. Sixty years before, such a tactic was guaranteed to end in crash and burn.

More than anything, that thought promoted a sense of family. There was need of it when drivers would perish on an appallingly regular basis. It fostered camaraderie; a sense of belonging and support that is hardly necessary today.

Nonetheless, there were conflicts and jealousies many decades ago. Stirling Moss would irritate his rivals because, as a young upstart, he was fast – and he knew it. Moss fought for the 1958 championship with fellow Englishman, Mike Hawthorn. The duel lasted until the final race, Hawthorn becoming the first British World Champion – but only after the stewards at the Portuguese Grand Prix unsuccessfully tried to exclude Hawthorn on a technicality and, remarkably, Moss had come to his defence. That was the height of 'rivalry' then.

Such gentlemanly conduct continued into the 1960s, particularly at the conclusion of the 1964 championship, which was won by the Briton, John Surtees, after his Ferrari team-mate had hit the back of one of Surtees' rivals. This was accepted, albeit reluctantly, by the aggrieved party as an accident and no more was said in public. Today, there would be stewards' inquiries, court cases and endless social media opinion.

Left
Stirling Moss.

Overleaf
Fellow countrymen tended to stay close. Juan Manuel Fangio *(right)* **and Carlos Menditeguy of Argentina chat before the 1957 French Grand Prix at Rouen-les-Essarts.**

A sharper, potentially corrosive element did not appear until the 1980s, significantly at McLaren when the legendary Ayrton Senna became team-mate to Alain Prost, considered to be one of the best drivers in this or any other decade.

A fight for the 1989 championship between the two ended in a collision while battling for the lead at the penultimate round in Japan. A year later, at the same circuit, Senna simply drove into the back of Prost – now racing for Ferrari – and shoved him off the road, becoming World Champion in the process.

The title battle between Michael Schumacher and Damon Hill in 1994 ended at the final race when the pair collided, popular opinion being that Schumacher caused the crash that eliminated both cars and gave him the championship. Schumacher would go some way to proving he was capable of such a tactic at the final race in 1997 when, once again, he collided with his championship rival, Jacques Villeneuve. This time, Schumacher came off worst in every sense, as he was stripped of his championship points, the title going to Villeneuve.

On each occasion, Schumacher drove for Ferrari, while his rivals Hill and Villeneuve raced for Williams. In 2014 and 2015, rivalry returned to within one team as Lewis Hamilton and Nico Rosberg made the most of their technically superior Mercedes to engage in a battle that became increasingly intense. It resulted in a clash of wheels on the track and a frigid atmosphere off it.

At Spa-Francorchamps in 2014, Rosberg was adjudged to have hit the back of Hamilton's car, causing a puncture. A year later, while dominating the championship once more, the pair had edgy moments as they ran wheel-to-wheel on the track – and sometimes off it. Rosberg was not happy when Hamilton cut across to take the lead on the first lap in Japan. The German was even less impressed when the two touched at the first corner of the US Grand Prix, Rosberg being forced to run off the road. Gathering himself together, Rosberg eventually got back in front – only to throw away the lead with an elementary error.

The timing was unfortunate, since the mistake allowed Hamilton to win his second championship in succession. The pair may have been team-mates but there was clearly no love lost in the pre-podium cool-down room when Hamilton playfully threw the cap for second place in Rosberg's direction, only to have it flicked back with barely concealed frustration.

That simple impulsive reaction said everything about Rosberg's effort and focus of the previous six months amounting to nothing. Suddenly he was faced with having to do it all over again in 2016. Each race must have a winner and a loser in the same way that motor racing is predicated on conflict and barely concealed enmity – just like any other sport.

The fight between Rosberg and Hamilton is nothing new. The difference these days is that the risk element is massively reduced compared to forty years ago. Added to which, the associated action on the track is far more accessible and public than it was in the era virtually free from live television, when drivers might have a difference of opinion, but then politely agree to say no more about it.

But the fact remains that high-fuelled rivalries unique to F1 continue to be at the very core of the sport, as drivers deal with danger while pursuing excellence. Rivalry exists – as it always has done. It's just that the terms of engagement tend to be more dramatically defined at 200mph.

Above left
Signs of the uneasy relationship between McLaren drivers Ayrton Senna *(right)* **and Alain Prost after finishing first and second in the 1988 Hungarian Grand Prix.**

Above right
Team-mates but rivals: Lewis Hamilton *(left)* **and Nico Rosberg of Mercedes stand to attention before a start at Monza in 2015.**

Opposite
The start of an intense and ultimately respectful rivalry as James Hunt scores his first Grand Prix win for Hesketh in the 1975 Dutch Grand Prix, beating the Ferraris of Niki Lauda *(left)* **and Clay Regazzoni.**

Overleaf
There was no rivalry as intense as the in-house fight between McLaren drivers Ayrton Senna (1) and Alain Prost during 1989. The Brazilian leads the Frenchman at Monaco.

■ ASCARI–FARINA
1951

Alberto Ascari and Giuseppe 'Nino' Farina were never great rivals as such, since Ascari usually had the upper hand when racing against a fellow Italian twelve years his senior. The latter part of Farina's career was affected by the intervention of the Second World War, but he did become the first World Champion when the title was established in 1950. Ascari won it in 1952 and 1953. During this period, Farina won five Grands Prix, Ascari twenty, including the Dutch Grand Prix in 1953 *(left)*. The two are pictured together in the pits at Spa-Francorchamps in 1954 *(below)*. Ascari *(right)* was not racing that weekend because his car was not ready. He did race at Monaco in 1955 *(below, left)* and famously crashed this Lancia-Ferrari into the harbour while leading. He swam to safety. Four days later, the great Italian hero was killed during a test session at Monza.

■ FANGIO–MOSS
1955

This was not so much 'Rivalry' as 'Master and Pupil'. Moss, eighteen years the Argentine driver's junior, was only too happy to follow in the wheel tracks of the double World Champion when they raced for Mercedes in 1954 and 1955. Moss would say that watching the maestro from close quarters was the best education a young driver could have. Both drivers were trusted by the legendary Mercedes team manager Alfred Neubauer *(top row, left)* to race each other, the rare occasion when Moss (number 12) beat his team-mate being the 1955 British Grand Prix at Aintree *(bottom, right)*. Moss never did find out if Fangio allowed the young Englishman the honour of winning at home.

Having moved on from being team-mates at Mercedes, Moss and Fangio were up against each other in 1957 when driving for Vanwall and Maserati respectively. The friends and rivals, confer *(top, left)* after a hard afternoon's racing in Italian heat, Moss having beaten Fangio at Pescara. At Monza *(top, right)* Fangio's over-steering 250F leads the Vanwall. In the 1956 Championships *(left)*, Moss congratulates Fangio, who knew he had been fortunate to win the British Grand Prix in his Ferrari after Moss's Maserati had run into trouble in the closing stages.

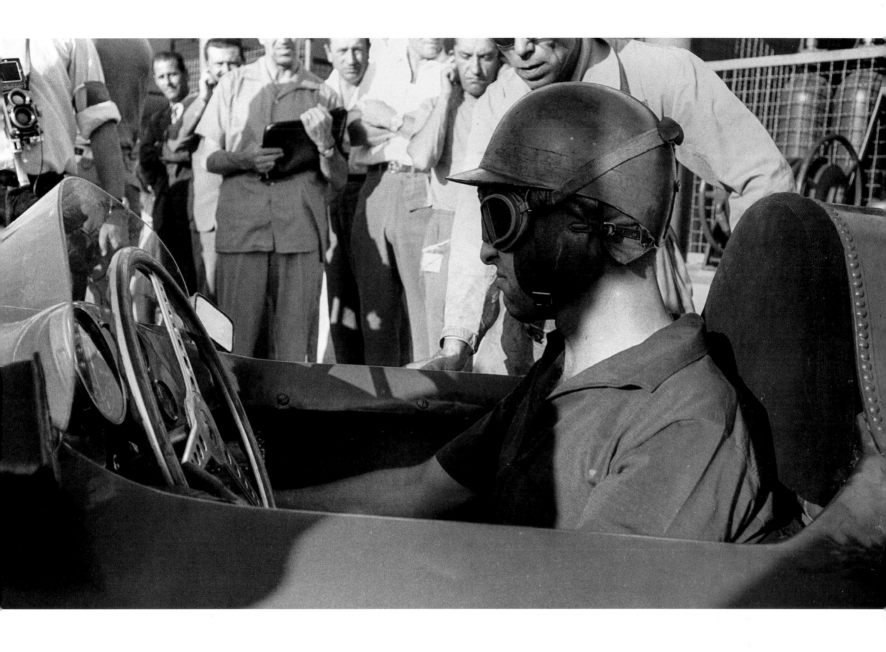

■ FANGIO–COLLINS
1956

Respect rather than rivalry as Juan Manuel Fangio and Peter Collins *(top row, right)* drove for Ferrari in 1956. Collins won the warm approval not only of Fangio but also Enzo Ferrari at Monza when he stopped of his own accord during the Italian Grand Prix and handed his car over to the Argentine. Fangio's Ferrari had failed and this selfless act not only allowed him to become champion for a fourth time, but it also denied Collins the chance to take a title he was destined never to win. The Englishman (number 2) lines up alongside Fangio's Lancia-Ferrari before the start of the 1956 German Grand Prix *(top row, left)*. Communication between the two was difficult, as Fangio did not speak English and Collins was not fluent in Spanish.

■ COLLINS–FANGIO–HAWTHORN
1958

Mike Hawthorn, an archetypal Englishman with a trademark bow tie, shot to prominence by beating Fangio in an epic wheel-to-wheel battle in the 1953 French Grand Prix at Reims. Even though Fangio usually had the upper hand, they remained rivals for many years, the classic confrontation coming at the Nürburgring in 1957 when Hawthorn and Peter Collins drove for Ferrari. The Britons appeared to have the race under control when Fangio made a pit stop. But the Maserati driver then produced the performance of his life on this long and difficult track, catching and passing them both *(above)*. Collins would be killed on the same circuit a year later, Hawthorn *(above right, right)* losing his life in a road accident after becoming the first British World Champion in 1958. Fangio *(above right, left)* retired in the same year and passed away in 1995, aged eighty-four.

■ MOSS–HAWTHORN
1958

Although great championship rivals in 1958 when Stirling Moss drove for the British Vanwall team and Mike Hawthorn represented Ferrari, the actions of Moss *(above left, right)* during the Portuguese Grand Prix defined sportsmanship at the time. When Hawthorn was threatened with disqualification for going against the race traffic while recovering from a spin on the street circuit, it was Moss who pointed out that his rival had been on the pavement and therefore not on the track at all. Hawthorn kept his six points – and, two races later, beat Moss to the championship by one point despite Moss winning the race in Porto *(above, right)*. One of the fittest and most professional of drivers, Moss was destined to never win the title.

■ PHIL HILL–VON TRIPS
1961

At the start of a new formula for Grand Prix racing in 1961, Ferrari produced a car that would have no equal that year. The 'Sharknose' – so called because of the distinctive twin-nostril air intakes in the nose – won five championship races, allowing Phil Hill of the USA and Wolfgang von Trips to fight for the title. The highly strung but thoughtful American *(above)* had little in common with the cool, aristocratic German who led the championship when it reached the penultimate round in Italy. By finishing third or higher at Monza, von

Trips *(below, right)* would have been crowned champion, but his Ferrari collided with another car and spun off at high speed, killing himself and fifteen spectators. Hill became the first American to win the title and retired from F1 in 1964. He died, aged eighty-one, in California in 2008.

■ SURTEES-HILL-CLARK
1962-64

All three British drivers were in contention when the 1964 championship reached the final round in Mexico. To take the title for the second year in succession, Jim Clark (right) needed to win the race, with Graham Hill lower than third and John Surtees lower than second. With Surtees having to finish first or second, Hill was the favourite because he would automatically become champion if the other two did not finish well. There was controversy when Hill, lying third, was hit from behind by Surtees' team-mate Lorenzo Bandini. When Clark's Lotus retired from the lead with engine failure, Surtees (left) only had bring his Ferrari home second – which he duly did to become the only man to win World Championships on two wheels and four. Clark and Hill had battled before. As the more senior of the two Britons, Hill had the edge on experience, if not out-and-out speed. Hill, driving for BRM, went head-to-head with Clark for the championship in 1962 (p.42), Hill taking the title when Clark's Lotus ran out of oil during the last race. Clark would have his day in 1963 and 1965, the two then joining forces to make a powerful combination at Lotus in 1967.

Clark brought a sublime skill
to F1 when the quiet Scotsman
struck up a winning relationship
with Colin Chapman, the design
genius behind Lotus. Hill, driving
for BRM, went head-to-head
with Clark for the championship
in 1962 (Clark leads Hill in
Holland, *below*; the pair are
neck-and-neck, centre and left
of the grid in France, *below
right*), Hill's BRM leads Surtees
at Monaco in 1963 *(right)*, the
Ferrari driver going on to win in
Germany *(far right)*.

■ RINDT–STEWART
1969

Rivals, but friends and neighbours in Switzerland, Jackie Stewart and Jochen Rindt engaged in some classic battles, particularly the 1969 British Grand Prix when they swapped the lead many times during an epic contest, victory eventually going to Stewart's Matra-Ford. Stewart won the championship that year, but in 1970 Rindt had the upper hand with his Lotus-Ford. The Austrian was killed during practice for the Italian Grand Prix, but had scored enough points to become Grand Prix racing's only posthumous World Champion. Stewart was devastated, he and his wife Helen *(below left, after Stewart had won the 1969 Dutch GP)* having been close to Jochen and his wife Nina *(below)*. Rindt is best remembered by fans for his spectacular driving style and a fairy-tale victory at Monaco in 1970 after the erstwhile leader, Jack Brabham, had crashed at the final corner when under pressure from the flying Rindt.

■ FITTIPALDI–STEWART
1972–73

Emerson Fittipaldi's *(above right)* meteoric rise in motorsport continued after winning only his fourth F1 race – the 1970 United States Grand Prix – and going on to challenge Jackie Stewart *(above left)* for the championship two years later. Fittipaldi made the most of the all-conquering Lotus-Ford to take his first title in 1972, but had a much harder fight with Stewart and his Tyrrell-Ford during the following season. Fittipaldi won the first two races, including his home Grand Prix in Brazil, but had to give best to the Scotsman, a driver he much admired. Stewart, having won his third championship, retired at the end of 1973.

■ FITTIPALDI-REGAZZONI
1974

Emerson Fittipaldi moved from Lotus to McLaren *(right)* for 1974 and immediately won the Brazilian Grand Prix. After a challenge from Niki Lauda, Fittipaldi's championship rival would turn out to be Lauda's Ferrari team-mate, Clay Regazzoni *(above)*. The Swiss and the Brazilian were in a shoot-out at the final race in the United States, the two running wheel-to-wheel on the opening lap, with Fittipaldi being forced to put two wheels on the grass at over 160 mph. The McLaren driver did not back off and went on to win his second title. Fittipaldi left McLaren at the end of 1975 to start up an all-Brazilian F1 team, before enjoying much more success by moving into IndyCar racing in the United States and winning the Indianapolis 500 twice. He retired from full-time racing in 1996.

■ HUNT–LAUDA
1976

A rivalry so intense and powerful that it provided the basis of *Rush*, a full-length feature film covering the 1976 season. James Hunt, a dashing young Englishman enjoying his first proper break with a top team, drove for McLaren-Ford *(above, left)*. Lauda, a wily and more seasoned campaigner, having won the title in 1975, raced for Ferrari. A year of protests and controversy would have two key moments: supported by his wife Marlene *(bottom, right)*, Lauda made a remarkable comeback after being badly burned and close to death when his car crashed and caught fire in Germany *(above, right)*. The Austrian then pulled out of the final race in Japan when he considered the streaming-wet conditions too dangerous, allowing Hunt to win the title. Lauda *(overleaf, in middle, talking to Ronnie Peterson)* would go on to win a second championship in 1977 before retiring abruptly, only to return and win a third in 1984. Hunt *(overleaf, left)* retired in 1979, eventually becoming a TV commentator before dying suddenly at the age of 45 in 1993.

THE PURSUIT OF SPEED: A PHOTOGRAPHIC CELEBRATION OF F1'S GREATEST MOMENTS

■ SCHECKTER-VILLENEUVE
1979

Gilles Villeneuve gave a perfect demonstration of team loyalty in 1979 when he supported Jody Scheckter's successful championship bid, even though the talented French-Canadian was faster at times than the South African. Villeneuve had already been with Ferrari for one season (winning his home Grand Prix in Montreal in 1978) when Scheckter arrived from Wolf as team-leader. They each won three races *(above right, Villeneuve at Watkins Glen in the United States)* but Villeneuve dutifully remained in Scheckter's wheel tracks *(above left)* when requested, allowing his team-mate to take the title at Monza, Ferrari's home ground. Scheckter would retire from motorsport at the end of 1980 and go on to start successful businesses in firearms training simulators in the USA and organic farming in England.

■ JONES–PIQUET
1980

Alan Jones did not have a lot of time for South American drivers' style of racing and Nelson Piquet in particular. When they ran head-to-head in the 1980 World Championship, with the impetus regularly swapping between the Brazilian and the Australian, it was bound to end in tears. As if it had been scripted, the pair were side-by-side on the front of the grid for the penultimate race in Canada. Piquet's Brabham-Ford was on pole position, on the inside on the right. When Jones made a slightly better getaway and aimed his Williams-Ford for the right-hand curve immediately after the start, the resulting collision did more damage to the Brabham than the Williams, Piquet having made contact with the concrete wall. When the race was re-started – several cars had been involved in the resulting pile-up – Piquet had to use his back-up machine, which was not as well-prepared as his favoured car. After the Brabham's engine blew up, Jones sailed to the championship. Piquet *(below, right)* sprays the champagne after finishing second in the 1980 British Grand Prix *(below, left)* while Jones holds the winner's trophy.

JONES–REUTEMANN
1981

Carlos Reutemann's serious expression *(far right)* sums up the relationship with Alan Jones when the Argentine driver was the Australian's team-mate at Williams in 1981. As reigning World Champion and having enjoyed a comfortable history with the team, Jones was the de facto number-one driver and was supposed to be allowed to win the Brazilian Grand Prix early in the year. When Reutemann ignored team orders and took the victory, an icy atmosphere set in for the remainder of the season. Reutemann, through first-class performances such as his win in Belgium *(below, leading Piquet's Brabham)*, got himself into the lead of the championship, but lost his chance at the final race in Las Vegas after starting from pole and finishing out of the points. A commanding win for Jones *(right)* in the same race exacerbated Reutemann's disappointment as much as it quietly pleased his team-mate.

■ PROST-ARNOUX
1982

Despite fielding a competitive car, Renault's hopes of winning the championship for the first time in 1982 were compromised by the disorderly behaviour of René Arnoux *(above)*. The Frenchman agreed to allow Alain Prost *(right)* to win their home Grand Prix because his fellow-countryman had a better chance of taking the title thanks to scoring more points thus far. When Arnoux took an early lead, Prost was happy to conserve his car and tyres, knowing he would be allowed to take command later in the race. But Arnoux never let up and ignored pit signals reminding him of the agreement. Prost's fury multiplied when the Renault management failed to tell the world what had been agreed, giving the false impression that Prost was being a bad loser when he said he could have won the race had he known from the outset that he was racing his team-mate. Renault did not win the championship and it took several years before the French drivers spoke amicably again.

■ PIRONI-VILLENEUVE
1982

The story of a short but bitter rivalry with a tragic conclusion. Gilles Villeneuve had become a stalwart at Ferrari when Didier Pironi joined the Italian team in 1982. Villeneuve had no need of team orders, but it seemed a good idea when the potentially fragile Ferraris had no opposition to speak of in the San Marino Grand Prix. Rather than race each other to destruction, it was agreed that whoever was in front in the early going would be allowed to stay there until the finish. When Pironi overtook Villeneuve and led during the closing stages *(right)*, Villeneuve assumed it was for show, to keep the Ferrari fans amused. But rather than put on an act, Pironi was serious about winning and stayed out of Villeneuve's reach. The French-Canadian was livid, spoke of Pironi's duplicity and vowed never to speak to the Frenchman again. It was a threat with a terrible resonance. Two weeks later, while trying to better Pironi's qualifying time for the Belgian Grand Prix *(below)*, Villeneuve collided with a slower car that had inadvertently moved into his path. Villeneuve died of injuries received when thrown from the cockpit of the cavorting Ferrari.

■ PIQUET–PROST
1983

The story of 1983 was not so much that Nelson Piquet *(right)* had won the World Championship, but that Alain Prost had lost it. Prost and Renault *(above)* had been the favourites but, not for the first time, their chances had been frittered away as they came under increasing threat from Piquet and Brabham-BMW. Prost won four races to Piquet's three, the pair colliding in Holland after Prost had misjudged an overtaking move, all of which turned up the pressure another notch. Going into the final race in South Africa, Prost led by two points. Believing they were about to witness the crowning of their first World Champion, the French media descended on Kyalami in their droves – only to be stunned when the Renault, never in the hunt, broke down. Prost was heavily criticised by the French reporters, the majority of whom did not understand how F1 worked. He left Renault almost immediately and joined McLaren. Piquet, with a second title under his belt, stayed with Brabham before moving on to Williams.

■ PROST–LAUDA
1984

Finding themselves with the best car – the McLaren-TAG Turbo – Alain Prost and Niki Lauda were free to race each other for the title. It would turn out to be the closest finish in the history of the championship, Lauda *(above left, on the right)* beating Prost by half a point (the anomaly of the half-point created by the Monaco Grand Prix having been stopped early because of heavy rain and half-points awarded, Prost receiving 4.5 points instead of nine for winning). Lauda was in the twilight of a distinguished F1 career but no less canny for that. Realising that his young team-mate was faster, Lauda used his guile and experience to focus on collecting points rather than being fastest all the time. Each driver had great respect for the other, making it one of the most productive, amicable and yet seriously competitive partnerships in the history of the F1 championship. Prost, as Lauda predicted, went on to win four world titles, while the Austrian retired for a second time at the end of the following year.

■ MANSELL–SENNA
1985–89

The enmity between Nigel Mansell and Ayrton Senna took hold in 1985 and would run in two phases into the 1990s. It started when both drivers, united only by an iron will to win, scored maiden wins in 1985, the year Senna replaced Mansell in the John Player Special Lotus *(right)*. Mansell was much more at home with Williams-Honda and the raging impulse to beat each other continued into 1987, reaching its most dramatic peak in Belgium when the pair collided, Mansell later attempting to throttle his rival in the Lotus garage. Even after Senna *(below)* switched to McLaren-Honda and Mansell to Ferrari, the animosity continued when they collided yet again during the 1989 Portuguese Grand Prix, as Mansell tried an ambitious move that added fuel to a fire started when he ignored a black flag signalling him to stop for an earlier indiscretion. It fostered a deep-seated antagonism that would resume a few years later.

■ MANSELL-PIQUET
1986–87

Sharing the competitiveness of the Williams-Honda in 1986 and 1987, Nigel Mansell and Nelson Piquet may have been in the same team but were never on the same side. The mutual antipathy was evident from the outset as the Brazilian poked fun at his very British counterpart. In the absence of team orders, it was every man for himself – as was proved in Hungary *(opposite, top, left)* when Piquet found a performance tweak for his car that he didn't share with his team-mate. Mansell *(opposite, bottom, right)* found out about it when lapped by Piquet's winning car. Mansell gained more impressive high ground in 1987 when, in a straight fight, he beat Piquet by pulling off a brave overtaking move to win the British Grand Prix *(above)*. Piquet *(opposite, top, right)* had the last laugh by winning the championship that year, unlike 1986, when the pair had run neck-and-neck and taken enough points off each other to allow Alain Prost to slip through and take the championship at the final race.

■ SENNA–PROST
1988–90

The most infamous rivalry of them all. Ayrton Senna *(bottom row, middle)* joined McLaren-Honda in 1988 knowing that Alain Prost *(middle row, centre)*, with the team since 1984, was considered to be the best driver of the era. Senna's intense desire to prove himself by beating the Frenchman began to surface in Portugal near the end of 1988 when he eased Prost towards the pit wall at 175mph. It really got going the following year when a row blew up after Senna had broken a private agreement with Prost and taken victory in the San Marino Grand Prix. When the championship boiled down to these two drivers, the inevitable collision took place at the penultimate race as they fought for the lead, the title going to Prost. Infuriated over what he perceived to be unjust treatment, Senna took the law into his own hands at the same race a year later and drove Prost, now with Ferrari *(top row, right)* off the road, winning the championship in the process. They battled less often in 1993 when Prost switched to Williams-Renault *(overleaf)*, and there would be an unexpected and complete rapprochement when Prost retired at the end of that year, six months before Senna was killed at Imola.

■ MANSELL–SENNA
1991–92

The rivalry between the Brazilian and the Englishman picked up again in 1991 when Mansell once more had a very competitive car at his disposal. With maturity and experience came a grudging respect that saw Mansell give Senna a lift on his victorious Williams-Renault after Senna's McLaren-Honda had broken down during the 1991 British Grand Prix. The sight of the pair running within inches of each other – and without contact – at 190 mph while fighting for the lead in Barcelona later that year remains one of the sport's most iconic images. Mansell would win the world crown in 1992, but not before Senna had used his guile to win in Monaco *(right)* and sucker Mansell into a crash as they fought for position during the Canadian Grand Prix. Mansell would switch to IndyCar racing in 1993, making a brief return to F1 in 1994 and in 1995 after Senna's fatal accident in the San Marino Grand Prix.

■ SCHUMACHER–HILL
1994–95

When Ayrton Senna was killed at Imola in May 1994, Damon Hill *(below and bottom row, left and right)* found himself elevated to team leader at Williams-Renault – and straight into conflict with Benetton's Michael Schumacher *(second row)*. The German would become Hill's nemesis in a championship battle that saw Hill score classy wins (particularly in Japan) and would run until the last race when they collided while disputing the lead of the Australian Grand Prix. Both were out but the title went to Schumacher. The following year, Hill was consistently beaten (they collided twice more) as Schumacher won his second championship, but the Englishman regrouped in 1996 to take the title after Schumacher had switched to the uncompetitive Ferrari team. They never did become the best of friends, not even after Hill retired in 1999 following stints with Arrows and Jordan.

■ SCHUMACHER–VILLENEUVE
1997

After a shaky start as Ferrari reorganised in 1996, the combination of the Italian team and Schumacher *(above, and below left)* began to come good the following year and to lock into battle with the Williams-Renault of Jacques Villeneuve. As in 1994, the championship went down to the wire, but this time Schumacher lost out following another collision with his rival in the last race. When Villeneuve *(above right, bottom right)* tried to overtake during the European Grand Prix at Jerez in Spain, the French-Canadian (son of Gilles Villeneuve) found the Ferrari turning in on him. The deliberate move by Schumacher raised questions about the part he had played in Hill's demise three years before and also earned a reprimand, Schumacher being stripped of his 1997 championship points. Villeneuve would spend another eight seasons in F1, but would never enjoy the same level of competitiveness.

■ SCHUMACHER-HAKKINEN
1998-2000

Ferrari's bid to win the championship with Schumacher for the first time since Jody Scheckter in 1979 was heavily compromised by the energetic presence of Mika Hakkinen and McLaren-Mercedes *(above)*, the Finn edging out his rivals by narrow margins in 1998 and 1999. By and large, the contest was clean. Schumacher would learn the hard way that his rival was not a driver to be messed with when, in a pass of spine-tingling commitment and bravery at Spa-Francorchamps, Hakkinen went one side of a backmarker while Schumacher went the other as they braked from 200mph for the following corner. The move gave Hakkinen the lead; fair reward he felt for having had Schumacher cut in front of him at the same spot a lap earlier. This was in 2000, the year Schumacher and Ferrari finally became champions. Hakkinen would quit F1 at the end of the following year.

(Opposite, clockwise from top left)
In 1998, Schumacher celebrates
victory at Monza, heads for
another win at a wet Silverstone
and points the Ferrari towards
a podium finish in Austria.
(Above) Schumacher prepares to
evacuate the cockpit in Germany.

■ IRVINE-HAKKINEN
1999

Marked out to play a supporting role to his Ferrari team-mate, Eddie Irvine *(below right)* was thrust into the championship equation halfway through the 1999 season when Schumacher crashed and broke a leg during the British Grand Prix. When the German made a return for the last two races, roles were reversed as he did what he could to assist Irvine's fight with McLaren's Mika Hakkinen *(below left)*. The Ulsterman eased into the reckoning by winning the penultimate round in Malaysia, with Schumacher demoting Hakkinen to third. But, in the final race in Japan, Irvine was sidelined with a mysterious handling problem, allowing Hakkinen to win both the race and the title. Irvine would never come so close again during three seasons with Jaguar before retiring at the end of 2002.

■ ALONSO–SCHUMACHER
2006

Fernando Alonso *(above)* and Michael Schumacher dominated the 2006 World Championship, each winning seven races for Renault and Ferrari respectively. A very strong first half of the season kept Alonso ahead but Schumacher fought back, victory in China putting the German in front in the title race for the first time with two races to go. A first and a second in Japan and Brazil were enough to make Alonso the youngest driver to win back-to-back World Championships. Schumacher would quit F1 at the end of the season, making a return with Mercedes in 2010 but showing none of the dominance that had effectively been ended by Alonso's two strong seasons.

■ HAMILTON–ALONSO
2007

Fernando Alonso joined McLaren-Mercedes for 2007 to lead Lewis Hamilton in his first F1 season. It was a dream team that turned into a nightmare thanks to the young Englishman's precocious performances and Alonso's increasing paranoia when, in his view, Hamilton's speed should have been kept in check by McLaren management. Alonso led the championship after winning the second race in Malaysia and the fifth in Monaco, but then had to give best to his team-mate as Hamilton *(bottom, right)* won

two races and led the title race all the way to the final round – by which time the relationship had deteriorated to the point where Alonso, despite winning in Italy *(below)*, had become a disgruntled loose cannon. Added to which, McLaren had to deal with the damage created by allegations of spying by Ferrari, whose driver, Kimi Räikkönen, lifted the championship at the final race, having led only briefly early on. Alonso left immediately, while Hamilton stayed on for another five years.

RIVALRIES: THE LEGENDS OF F1 **99**

■ HAMILTON–MASSA
2008

In one of the greatest cliff-hangers in the history of the World Championship, Lewis Hamilton *(near right, and far right columns)* won the title at the last corner of the last race in Brazil. For ten seconds, Felipe Massa *(middle column)*, having won his home race, thought he was champion, until Hamilton made up one crucial position a quarter of a mile from the finish. It summed up a hugely dramatic season as Massa led the title chase halfway through before Hamilton began a run of high point-scoring, only to be taken out by a collision with Massa three races from the end. Massa had his share of bad luck while leading in Singapore only to be waved away from a pit stop with the fuel line still attached. It would be the closest Massa has yet come to winning the title; he survived a potentially fatal injury in 2009 and was still racing in F1 in 2016.

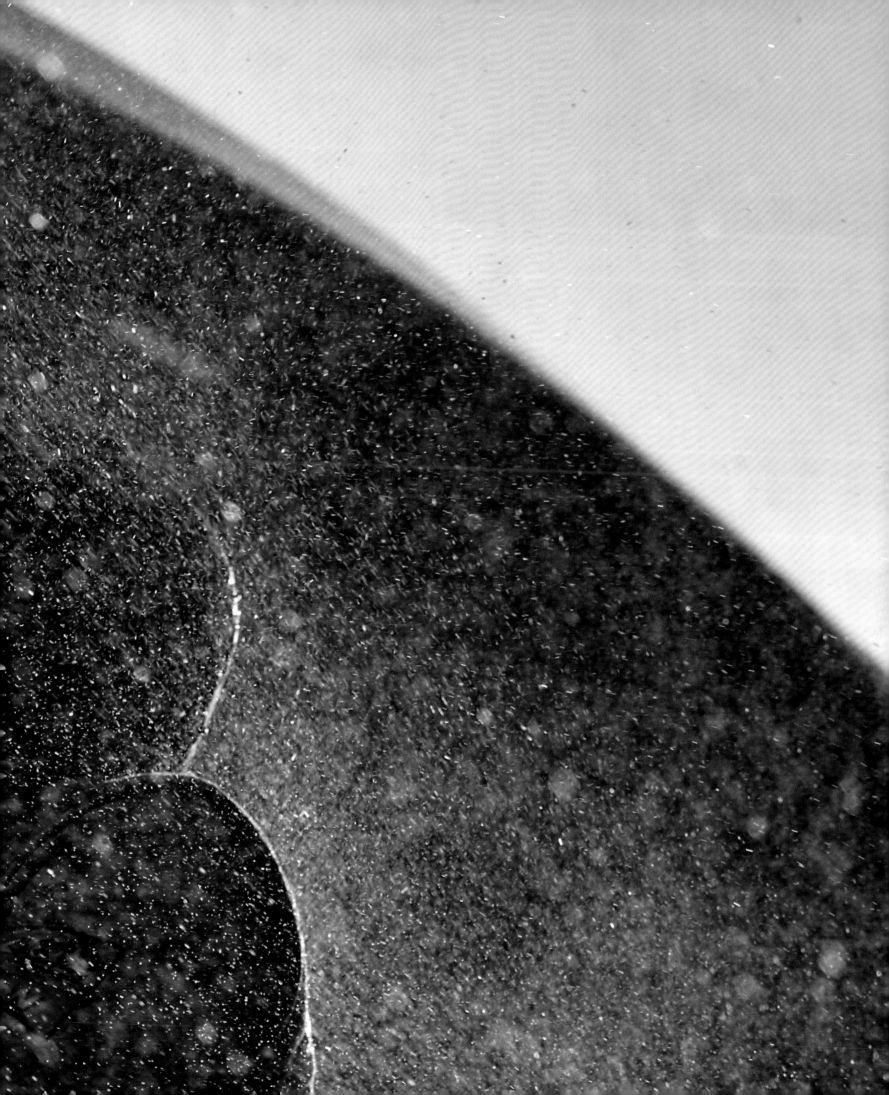

■ VETTEL-WEBBER
2010–13

Sebastian Vettel *(above)* won four championships in succession between 2010 and 2013, the early years in particular being enlivened by an increasingly tense battle with his Red Bull team-mate, Mark Webber *(opposite top, left)*. There was little love lost between the Australian and Vettel, particularly in 2010 when the pair collided as the German tried to take the lead in Turkey. Vettel had become edgy after Webber's victories in the previous two races, including the difficult and prestigious Monaco Grand Prix. Webber was ahead of Vettel on points going into the final race in Abu Dhabi but pole position for Vettel and a clean race gave him the title as Webber became bogged down in traffic. Webber would never get a better opportunity during his remaining three years in F1 before switching to become World Endurance Champion in 2015.

■ HAMILTON–ROSBERG
2014–16

This has been the headline-grabbing rivalry of recent years as Lewis Hamilton made the move from McLaren to join Nico Rosberg *(below, left)* at Mercedes for 2014. Hamilton knew the German well, the pair having grown up together through karting and the junior formulae. Their lap times in the dominant Mercedes were frequently separated by fractions of a second – the click of a finger. But when it came to the ruthless bare-knuckle fight needed to succeed in such a situation, Hamilton would usually come out on top. Frustrated by his team-mate's aggression, Rosberg's attempt at resisting a pass in Belgium resulted in Hamilton's left-rear tyre being punctured – and Rosberg being further upset by the criticism that came his way. Hamilton won the title at the final race of 2014 and, emboldened by his second championship, drove better than ever and took a third before the end of the 2015 season. But not before more controversy as he eased Rosberg off the road in the US Grand Prix. Released from the pressure of the championship, Rosberg then moved onto a higher plane – with Hamilton possibly relaxing a little – and won the final three races in truly dominant style, thus setting the scene for 2016.

A pensive Lewis Hamilton (left)
as Rosberg (right) has his share
of spraying victory champagne.

TEAMS AND CARS
A DESIRE FOR SPEED

M otorsport fans are intensely loyal. But while many attach their allegiance to a particular driver, others remain devoted to a single team. The cult of family and passion generated by an established team will often outweigh dedication to the star performer. The driver is transient; enjoying his moment before either moving on or retiring. The team will be there, if not forever, then for quite some time. That, at least, is the plan. A glance at the historical register of F1 teams, however, shows just how difficult that can be.

Since the start of the F1 World Championship in 1950, more than sixty-five teams have taken part. Only one – Ferrari – has stayed the course. Of the current teams, McLaren has been in F1 since 1966; Williams, in various guises, since 1973. The rest vary from twenty-five years to novice, as demonstrated by the Haas team entering F1 in 2016.

The American name has been added to a list that actually began long before the World Championship was invented sixty-six years ago. In fact, the origins of the sport demonstrate the importance of machine over man, as the first motor races at the turn of the twentieth century allowed one motor manufacturer to show its superiority over another. The race from Paris to Rouen in 1894 was all about Peugeot against Panhard and other car companies rather than the skill of the drivers coping with these spindly machines on rutted and dusty roads.

The trend would continue until the Second World War interrupted dramatic battles between Auto Union and Mercedes-Benz who fought for supremacy, not just in Germany but internationally. When sport resumed in the mid-1940s, the value of racing continued to be of interest to car companies, the Italians joining the fray with teams from Maserati, Alfa Romeo and, significantly, Ferrari.

Enzo Ferrari may have started out as a driver, but he was astute enough to see racing as a means of advertising his exotic road-going sports cars, the sale of which funded his motor racing. Ferrari was living for the moment and, much as he would have enjoyed the thought, it's a fair bet he did not dream of his racing team being viewed as a motorsport icon several decades later.

He did, however, live through an era of change, one that would accelerate even more dramatically in the years following his death at the age of ninety in 1988. Before then, however, Ferrari had done more than any other entrant to perpetuate the dramatic image and raison d'être of a team pursuing motor racing at the highest level.

The undeniable fact is that much of the melodrama was created by the Italian autocrat setting his drivers against each other at a time when safety was not a priority and fatalities were common. In the view of Enzo Ferrari, the best drivers may have been brilliant but they had to be regarded as expendable. Indeed, in his openly expressed opinion, they were lucky to be racing for Ferrari.

There is a certain amount of truth in the fact that a top driver is impotent without a fast and reliable car but, equally, many promising careers could be wrecked by a top team enduring a single season of uncompetitiveness. In this cyclical business, Ferrari had several of those, even though his personal desire for speed remained undiminished. But when his crafty gamesmanship blended with clever technology, Ferrari's unstoppable force would add another chapter to the growing legend.

His handling of a change of engine formula for the 1961 season was a perfect example of adroit political subterfuge. While the British teams bemoaned the new formula, threatening boycotts and talking of lobbying for a more attractive alternative, Enzo Ferrari agreed with them. But all the while, his team was beavering away at being fully prepared for the latest regulations as soon as the season started. While the British wrung their hands and cried unfair, Ferrari dominated the championship. When the opposition caught up in 1962, the Ferrari team was nowhere. Such is the roller-coaster intrigue of F1.

Being one step ahead has always been the yardstick. When the formula changed again in 1966, Jack Brabham was prepared. Instead of investing in complex plans for the latest engines, the wily Australian developed a unit based on a tried and trusted V8 from America. It may not have been the most advanced engine ever seen in F1 but it was reliable – and ready. His cars won the championship for two successive seasons.

As the years went by and technology advanced rapidly, Colin Chapman tapped into it better than most. The mercurial genius dreamed up the wedge-shaped Lotus 72 that would dominate the scene in the early 1970s. Not satisfied with that, Chapman took a huge step forward when he invented so-called 'ground effect', a development that effectively sucked the car to the track and allowed Mario Andretti to destroy the opposition in 1978.

In between, there had been a bad patch for Lotus – as would happen to Williams after their cars had been a major force throughout the early 1980s. Williams, in turn,

were usurped by McLaren, as the team from Surrey mated a purpose-built engine from Porsche with an equally competitive chassis made from carbon fibre, a material that McLaren had used to revolutionise F1 not long before. But unlike its rivals, McLaren kept the ball rolling into the 1990s with a timely switch to Honda engines and an equally powerful driving pairing of Ayrton Senna and Alain Prost.

And so it continued, the impetus shifting back to Williams, then on to the newly formed Benetton team, back to McLaren (now with Mercedes engines), followed by a long run for Michael Schumacher and the ever-present red cars from Ferrari at the start of the 2000s. A brief period for Renault led to a four-year domination by Red Bull until another change of engine formula for 2014 saw Mercedes – now running their own team instead of just supplying engines – being better prepared than most.

It has been a dictum of motor racing that Mercedes understood through past experience. In 1954, the German team had returned to F1 and steamrollered the opposition from the word go with their superior silver machines. It was eloquent proof that the desire for speed has never changed, no matter the colour of the car or who may be driving it – as any F1 fan will confirm.

■ McLAREN

Founded by Bruce McLaren *(right)* in 1963, the early days of McLaren Racing are encapsulated by the images above. The two cars parked randomly *(above)* with drivers Denny Hulme *(left)* and McLaren sitting on the front wheels, casually preparing for a photo call in the pit lane at Jarama, sum up the relaxed small-team atmosphere in 1968. As does the shot *(top right)* of Hulme sprawled across the front of the car driven by his boss and Kiwi mate, Bruce. The cars were originally sprayed orange when Gulf represented the leading sponsor, prior to the arrival of Marlboro in the late 1970s. Alain Prost, in the foreground *(bottom right, middle)*, waits in the pit lane at Monza in 1985, the way barred by the JPS Lotus of Ayrton Senna before the Brazilian joined Prost at McLaren. The pair would win championships for McLaren before the arrival of Mika Häkkinen *(p.126)* and Lewis Hamilton *(p.127)*.

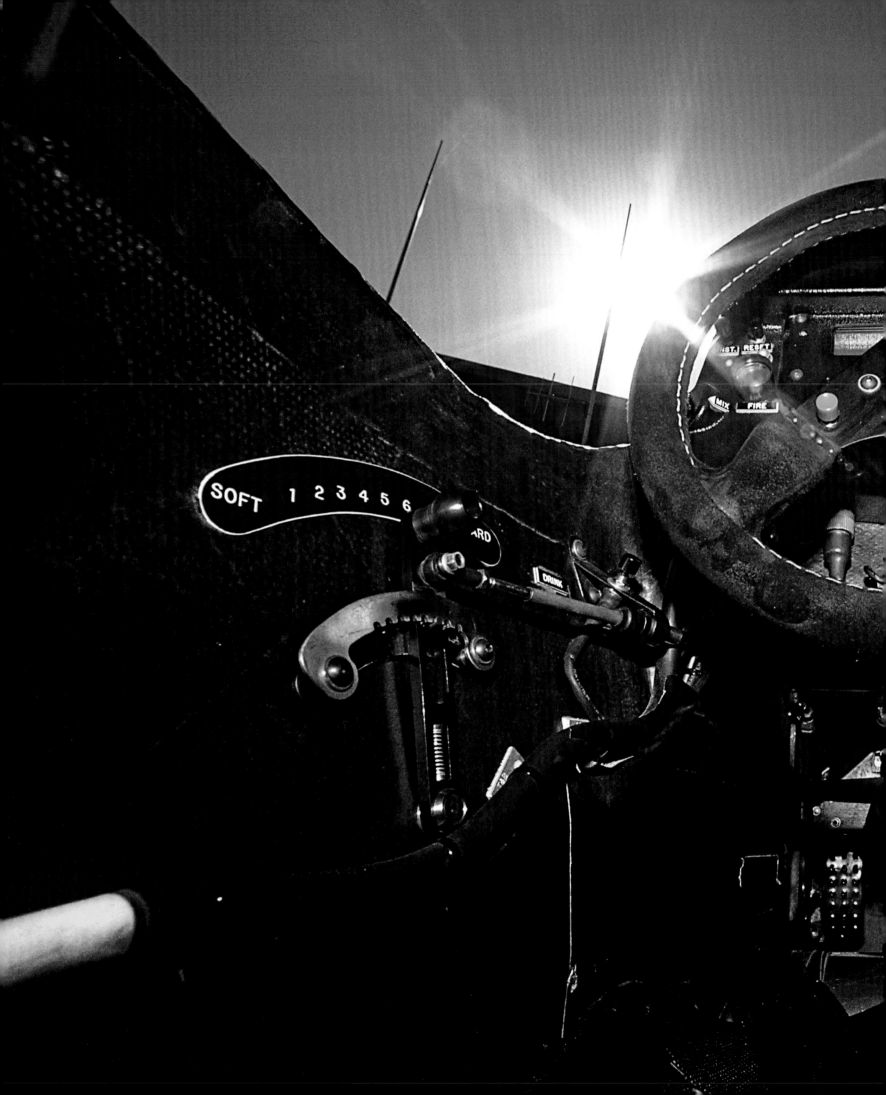

Mika Hakkinen   Lewis Hamilton

Fernando Alonso

■ FERRARI

The images on the following pages illustrate the many shapes but consistently charismatic red of Ferrari through the decades, as befits the longest-serving team in F1. From the front-engine machines of the 1950s *(Phil Hill above, left)* to the chisel-nose profile of cars three decades later *(above, right)*, all have carried the famous Prancing Horse insignia that represents the most famous name in motorsport. The story of this great team abounds with personalities, starting with Enzo Ferrari himself *(p.130 bottom, far left, talking to Phil Hill)* and moving through drivers such as Froilán González, winner of Ferrari's first championship Grand Prix *(top, left)* to Giuseppi Farina *(top, centre)*, John Surtees *(bottom, far right)* and Mike Hawthorn *(chasing the Vanwall of Tony Brooks at the Nürburgring in 1958, centre)* with brilliant engineers including a pensive Mauro Forghieri, seated in the 1963 Ferrari at Silverstone *(top and centre, right)*.

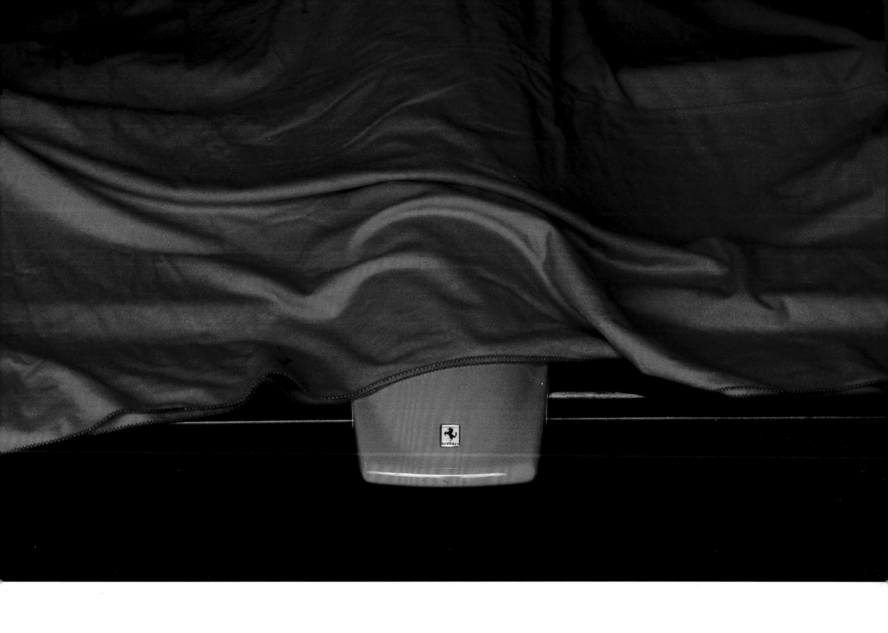

Little can match the imposing sight of five Lancia-Ferraris, waiting for the start of practice at Monza in 1956.

Niki Lauda and Carlos
Reutemann: Monza 1977.

Patrick Tambay : Detroit 1983.

Mechanics at work: Estoril 1988
(top) and Interlagos 1991.

Kimi Raikkonen : Silverstone 2007.

Gerhard Berger : Argentina 1995.

Rubens Barrichello: Imola 2004.

Michael Schumacher's Ferrari:
post-race Bahrain 2004.

Overleaf
Gilles Villeneuve in typical
power-sliding pose with his
Ferrari during the 1980 French
Grand Prix at Paul Ricard.

Michael Schumacher at Magny-Cours in France after one of his seventy-two wins for the team.

■ MATRA

The aerospace company was in the vanguard of a French invasion of F1 in the late 1960s. Using aero industry techniques, Matra built chassis notable for their stiffness and precise handling. The attack on F1 was two-pronged. A works car, in the hands of Jean-Pierre Beltoise and powered by a glorious-sounding V12 engine, made its debut at Monaco *(above)* in 1968. Matra's principal success came with chassis – powered by a Ford V8 – farmed out to the British Tyrrell team and their driver, Jackie Stewart. The Scotsman scored an outstanding victory with the Matra-Ford MS10 in the 1968 German Grand Prix run in appalling conditions *(above, right)* and went on to win the championship for Tyrrell-Matra the following year with the MS80 *(right)*. That would be the high point of Matra's success. They lost the association with Tyrrell thanks to an insistence on running their own car and V12 engine, before withdrawing from F1 at the end of 1972.

■ JORDAN

This was a small but colourful team that arrived in F1 in 1991 after the owner, Eddie Jordan, had won championships in the junior ranks. After almost winning a Grand Prix during their first season, Jordan finished a creditable fifth in the championship. Sometimes handicapped by switching engine supplier in a bid to find the best deal, it would take Jordan until 1998 to win their first Grand Prix, with two more the following year bringing the British-based team within striking distance of the title. It was a gradual downhill decline from there until the team was sold in 2005 but, throughout, Jordan maintained a lively presence by giving full value to sponsors, principally the tobacco company Benson and Hedges *(left, Martin Brundle at the wheel of the gold-painted Jordan-Peugeot in 1996).* Jordan is likely to remain one of the last of the small teams ever to win a Grand Prix.

■ RENAULT

The French automotive giant has been in F1 in many guises over four decades. Initially as a pioneer of turbocharged engines in their own car in 1977, Renault won Grands Prix but narrowly missed out on championships, before withdrawing as a team to act as engine supplier for others. They returned in 2002 to take over Benetton and went on to score great success in 2005 and 2006 when Fernando Alonso *(left)* won back-to-back championships. Then there followed a decline not helped by the global financial recession and a reputation tarnished by allegations of race fixing by team management in the 2008 Singapore Grand Prix. Renault focussed solely on engine supply once more from 2012, before making a return as an entrant by taking over their former team for 2016.

■ TYRRELL

Arguably the most successful new arrival of any small manufacturer, Ken Tyrrell was forced to build his own car in 1970 when other car makers were reluctant to supply a chassis to the reigning champion. Built in a wood yard in Surrey, the first Tyrrell-Ford led its debut Grand Prix at the end of 1970 and went on to provide the basis for Jackie Stewart's second championship the following year. With continuous backing from Elf, Stewart and Tyrrell-Ford dominated again in 1973 *(above)*. François Cevert *(far left, left)* was due to take over from Stewart as number one when the Scotsman retired at the end of the year, but the Frenchman was killed during practice for the final race at Watkins Glen in the USA. Tyrrell produced a revolutionary six-wheel car *(p.149)* and went on to win a few more Grand Prixs with Jody Scheckter and Patrick Depailler *(left)* but it was to mark the start of a slow and, at times, painful decline for this very British team before being bought by British American Tobacco in 1998.

Left
Patrick Depailler

Above
Tyrrell produced a revolutionary six-wheel car.

■ LOTUS

Lotus is second only to Ferrari as an iconic name in F1 thanks to entering F1 in 1958 and winning several championships, notably with Jim Clark in the 1960s. The quiet Scot *(bottom, middle)* made the most of the pioneering cars designed by Colin Chapman *(peaked cap, top left)*, one of the outstanding combinations being Clark and the Lotus-Ford 49 *(above, right)*. Clark was killed in 1968 before he could make full use of this car and carry on great battles with his fellow countryman, Jackie Stewart *(with Clark, overleaf)*. Chapman went on to win more titles with Jochen Rindt *(p.154)* and Emerson Fittipaldi *(p.155)* after breaking further new ground with the Lotus-Ford 72 *(p.156; Ronnie Peterson at Monaco in 1973)*. When Chapman died suddenly in 1982, the team lost momentum briefly and failed to give Elio de Angelis *(p.157)* the chance he deserved. The arrival of Ayrton Senna in 1985 helped regain the impetus, as Lotus won more Grands Prix and were in the running for the title. The decline was sudden in the early 1990s, the famous name being bought and used by other teams to no lasting effect.

Left
Jochen Rindt

Below
Jochen Rindt with Colin Chapman

Right
Emerson Fittipaldi

Far right
Emerson Fittipaldi with Colin Chapman

Below right
Emerson Fittipaldi

Ronnie Peterson with the Lotus
72 at Monaco in 1973.

Elio de Angelis

■ EAGLE

The American Dan Gurney *(right)* created one of the most beautiful cars in F1 when he built the Eagle, which he then took to victory in the 1967 Belgian Grand Prix *(above)*. Powered by a Weslake V12 engine, this car, entered by All American Racers (AAR), would be the highlight of the team's relatively brief association with F1. Initially intending to compete in the Indianapolis 500 as well as F1, Gurney saw a change of engine formula in 1966 as an advantageous moment. A smart engineer as well as a world-class driver, Gurney used a stopgap 4-cylinder Climax engine while waiting for the V12 to be completed by Weslake in Sussex, England. The combination won the non-championship Race of Champions at Brands Hatch in March 1967 before encountering various difficulties in subsequent Grands Prix. It all came good in Belgium, the victory at Spa-Francorchamps being the zenith of Gurney's efforts with the Eagle before AAR bowed out of F1 in 1969.

■ LIGIER

The French team was founded by Guy Ligier, a former international rugby player who used money made in the construction business to fund his passion for motorsport. A former private entrant and driver in F1, Ligier created a team to successfully race sports cars before moving into Grand Prix racing in 1976. Over the next twenty years, Ligier would use a succession of engines, ranging from Matra and Renault to Lamborghini. His greatest success came with Ford-V8-powered cars in 1979 when victories with the JS11 in South America put Ligier at the forefront, only to lose the championship because the drivers, Jacques Laffite *(left)* and Patrick Depailler, had joint number one status and took points off each other. Laffite *(above, in the 1982 Swiss Grand Prix at Dijon)* remained a stalwart of the team over nine seasons and scored Ligier's maiden victory with a Matra-powered JS7 in the 1977 Swedish Grand Prix. Ligier claimed nine Grands Prix wins in total, the last being an unexpected victory in changeable conditions at Monaco in 1996. Guy Ligier sold the team at the end of the year.

■ JAGUAR

The Ford Motor Company brought the Jaguar name into F1 in 2000 by buying Stewart Grand Prix, a team founded three years earlier by former champion, Sir Jackie Stewart. Whereas Stewart had won a Grand Prix during their brief existence, Jaguar would fail thanks to dysfunctional management during the course of eighty-five Grands Prix, the highlights being third places for Eddie Irvine *(above right)* in Monaco in 2001 and in Italy the following year. Mark Webber replaced Irvine *(above, storming away from a pit stop in Spain in 2001)* for the final two seasons, by which time new management had begun to bring improvements – but no results worth speaking of for the Ford-powered car. Having ventured into F1 to promote the premium Jaguar brand, Ford did not feel the expenditure was justified and called a halt at the end of 2004.

■ RED BULL

The Austrian energy drinks company bought the Jaguar F1 team in November 2004 and renamed it Red Bull Racing (RBR). Investment began to pay off in the first year when RBR won more championship points than Jaguar had managed in the previous two seasons. A major turning point came at the end of the year with the hiring of Adrian Newey as technical chief and, for 2009, the promotion of Sebastian Vettel from Toro Rosso, effectively a junior team for RBR. The combination took its maiden win in China, a prelude to Vettel scoring four successive world titles between 2010 and 2013, ending Ferrari's dominance *(above left, Vettel shakes hands with Fernando Alonso after the 2013 Singapore Grand Prix)*. Along the way, Vettel also faced strong opposition from his team-mate, Mark Webber *(left and above)*. Having briefly used Ford and Ferrari engines in the early years, RBR's success had come through close ties with Renault, but the relationship came under strain following the engine manufacturer's failure to meet the demands of new and complex technical regulations for 2014. For the first time in six years, Red Bull failed to win a race in 2015.

■ COOPER

Cooper is best remembered for pioneering work in the late 1950s when the British team set the trend by moving the engine from the front to the rear of the car. Jack Brabham won successive championships in 1959 and 1960. The Australian is pictured *(above, right)* with Bruce McLaren, who also won for Cooper in 1959 before starting his own eponymous team. As others caught up with Cooper's technical advances, success became sporadic. Despite the sometimes spectacular efforts of Jochen Rindt *(near left)* with the hefty Maserati-powered car, it was Pedro Rodriguez *(far left)* who scored Cooper's last win in the 1967 South African Grand Prix. After sixteen wins, Cooper withdrew from Grand Prix racing in 1969.

■ MASERATI

Maserati competed in Grand Prix racing in the 1940s and 50s. The Italian firm produced three classic Grand Prix cars, the most famous – and certainly most enjoyed by its drivers – being the 250F. Luigi Musso prepares to leave the pits at Spa in 1955 *(above)* while Juan Manuel Fangio *(top right, and right)* used this sleek front-engine classic to win the last of his five world titles in 1957, shortly before financial difficulties forced Maserati to close its racing team. Privateers continued to campaign the 250F and Maserati had a presence in F1 thanks to supplying engines to the Cooper team in 1966 and 1967. Maserati competed in sixty-eight championship Grands Prix and won nine of them.

■ BRABHAM

Jack Brabham *(above, and near right)* became the first man to win a race and then a World Championship driving a car bearing his name. Having won championships with Cooper, Brabham left to build and race his own cars in 1962 and really came into his own in 1966 when a new formula was introduced. Better prepared than most, Brabham won four races to take the title, his team-mate Denny Hulme *(far right)* winning the championship the following year. Not long after Brabham retired at the end of 1970, his team was bought by Bernie Ecclestone, who kept the name and went on to win races and championships in the early 1980s. Along the way, the team caused uproar during 1978 when Niki Lauda won the Swedish Grand Prix *(above, right)* with a car fitted at the rear with a huge fan that helped suck the car to the ground. Victory in the 1985 French Grand Prix would be the last for Brabham before the team changed hands and went into rapid decline.

■ WILLIAMS

This is a British team much admired and respected, largely through the dogged determination and relentless efforts of its founder, Sir Frank Williams. Having lived hand-to-mouth in the early 1970s, Williams turned a corner in 1977 when he won sponsorship from the Middle East. He rebuilt his team into a race winner, the first being the British Grand Prix in 1979, one year before Williams' Alan Jones became World Champion, the team also winning the constructors' title. Further titles followed with Keke Rosberg in 1982 and Damon Hill in 1996 *(p.174)*. Many top drivers have passed through the team, including David Coulthard and Juan Pablo Montoya. But perhaps the best remembered for more unfortunate reasons is Ayrton Senna *(below)* whose tenure was brief in 1994 before a fatal accident at Imola. Williams have won seven drivers' titles and more than 110 races and continue to play a leading role in F1 today.

Keke Rosberg

David Coulthard

The Williams of Carlos Reutemann
chases the Brabham of Nelson
Piquet during the 1980 Dutch
Grand Prix.

Damon Hill

Juan Pablo Montoya

■ MERCEDES

The reigning World Champions have a racing heritage stretching back not only to the 1950s but, before the start of the World Championship in 1950, to the 1930s. Having been absent since the end of the Second World War, Mercedes returned halfway through the 1954 season and wiped the floor with his opponents, using streamlined cars that were peerless during the French Grand Prix on the fast straights of Reims *(this page)*. Following a tragedy in the 1955 Le Mans 24-Hours sports car race, Mercedes withdrew from motor racing, but not before Juan Manuel Fangio had dominated the championship. The German firm returned as an engine supplier in the 1990s, winning championships with McLaren before becoming a team in their own right once more in 2010. Fully prepared for a change in regulations at the start of 2014, Mercedes dominated F1 with Lewis Hamilton *(overleaf right)* winning back-to-back titles.

Michael Schumacher: Malaysia 2012

Lewis Hamilton: Abu Dhabi 2014

■ BENETTON

Having sponsored Tyrrell and Alfa Romeo, the Italian fashion family bought into F1 in a major way in 1985 by purchasing Toleman and transforming the small British team. Benetton, powered by BMW engines, scored their first win in Mexico in 1986, a one-off result largely through being on superior tyres on the day. Nelson Piquet *(right)* brought limited success, but it was not until a restructured team and the arrival of Michael Schumacher *(above right)* in late 1991 that Benetton began to enjoy consistent success. The German driver won the first of two back-to-back titles in 1994, the team boosted by a pair of wins for Johnny Herbert *(above left)* in 1994 and 1995. After accounting for nineteen of Benetton's twenty-seven victories, Schumacher's departure to Ferrari for 1996 marked the beginning of a decline in fortune for Benetton, the family selling out to Renault at the end of 2001.

THE CIRCUITS
TRIUMPH AND TRAGEDY ON F1'S COURSES

Previous pages
Best of both worlds for Ferrari at Suzuka in 2003 after Rubens Barrichello (with crash helmet) has won the Japanese Grand Prix and Michael Schumacher has become World Champion.

Left
Monaco: the most famous of them all. Mika Hakkinen locks his brakes behind Michael Schumacher as the Ferrari and McLaren-Mercedes lead the pack into the first corner at the start of the 1999 Monaco Grand Prix.

Overleaf
Top left **The starting grid at Monaco (shown in 1957) used to be on the straight that is now the pit lane run in the reverse direction.**

Top right **Heading off to the seaside: the first lap of the 1960 Dutch Grand Prix at Zandvoort.**

Bottom left **Riverside in California was used just once to stage the United States Grand Prix. The race gets under way in 1960.**

Bottom right **Spa-Francorchamps in Belgium is notorious for fickle weather. Jim Clark heads for victory with his Lotus-Climax in 1963.**

There have been more than seventy different race tracks used to stage Grands Prix since the start of the World Championship in 1950. Some have been used just once. Others, such as Monaco and Monza, have provided a perpetual showcase just as intoxicating and passionate as the sport itself.

The striking difference between these two traditional venues sums up the variety that makes F1 what it is. And the fact that both Monza and Monaco have been responsible for the writing of racing drivers' obituaries also underscores the tragedy that occasionally stalks the sport and tarnishes its best intentions, no matter where or what form the track may take.

Monza is a purpose-built high-speed circuit, established in 1922 in the Royal Park within a suburb of Milan. Monaco is the slowest on the F1 calendar thanks to the racing being constricted by narrow streets that make up arguably the best-known Grand Prix track in the world. The contrast may be stark and the challenge diverse but the end game is the same as it has always been; to finish first and score maximum championship points. Then move on to the next race track. And the one after that.

Variety has always been an essential part of F1's fabric. The first motoring competitions were staged more than 100 years ago with races from city to city. The inherent danger to spectators brought an awareness of the need for more control in the shape of a circuit that could be more easily managed and provide some form of crowd constraint. That said, public highways and byways continued to provide the easiest, if not the most socially convenient, form of race track, but permanent venues soon became popular and offered more potential for profit.

Nonetheless, when the World Championship was introduced, the seven-race calendar in 1950 was dominated, not by permanent fixtures, but by road and street tracks such as Spa-Francorchamps, Reims, Berne and, of course, Monaco. The diversity presented by these four ensured their presence: Spa utilising nine undulating miles of roads sweeping through the Belgian Ardennes; Reims being a flat and very fast triangle of straight roads amid corn fields to the west of the French city; Berne, a scary and relentless sequence of curves and high-speed corners through woods on the northern outskirts of the Swiss capital; and Monaco has been described above.

By their very nature, all four were bound to cause casualties. But, even allowing for a more relaxed approach to safety in the decade following the Second World War,

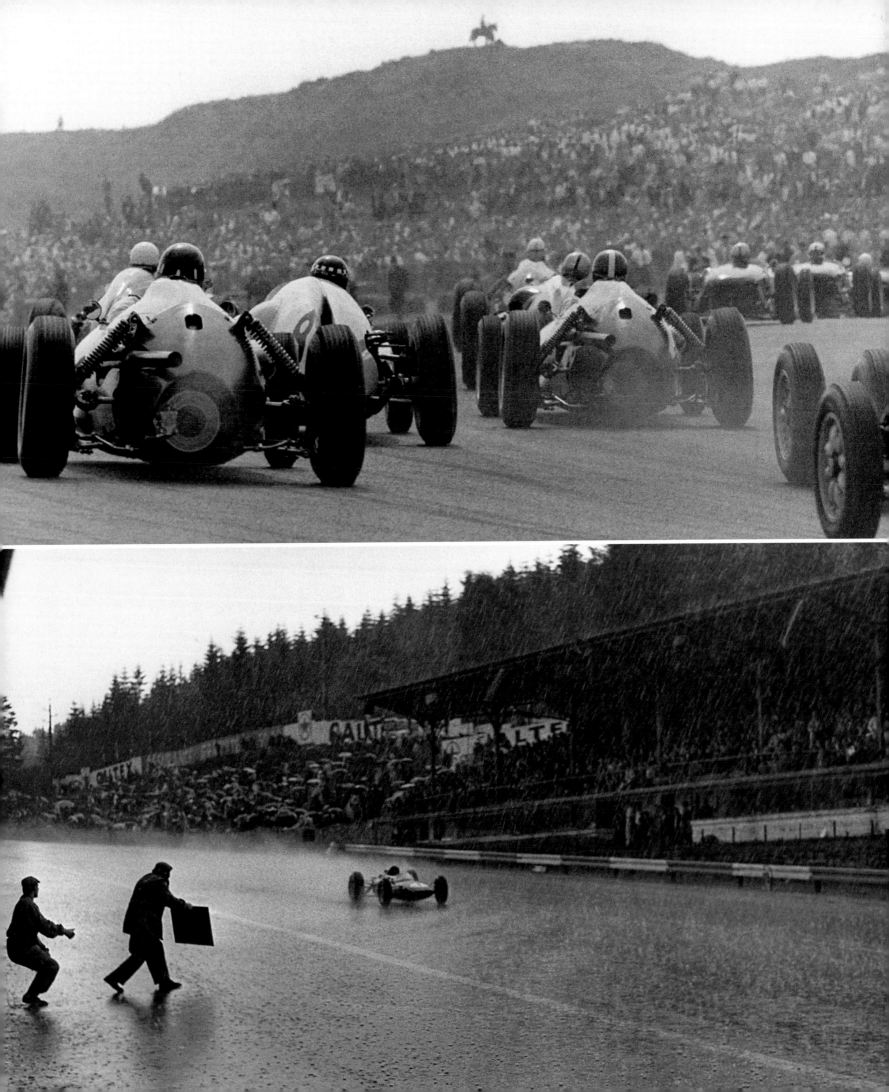

Above
**Nigel Mansell sweeps through
the exit of Paddock Hill Bend
on his way to victory with the
Williams-Honda at Brands Hatch
in 1985.**

Opposite
**Ayrton Senna's Lotus-Renault
charges down the hill at Spa-
Francorchamps in 1985 and
prepares to tackle Eau Rouge,
one of the classic corners in F1.**

Berne in particular was considered excessively dangerous. The end of Grand Prix racing in Berne in 1955, however, was not due to the inherent risks but because motor racing was banned in Switzerland following the death of more than eighty spectators that year in the Le Mans 24-Hour sports car race.

Danger was not confined to circuits on public highways passing between trees. The Nürburgring, thought to be one of the greatest race tracks ever built when opened in 1926, was also one of the most hazardous. It could hardly be otherwise given that this leviathan snaked its way through the Eifel mountains for fourteen tortuous miles, with no two of more than 170 corners being the same. Not a year would pass without casualties, the situation made worse by the impossible task of marshalling this giant of a race track.

The same applied, albeit to a lesser degree, through the fast curves of Spa, and yet each track survived through the 1960s, despite a litany of sorrow. This in itself summed up the conflict of emotion that attended such majestic tracks. Paradoxically, the knowledge that an error could be severely punished brought a frisson of excitement as a driver measured up to the challenge of getting through these corners faster than anyone else. They were racing against the track just as much as their competitors.

Under different circumstances because of lower speeds, the same test of daring nevertheless applied to Monaco, where a wheel a fraction out of line would bring instant retirement against a wall or kerb. The wide grassy expanse of Silverstone – a former airfield – this most certainly was not.

It was an immediate means of measuring a driver's skill and precision – with the added ingredient of maintaining concentration throughout a race lasting, in the 1950s and 1960s, at least, for more than two hours, often in searing heat. The price of the smallest misjudgement could be horrific.

At Monaco in 1967, Lorenzo Bandini was carrying the hopes of Ferrari – and by association, the whole of Italy – as he chased the leader with 19 of the 100 laps remaining. A tiny miscalculation had massive consequences as he clipped the high-speed chicane leading to the harbour front. Thrown from its course, the Ferrari hit straw bales lining the outside of the corner, overturned and caught fire. Even with marshals in close proximity, Bandini could not be extricated and died in hospital days later. There have been no fatalities at Monaco since.

In fact, the sport's terrible record improved massively as F1 came to terms with the fact that race tracks needed to offer the best possible protection and medical support should a driver crash – not necessarily through any fault of his own. From having close to one fatality every month during the 1968 season, Grands Prix ran for twelve years without tragedy until the 1994 San Marino Grand Prix when two drivers were killed. The fact that one of them was Ayrton Senna, a three-time World Champion and six-time winner at Monaco, brought home the fact that circuits could never be completely safe.

But that has not stopped the search for perfection. If anything, it has accelerated it. The sport's governing body, the FIA, examines every detail of every accident, fatal or not. Circuits and facilities are improved continuously.

Spa-Francorchamps remains proof that this can be done without compromising the very reason a driver snuggles into the cockpit, has his seat harness pulled painfully tight, closes his visor, grips the wheel and prepares to take on the race track. Spa was heavily revised in 1983 and yet retains much of its original character. It is a place where a hint of sweat on a driver's brow and a wide-eyed expression says everything about man and machine versus race track. It's about flirting with danger and embracing triumph. Just as it always was.

■ FRANCE

There have been more Grand Prix tracks in France than in any other European country. Reims *(left and p.194 bottom)* was an obvious choice when the championship was instigated in 1950, the flat triangle of public roads having been used for racing since 1932. Jim Clark and Lotus won in 1963 *(p.195, bottom and top right)*, three years before Reims was deemed unsafe because of the extremely high speeds. Rouen, a fast but very different type of road circuit, was first used in 1952 *(Ascari's winning Ferrari pictured p.194, top right)*, the cobbled hairpin being a feature of this picturesque but dangerous track *(Fangio's Maserati negotiates the hairpin p.194, top left, on his way to victory in 1957)*. When introduced to the F1 calendar in 1965, stunning roads around an extinct volcano above Clermont-Ferrand were popular among drivers, if not the mechanics, forced to use a rudimentary paddock. Here you see the March and BRM teams cheek by jowl *(p.196)* in 1970, two years before the final Grand Prix was dominated by Chris Amon's Matra *(p.197)* until the luckless New Zealander suffered a puncture. A purpose-built circuit at Paul Ricard may have been considered safer when first used in 1971 but the track, high above the Mediterranean coast, produced a spectacular incident in 1989 *(p.198)* when Mauricio Gugelmin misjudged his braking at the first corner and became airborne, the turquoise March wiping off the rear wing from Nigel Mansell's Ferrari as Thierry Boutsen's Williams-Renault (number 5) locked a front brake in avoidance. No one was hurt.

The March and BRM teams cheek
by jowl at Clermont-Ferrand in 1970.

Chris Amon's Matra

Overleaf
The 1971 purpose built track
at Paul Ricard that produced
a serious crash in 1989 –
fortunately no one was hurt.

■ MONACO

This is the most famous race track in the world, if only because 70 per cent of what you see today was used for the first Grand Prix in 1929. The setting could not be more glamorous, from the steep climb towards the Hotel de Paris and the Casino, to the tunnel and the dash along the waterfront, the entire glittering scene overlooked by the Royal Palace.

The Mercedes of Stirling Moss (6) and Juan Manuel Fangio lead the pack through Gasworks Hairpin, the first corner in 1955.

Graham Hill tweaks his famous moustache with the bearded Jo Bonnier and Raymond Mays, the boss of BRM, in the background.

Moss looks on as Mike Hawthorn receives a light.

Surtees, Hill and Bandini in 1965.

Jackie Stewart congratulates his BRM team-mate Hill after winning in 1965.

The Maserati (28) of eventual winner Stirling Moss fights with the Ferrari (22) of Eugenio Castellotti from the start in 1956 *(above)*.

The backdrop may have changed, but the hairpin remains exactly as it was; the Ferraris of Lorenzo Bandini and John Surtees negotiate the tightest corner in F1 in 1965 *(top left)* and Chris Amon's March leads the Brabham of Jack Brabham, Jacky Ickx's Ferrari and the Matra of Jean-Pierre Beltoise away from the hairpin in 1970 *(top right)*.

Hill's winning Lotus is parked by the kerb in what was the pit lane in 1968 *(right)*. The original track was shorter than today, the start and finish area being where the pit lane is presently located. The addition around the swimming pool in 1973 began just after Tabac *(middle left, being negotiated by Luigi Musso's Ferrari in 1958)* and allowed the pits to be removed to safety from the side of the main start and finish straight.

Ayrton Senna's McLaren-Ford climbs the hill in 1993 on his way to the last of a record six wins at Monaco.

David Coulthard won twice in the Principality.

Nico Rosberg points his Mercedes up the hill towards Casino.

The Williams of Valtteri Bottas kicks up sparks.

Kimi Räikkönen's Ferrari tackles
Tabac in 2015.

■ ITALY

The Italian Grand Prix is all about the madness of Monza, captured perfectly in 1970 as Clay Regazzoni's winning Ferrari was engulfed as an enthusiastic mob invaded the track *(below)*, the huge numbers indicating many had actually climbed the fence before the race had finished. This shot also catches the historic sense of the famous autodrome, opened in 1922 with the banking, no longer used, arcing across the background. The flat-out nature of the long straights has produced epic battles with Italian red cars usually in the midst of them.

Juan Manuel Fangio's Maserati
leads the Ferraris of Alberto Ascari
and Giuseppe Farina in 1953.

A happy Jim Clark, victor at Monza
in 1963.

Fangio drifts his Maserati 250F
while chasing the Vanwall of Tony
Brooks in 1957, the same pair
poised on the grid before the start.

Overleaf
A study in concentration as Stirling
Moss prepares to start the same
race in his Vanwall.

Sebastian Vettel prepares for
the start at Monza in 2015.
The emergence of Imola as an
alternative saw the Italian Grand
Prix shift to the picturesque track
in the province of Bologna in
1980 before assuming the title
San Marino Grand Prix in 1981.

The atmosphere was no less
passionate despite Ferrari not
being part of a battle between
the McLaren-Hondas of Ayrton
Senna and Alain Prost in 1988.

Ferrari adulation at the exit of
Imola's Tosa corner.

Overleaf
There was little in motorsport to
match the pulsating atmosphere
on the hillside at Imola.

Jenson Button produced stirring performances in the BAR-Honda at Imola.

Sadly, Imola will also be remembered for the death of Senna. Memorabilia in tribute adorns the fence at Tamburello, the corner where the Brazilian's Williams-Renault crashed on 1 May 1994.

Michael Schumacher brought joy to the home crowd with no fewer than six wins for Ferrari.

■ HOLLAND

The seaside track at Zandvoort was hugely popular from the moment it hosted the first Dutch Grand Prix in 1952, the sand dunes forming excellent viewing points. Located a train ride from Amsterdam, the race became a regular feature of the F1 calendar and attracted spectators from France, Belgium and Germany, as well as from across the English Channel. British fans were thrilled to witness James Hunt score his first Grand Prix win after his Hesketh-Ford held off Niki Lauda's Ferrari in 1975. The long main straight, illustrated in the start shot from 1965 *(top left)*, contributed to close racing as cars braked heavily for the first corner. In 1966 Jack Brabham led Jim Clark away from that corner *(top, middle)*. Twelve years later, Mario Andretti and Lotus team-mate Ronnie Peterson dominated the race, 1985 providing a livelier Grand Prix as Alain Prost *(middle)* battled with his McLaren team-mate Niki Lauda. René Arnoux's Renault led the field at the start in 1980 *(bottom, right)*.

■ PORTUGAL

Jim Clark's set expression *(right)* summed up a rare driving error as the Scotsman walked away from his damaged Lotus in Porto in 1960. Attempting to take the first corner flat out during practice while avoiding the tramlines that were part of the street circuit, Clark clipped a kerb and spun into the straw bales. The car was patched up and Clark went on to score his first podium finish the next day. The street circuit, with its mixed surfaces and cobblestones, was only used twice, one more time than a road circuit at Monsanto near Lisbon where Dan Gurney is pictured *(above)* in his Ferrari on his way to third place in 1959. Portugal would be without a Grand Prix until the upgrading of Estoril in 1984. This permanent track would stage thirteen Grands Prix and prove popular for testing.

Niki Lauda raises an arm in triumph at Estoril in 1984, second place being good enough to give the McLaren driver the championship by half a point.

The Benettons of Alessandro Nannini and Thierry Boutsen are prepared in the cramped garages in 1988.

Gerhard Berger's Ferrari raises sparks on the narrow and bumpy main straight in 1989.

■ HUNGARY

F1's first venture into an Eastern bloc country in 1986 saw the introduction of the Hungarian Grand Prix at the Hungaroring. The purpose-built track was tight and twisting, the only overtaking place of note being into the first corner, where the Ferraris of Rubens Barrichello and Michael Schumacher led the Williams-BMW of Ralf Schumacher in 2002 *(right)*. Although the races tend to be processional, the Hungaroring has set statistical landmarks by settling the championship twice (Nigel Mansell in 1992 and Michael Schumacher 2001) as well as listing several first-time winners (Damon Hill in 1993, Fernando Alonso in 2003, Jenson Button in 2006 and Heikki Kovalainen in 2008).

■ GERMANY

The German Grand Prix has been staged on four different circuits, none more infamous than the Nürburgring Nordschleife, twisting and turning for fourteen miles through the Eifel mountains. Opened in 1926, the circuit joined the World Championship trail in 1951 and remained on it until deemed too dangerous following Niki Lauda's near-fatal crash in 1976. In 1957 the race produced one of the most mesmeric performances of all when Juan Manuel Fangio *(below)* chased, caught and overtook the Ferraris of Peter Collins and Mike Hawthorn after making a pit stop. Fangio posed in his Maserati (number 1) alongside Hawthorn's Ferrari *(left)* before the start. The field gets away in 1956 *(far left)* and John Surtees takes his first Grand Prix victory for Ferrari in 1963 *(below, left)*.

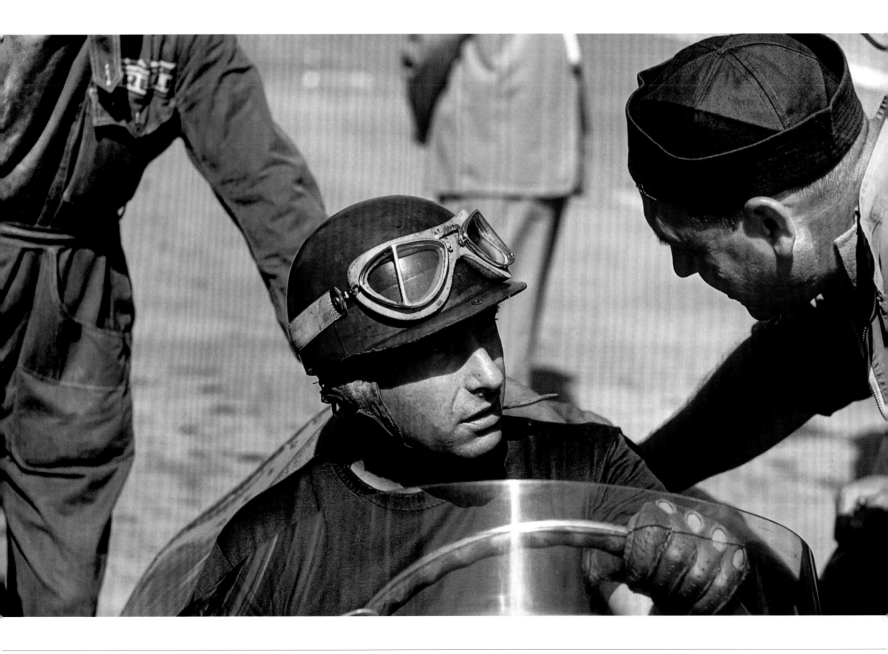

Jim Clark (1) leads Graham Hill's
BRM into the first corner of the
1965 Grand Prix (above), Clark
going on to win, his Lotus-Climax
casting a shadow in 1964 as the
circuit weaves its way through
the forest (right).

overleaf
When the Nordschleife fell from favour, and before a new track was built alongside, the Grand Prix moved to Hockenheim, where Rubens Barrichello scored an emotional maiden victory in his Ferrari in 2000.

■ SPAIN

Spain has been part of F1's fabric since the early days with no fewer than six different tracks staging the Grand Prix. Jarama, used nine times between 1968 and 1981 *(top row: left, centre left and centre right)*, was arguably the least popular, the 1970 race being marred by a fire when two cars collided, leaving victory to the blue March of Jackie Stewart. Gilles Villeneuve scored a spectacular and unexpected win in 1981 when he managed to withstand huge pressure and hold everyone back with the cumbersome Ferrari (number 27). Jerez *(top row, right; bottom row, left)* was used seven times between 1986 and 1997 before the Spanish race found a more permanent home outside Barcelona at Circuit de Catalunya. The Williams-Renault of Nigel Mansell and Ayrton Senna's McLaren-Honda engaged in an epic wheel-to-wheel contest at the first race in 1991 *(above)*. McLaren's Lewis Hamilton

and Fernando Alonso *(bottom row, centre right)* sprayed the champagne after finishing second and third in 2007, with happier times for the home hero as Alonso greeted his fans after winning for Ferrari in 2013 *(bottom row, right)*.

■ BELGIUM

Despite ten visits to Zolder, Spa-Francorchamps is considered to be the spiritual home of the Belgian Grand Prix. The awesome circuit in the Ardennes was first used for a Grand Prix in 1925, its nine-mile length causing havoc in 1966 when the race started in the dry and competitors ran into a rainstorm a quarter of the way round the first lap. It was wet for the start in 1965 *(opposite bottom left)* as the field left the downhill grid and headed into Eau Rouge before the steep, curving climb through the trees towards Les Combes. The Ferraris of Phil Hill and Ricardo Rodriguez fight it out in 1962 *(opposite top, left)*. The Cooper-Maserati of Jo Siffert crests the rise at Eau Rouge in 1967 *(opposite top, right)*. Spa had

become the fastest road circuit in use by 1960 when two British drivers were killed in separate accidents. Growing concern over safety brought a halt to Spa's inclusion on the calendar after the 1970 Grand Prix, but a first-rate piece of modernisation saw the race return in 1983. The circuit had virtually been cut in half but the atmosphere and challenge remained, particularly the swoop through Eau Rouge. The climb to Les Combes *(above)* had been straightened to allow speeds approaching 200 mph, contributing to Spa's continuing reputation as a fast and demanding track. Nigel Mansell *(top, right)*, heads back to the pits after retiring in 1991.

■ JAPAN

Japan has used three circuits: Suzuka, Mount Fuji and Aida. Suzuka stands head and shoulders above not only the other two Japanese venues but just about every other race track on the F1 calendar. It is unique in being the only figure-of-eight layout in Grand Prix racing thanks to a design generated in the early 1960s, one that made Suzuka a fascinating and difficult proposition for the drivers when the Grand Prix arrived in 1987. By comparison, Fuji is relatively simple and was used in 1976 and 1977, the first visit being famous for settling a season-long championship battle between James Hunt and Niki Lauda during a race run in atrocious conditions. There was heavy rain when the Grand Prix returned

in 2007 *(opposite, top)*, the following year being the final visit to Fuji before it reverted to Suzuka. Being at or near the end of the season, Suzuka has seen the crowning of several champions, often under controversial circumstances, none more so than in 1990 when Alain Prost and Ayrton Senna collided at the first corner *(top, right)*. Nigel Mansell and Williams team-mate Riccardo Patrese (6) run neck-and-neck into the first corner in 1992 *(bottom, right)*, Mansell having gone off at the same corner in 1991 *(bottom, left)*. Mansell's Williams chases the Ferrari of Jean Alesi in 1994 *(opposite, left)*. Mika Hakkinen wins the championship for McLaren in 1998 *(opposite, right)*.

■ CANADA

Canada has hosted a round of the championship since 1967, starting with Mosport Park and moving to Saint-Jovite the following year, where it ran twice. The race stayed at Mosport until 1977, by which time a new venue on a man-made island in the Saint Lawrence River was ready to become the permanent home for the Canadian Grand Prix. Despite a flat and straightforward profile, the Circuit Gilles Villeneuve (named after Canada's favourite motor racing son) is a tough proposition, mistakes being punished by the close proximity of concrete walls. It is a popular venue thanks to its location close by the city of Montreal and a knowledgeable and enthusiastic crowd. Originally placed at the end of the season, Montreal settled the championship in favour of Alan Jones in 1980, but a move to the summer months was favoured because of better weather conditions.

The Benetton of Michael
Schumacher *(right)* leads Damon
Hill's Williams *(left)* into the first
corner during their championship
battle in 1995.

Montreal was the scene of Lewis
Hamilton's first Grand Prix win
in 2007, and another victory in
2012. In 2005, Kimi Räikkönen
took his only victory in Canada,
the McLaren driver finishing
ahead of Ferrari's Michael
Schumacher (right).

■ AUSTRIA

A simple but fiercely bumpy airfield track at Zeltweg provided a spartan venue for Austria's first championship Grand Prix in 1964. The circuit was never used again and when a brand new track was built in the foothills overlooking the airfield, the comparison could not have been more dramatic. Ready for a Grand Prix in 1970, the Österreichring was a magnificent collection of fast, sweeping curves making full use of the natural majesty of its surroundings in Styria. Thousands of spectators from across the Italian border enjoyed a dream result when Jacky Ickx and Clay Regazzoni finished first and second for Ferrari. Eighteen Grands Prix were staged here until the track was considered too remote a location

and out of step with the changing commercial requirements of F1. The average speed had risen to more than 150 mph and concern had grown over the lack of run-off at quick corners such as the Bosch Kurve *(left)*. A ten-car pile up on the narrow pit straight at the start of the race in 1987 added to the pressure to have the race removed from the calendar. The Grand Prix returned ten years later to a shortened track known as the A1-Ring, where the race was staged until 2003 and included two wins for Michael Schumacher *(right)*. After much debate over future plans, the site was bought by Red Bull and upgraded in readiness for a round of the championship in 2014.

■ MEXICO

A passion for motorsport in Mexico was answered in 1961 by the building of an impressive track within Magdalena Mixhuca, a municipal park in the suburbs of Mexico City. Granted a round of the World Championship in 1963, the race soon established itself as a welcome part of the calendar *(above: Jo Siffert takes his Lotus-BRM to ninth place in 1963)*. The Mexican Grand Prix settled the championship in favour of John Surtees in 1964 and Graham Hill in 1968. Hill led Chris Amon's Ferrari on the first lap in 1967, but victory would go to Hill's Lotus team-mate, Jim Clark, lying third behind Amon *(right, above)*. The previous year's race was won by the Cooper-Maserati of Surtees, seen leading Jack Brabham's crossed-up Brabham-Repco at the hairpin *(right, below)*. The Mexican race would not be without its controversy, particularly in 1970 when the overenthusiastic crowd encroached onto the edge of the track and a large dog was fatally hit by Jackie Stewart's Tyrrell. Removed from the calendar, the race was revived on a shorter version of the track between 1986 and 1992, returning once more with further revisions in 2015.

■ BRAZIL

The emergence of Emerson Fittipaldi as Brazil's first World
Champion in 1972 accelerated the desire to stage a Grand Prix in
his home country. The obvious choice was Interlagos, a permanent
track opened in 1940 and twisting and turning within itself on
land on the edge of São Paulo's sprawling southwest suburbs
(above, Jean-Pierre Jarier's Shadow-Ford in 1975). Appropriately,
Fittipaldi's Lotus-Ford won the first championship Grand Prix in
1973, Interlagos staging the race until 1980, by which time it was
deemed to be too bumpy and dangerous. Jacarepaguá *(p.252, top
row, left)*, a new track near Rio de Janeiro, was favoured from 1981
until the rise of Ayrton Senna from São Paulo prompted a major
facelift at Interlagos in readiness for a return in 1990. The circuit
length had been reduced by almost half but the huge enthusiasm
of the Brazilian fans remained and often needed cooling down in
the torpid heat of race day *(left)*. Passion would run even higher
if a Brazilian driver was in the reckoning, as was the case when
Felipe Massa *(p.252, bottom right, and p.253)* fought with Lewis
Hamilton for the title in 2008, only to lose on the final lap.

Nigel Mansell heads for a
surprise victory for Ferrari at
Rio de Janeiro in 1989.

Michael Schumacher blasts his
Ferrari away from the pit box
at Interlagos in 1999.

The Williams of Damon Hill
(left) sits it out with Rubens
Barrichello's Jordan into the first
corner of the 1996 Brazilian
Grand Prix at Interlagos.

Felipe Massa savours the home
support after winning the 2006
Brazilian Grand Prix for Ferrari.

■ MALAYSIA

A desire to promote Malaysia as an international force led to the construction of a 3.4-mile track at Sepang, close by a new airport serving Kuala Lumpur. Costing 12 million US dollars, the venue was well received when the F1 teams arrived for the first Grand Prix in 1999. The track utilised the rolling landscape to include corners of every type and two wide straights with tight turns at the end of each to encourage overtaking. The first corner was unique in that it turned in on itself initially and offered drivers different lines to help promote close racing. Apart from the G-forces generated by several of the quick corners, drivers had to cope with high levels of humidity, making this one of the toughest races on the calendar.

Sebastian Vettel (below) **leads the Ferraris of Fernando Alonso and Felipe Massa at the start in 2013.**

Brands Hatch hosted the race
fourteen times, starting in 1964
and including 1986 *(below,
Nelson Piquet's Williams-Honda
leads the pack through Paddock
Hill Bend)*. **Donington Park** *(below,
left)* hosted a championship
round just once, the 1993
European Grand Prix being
memorable for a stunning drive
by Ayrton Senna. The Brazilian's
McLaren-Ford lay fourth behind
the Williams-Renaults of Alain
Prost and Damon Hill and Karl
Wendlinger's Sauber not long
after the start of the opening
lap. Senna would be leading
at the end of it. Jack Brabham
(above, left) won the British
Grand Prix for Cooper at Aintree
on his way to the first World
Championship for a rear-engine
car in 1959.

■ UNITED STATES

With no fewer than ten different venues since 1959, the United States Grand Prix has tried everything from permanent tracks to street circuits and an adaption of the famous Indianapolis 500 oval. Following brief visits to Sebring in Florida and Riverside in California, Watkins Glen became the most successful, the purpose-built track in New York State being used twenty times before it was no longer considered suitable in 1981. In 1982, there were three Grands Prix in the USA: on the streets of Long Beach and in a converted car park in Las Vegas in the west, and in downtown Detroit *(above)*, a street circuit that went on to host the US Grand Prix East seven times. For various reasons – mainly finance and an inability to meet required standards – all three faded, to be replaced by unsuccessful attempts on the streets of Phoenix and Dallas. Indianapolis, never totally satisfactory, lasted for eight years until, finally, a brand new circuit near Austin in Texas appeared to answer all the questions when introduced in 2012, the race being won by the McLaren-Mercedes of Lewis Hamilton *(right)*.

■ AUSTRALIA

Grands Prix in Australia may have been limited to just two
venues across more than thirty years but each has been
considered an outstanding success. Adelaide set new standards
for a temporary track when introduced to the calendar in 1985,
the South Australian venue settling the championship in a
spectacular manner for Benetton's Michael Schumacher in 1994. A
heavyweight political battle saw the state of Victoria wrench the
country's Grand Prix away from Adelaide to Melbourne in 1996,
switching from the end to the beginning of the year in the process.
Jacques Villeneuve *(left)* caused a sensation on his F1 debut by
taking pole position in his Williams-Renault in 1996, while Michael
Schumacher *(above, in 1999)* won four times for Ferrari.

■ SINGAPORE

Singapore delivered high standards when it arrived on the F1 scene in 2008 and not only established a challenging track on the streets of the business district alongside Marina Bay but also chose to become the first Grand Prix to be run at night. Powerful overhead lights successfully replicated daylight conditions for the drivers while producing a spectacular sight as the three-mile combination of boulevards and highways passed iconic landmarks such as the City Hall and the cricket ground, as well as crossing the ancient Anderson Bridge. A bumpy surface, angular corners and sapping humidity made this a tough test for the drivers in a race lasting an hour and three-quarters. A contract extended until 2017 was proof of the popularity and success of such a unique addition to the calendar.

INDEX

ACKNOWLEDGEMENTS

I would first like to thank my father, Bernard Cahier. This book is the result of a father and son collaboration, and even though my father is sadly no longer with us, he was by my side every day when working on this beautiful book. Searching through the negatives of the incredible, glorious days of Grand Prix Racing, I could feel his strong presence imbedded in the gelatine of the black and white films which I was scanning. He was behind the camera, and inside the film.

I would also like to thank Lucy Warburton from Aurum Press, my Editor, who was curious enough to search and discover the unique photographs from the Cahier Archive, and brave enough to push and make this book happen. What a great idea that was!

Finally, a big thank you to Sir Jackie Stewart for writing his heartfelt foreword to *Formula One: The Pursuit of Speed*. As it happened, I took my first photos of Formula 1 racing in Monza 1965, when I was a twelve-year-old boy and he won his first ever Grand Prix. Ever since those days, the Stewart and the Cahier families have remained friends, and nobody was in a better position to write the foreword than Jackie.

SIMPLY
NEW ZEALAND
A Culinary Journey

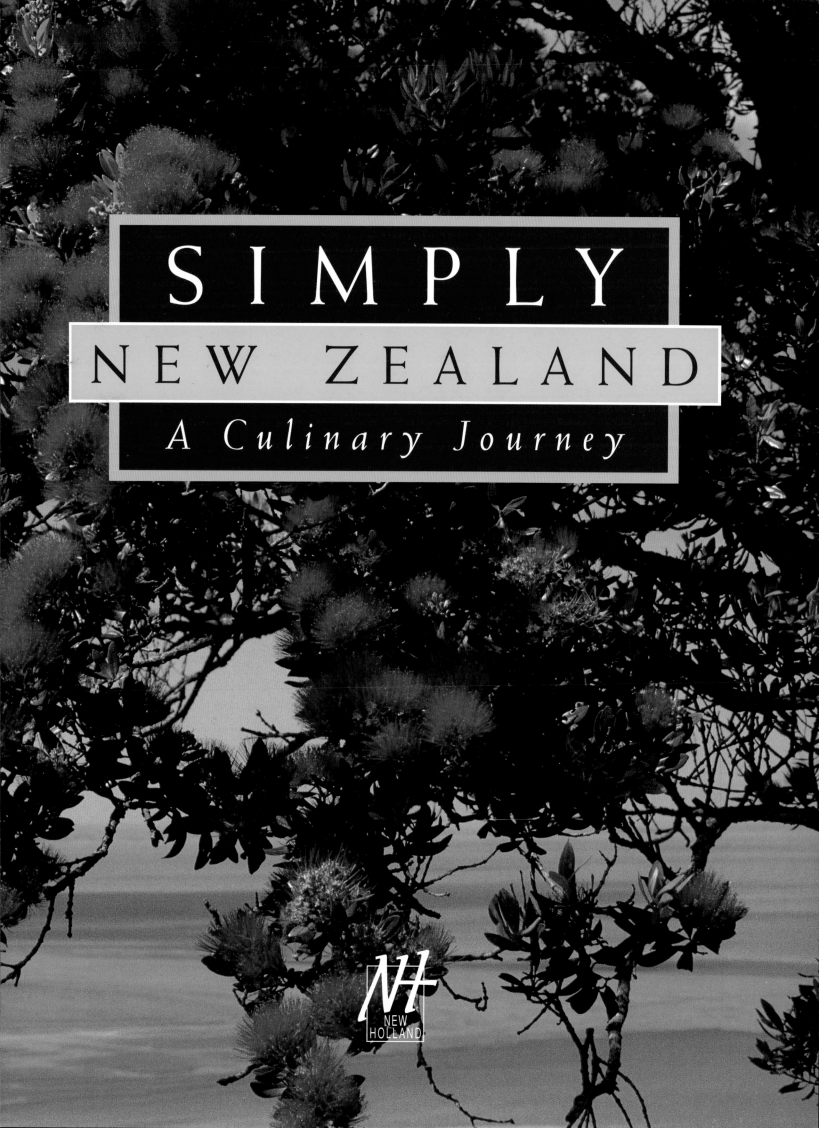

SIMPLY

NEW ZEALAND

A Culinary Journey

NH
NEW
HOLLAND

ACKNOWLEDGMENTS

In the course of producing this book, we visited many places that were not well known to us. We were dependent on word-of-mouth recommendations from local people to steer us in the direction of their favourite eating spots. We extend our warmest thanks for guiding us to what we think are some of the finest eateries in the country at this time. Special thanks go to Ian Baker for his enthusiasm and hard work in completing the photography and collecting (and tasting!) the recipes from the various restaurants and cafés.

To Jan Bilton, Dexter Fry, Pamela Parsons, Sue Attwood and to Mary Dobbyn, Jeannetta Josephs and Jeanne-Maree Fitzgerald, a sincere thanks. Most of all, our thanks go to the owners and chefs of the New Zealand restaurants who participated in our first culinary journey.

Cover photo: Canterbury Tales. This baked salmon recipe comes from Hamilton. See page 64.

Publisher: Cliff Josephs
Editor: Pamela Parsons
Food Editor: Jan Bilton
Editorial Assistant: Mary Dobbyn
Design and Production: Dexter Fry
Design Associate: Sue Attwood
Photography: Ian Baker and contributors
Printed by Bookbuilders, Hong Kong

First published in 1999 by New Holland Publishers (NZ) Ltd
Auckland • Sydney • London • Cape Town

www.newhollandpublishers.co.nz

218 Lake Road, Northcote, Auckland, New Zealand
14 Aquatic Drive, Frenchs Forest, NSW 2086, Australia
86–88 Edgware Road, London W2 2EA, United Kingdom
80 McKenzie Street, Cape Town 8001, South Africa

First edition published for Viking, an imprint of Penguin Books (NZ) Ltd, in 1997

ISBN: 1 877246 26 3

CONTENTS

THE NORTH ISLAND

THE SOUTH ISLAND

FOREWORD

THE VAST MAJORITY of our European ancestors were not given to the culinary arts. They were conservative, middle and working class English stock who came to New Zealand to better their lives. They did not come to make a fuss! Ergo – food was fuel not fun. Maori had their own remarkable gardens and New Zealand, a country with a small population, was rich in food resources. All in all we had nothing to worry about. Nor did we need to extend ourselves. It was enough that there were meat and three vegies on the table. Downplaying emotion, colour, humour and individuality, we Kiwis took it upon ourselves to make consistency in everything a virtue. Including our eating habits. Thank heavens those days are long gone. *Simply New Zealand* is entertaining proof that in our own unique culinary corner of the world, we can compete with the best. Food is fun not fuel. And fun is here to stay!

Gary McCormick

INTRODUCTION

GREAT FOOD! Stunning scenery! A refrain I constantly hear from overseas writers, reviewers and visitors. So we decided to publish an up-to-date cookbook/travel guide offering a wide selection of the country's best dishes discovered on a region-by-region culinary journey that ranged from the major cities to the most remote locations.

We were delighted with the reception that we received from restaurants, brasseries and cafés throughout the country. Owners and chefs were extremely obliging and helpful. We thank them sincerely for their valued contributions to *Simply New Zealand*.

In travelling around the country, we discovered that while certain local specialties are still popular (such as whitebait on the West Coast or lamb in Canterbury), we found that chefs are enthusiastic in their use of foods from other regions. (North Island restaurants may feature salmon farmed in the South Island or Bluff oysters as well as locally sourced meats, vegetables or seafood.) And the best chefs, both new and experienced, are ready to experiment with new varieties of fruits and vegetables, many of which are produced here. This results in food combinations that are deliciously unique.

Jan Bilton, our Food Editor, has adapted these chef-created recipes to ensure they are easy to follow and prepare. Her task was not an easy one, since many creative chefs prepare their recipes from memory and do not write them down!

Combining some of the most creative cooking in the country with magnificent scenic photography from Ian Baker and other contributors, *Simply New Zealand* is simply a little bit different — both a cook's travel guide and a traveller's cookbook.

Bon voyage and bon appetit!

The photographs on the previous pages are: (2-3) Pohutukawas, (4-5) Marlborough Sounds, (6-7) Martinborough. The map on the facing page is a regional guide to our culinary journey.

Cliff Josephs
Publisher

NORTHLAND & AUCKLAND

Cape Maria van Diemen

Waitangi • • Bay of Islands

• Whangarei

Kaipara Harbour
Whangaparaoa Peninsula
Muriwai •
Waitemata Harbour •
Auckland •
Manukau Harbour •
Hauraki Gulf • Port Jackson
• Waiheke Island
• Coromandel
• Firth of Thames
Thames • • Pauanui Beach

COROMANDEL, BAY OF PLENTY & EAST CAPE

Port Waikato
• Waihi
Bay of Plenty
Tauranga • • Mt. Maunganui
Raglan • • Hamilton • Te Puke
• Cambridge
• Rotorua
• East Cape

TARANAKI, KING COUNTRY & WAIKATO

Waitomo Caves •
Te Kuiti •

• Taupo
Lake Taupo
Tongariro National Park
Mt. Tongariro
New Plymouth • Mt. Ngauruhoe
Cape Egmont • Mt. Taranaki Mt. Ruapehu

Hawke Bay
Napier •
Hastings • • Cape Kidnappers

Palmerston North •

WAIRARAPA & HAWKE'S BAY

MANAWATU & WELLINGTON

Farewell Spit •
• Golden Bay
D'Urville Island
Abel Tasman National Park
Tasman Bay
Motueka •
Karamea • Nelson •
Murchison •
Nelson Lakes National Park
Westport •

Te Horo •
Waikanae •
Wellington •
Havelock •
Blenheim • Cloudy Bay

Masterton •
• Martinborough
Lake Wairarapa

• Cape Palliser

Cook Strait
Tararua Range
Rimutakas

Punakaiki •
Kaikoura Range
Kaikoura •

WEST COAST

MARLBOROUGH & NELSON

Greymouth •

Hokitika •

Southern Alps

KAIKOURA & CANTERBURY

CENTRAL OTAGO & FIORDLAND

Westland National Park
Franz Josef Glacier •
Fox Glacier •
Lake Paringa •
Haast • • Mt. Cook
• Haast Pass
Mt. Aspiring National Park

Canterbury Plains

Lyttelton • Christchurch
• Lyttelton Harbour
• Akaroa
Banks Peninsula

Ashburton •

• Timaru

Milford Sound Lake Wanaka •
Mitre Peak • • Wanaka
Lake Wakatipu •
Fiordland Queenstown • • Arrowtown
National Park • Clyde
Lake Te Anau •
Lake Manapouri •

The Remarkables

• Oamaru

• Otago Peninsula
• Dunedin

Gore • The Catlins • Balclutha
Invercargill • • Owaka
Foveaux Strait • Bluff
Toetoes Bay

OTAGO & SOUTHLAND

• Stewart Island

NORTHLAND & AUCKLAND

FROM PORT WAIKATO TO CAPE MARIA VAN DIEMEN (pictured here), Northland has been scooped out into great bays and harbours like the Bay of Islands, Whangarei and Hokianga Harbours and the largest harbour in New Zealand, the Kaipara. Surrounding Auckland are the Manukau and Waitemata Harbours, and to the east is the Firth of Thames. Our first stop was the Bay of Islands, where the weather is subtropical and the deep sea fishing first class, with marlin, tuna, kingfish and shark to be won. One of our recipes highlights this prized catch: seared game fish with a salad of ripe juicy tomatoes and quail eggs. Further south we visited the Whangaparaoa Peninsula, which juts into the Hauraki Gulf, and found other eating delights such as a creamy pineapple sable with chocolate mousse. The Gulf is home to everything marine - from great container ships and holiday cruise ships to fully-appointed yachts and commercial fishing boats as well as to windsurfers, waterskiers and sports fishermen. Auckland is located on the southwest side of the Hauraki Gulf, and is now New Zealand's largest urban centre. A city of sails, commerce, and miles of beaches, Auckland offers a happy mix of city amenities, suburban malls, outdoor sports and fine restaurants. In Auckland we found fresh John Dory fillets nested on a salad with honey and lime undertones and steamed mussels spiced with a Thai curry sauce. This is the tasty beginning of our culinary journey.

CHARGRILLED SMOKED VENISON SAUSAGE ON BAKED AUBERGINE WITH BLACKBERRY PICKLE & PEPPERED BRIE

BLACKBERRY PICKLE
1 small jar port wine jelly
200 ml each raspberry vinegar, red wine
vinegar
2 tablespoons brown sugar
1 cinnamon stick
2 bay leaves
3 cloves
200 ml red wine
500 g fresh or frozen blackberries

BAKED AUBERGINE
½ eggplant, sliced, salted and dried
butter
3 smoked venison sausages (from any good deli)
few slices Kapiti Peppered Brie cheese

To make the pickle, combine all ingredients except the blackberries in a saucepan and simmer for 5 minutes. Add blackberries and allow to cool. Makes enough for 8 servings. Bake eggplant in oven with a little butter. Chargrill venison sausage in griddle pan (or bake in oven). Arrange eggplant on plate, then venison sausage, then peppered brie. Finish with blackberry pickle and garnish with fresh garden herbs. Serves 1.

BISTRO 40, PAIHIA, BAY OF ISLANDS.

Preceding pages (14 & 15): Rawhiti Headlands, Bay of Islands. Rawhiti sits on the arm of Cape Brett, the lower part of the Bay of Islands, and looks across to the Kerikeri Inlet, the Purerua Peninsula and at inner bay islands such as Motukiekie, Urupukapuka and Waewaetoria. Urupukapuka in Otehei Bay is a sheltered island close to deep sea fishing zones and features an archaeological walk as well as marine life viewing from the Nautilus, a semi-submersible vessel.

WHERE TWO CULTURES MET

Below left is a vigorous carving from the Carrington Marae, Waitangi. Below: A waka at rest in the waters off Waitangi. Waitangi is best known as the place where in 1840 an agreement was signed between many Maori leaders and the British Crown. On the grounds of

the Treaty House, a Georgian-style edifice with part of its timber imported from Sydney, stands a meeting house or whare runanga. This meeting house is unique in having carvings provided by many different North Island tribes. Waitangi was one of New Zealand's earliest European settlements and Russell, which is near Waitangi and Paihia, was the first European town.

WARM SALAD OF SEARED GAME FISH WITH TOMATOES, QUAIL EGGS & POTATO

DRESSING
2 teaspoons cider vinegar
¼ cup olive oil
small bunch fresh basil
seasoning

SALAD
mixture of fancy lettuces
1 medium-sized potato,
scrubbed and boiled
2 tomatoes
8 quail eggs, boiled and peeled
8-10 capers
1 cucumber, sliced
2-3 slices each, red, green,
yellow capsicums

FISH
200 g game fish (tuna, swordfish, etc.)
100 ml soy sauce

To prepare dressing, blend all ingredients well. Arrange salad in a large bowl with sliced potatoes, tomatoes, quail eggs, capers, cucumber and capsicums. Slice game fish into 1 cm thick pieces and soak in soy sauce. Sear fish in smoking hot pan with a little olive oil until just underdone. Arrange fish in salad and drizzle dressing on the top.
Serves 1.

BISTRO 40, PAIHIA,
BAY OF ISLANDS.

PACIFIC HALF-SHELL OYSTERS TOPPED WITH MELON SALSA

MELON SALSA
¼ rock melon, finely diced
1 red chilli, seeded and finely diced
1 small red capsicum, finely diced
1 teaspoon chopped coriander
½ teaspoon Rose's Lime Juice
½ teaspoon fresh lime juice

OYSTERS
24 oysters in half shells
black pepper
shaved ice
rock salt
dried seaweed
2 limes to garnish
2 soft flour tortillas

To prepare melon salsa, combine rock melon, chilli, capsicum, coriander and lime juices in bowl. Allow flavours to mix for 30 minutes. Adjust seasoning, adding more lime juice if needed. Loosen oysters from shells. Season with black pepper. Top each oyster with ½ teaspoon melon salsa. On individual plates, scatter shaved ice and sprinkle with rock salt to stop ice melting. Scatter seaweed pieces on top of ice and salt and arrange 6 oysters in shells over the top. Garnish with lime wedges or twists and tortillas cut in wedges and deep fried.
Serves 4.

STANMORE COTTAGE
RESTAURANT, WHANGAPARAOA.

Islands in the Hauraki Gulf

PINEAPPLE SABLE WITH CHOCOLATE MOUSSE

SABLE

200 g butter
100 g caster sugar
2 eggs
zest of 1 lemon, 1 orange
3 drops vanilla essence
2 cups flour, sifted

Cream butter and sugar. Slowly add eggs a little at a time. Add zest and vanilla and fold in flour. Place in a container and refrigerate for 30 minutes. Dust work surface with flour and roll out dough. Using a cutter cut a large circle and place on a tray. Mark a centre line through diameter. When cold it will snap in half. Bake 180°C for 5-8 minutes until light in colour. Place on rack to cool. Store in an air-tight container.

CHOCOLATE MOUSSE

250 g chocolate
3 egg yolks
250 ml cream
2 egg whites
1 cup sugar
2 tablespoons rum

Melt chocolate in saucepan. Place egg yolks, cream and egg whites into separate bowls. Divide sugar evenly into each bowl. Add rum to egg yolks. Whip cream and refrigerate. Beat egg yolks until they form a stiff peak. Do the same with the egg whites. Fold chocolate into egg yolks. Fold in half the egg white, then add the cream. Lastly, fold in the remaining egg whites. Cover. Refrigerate overnight.

CANDIED PINEAPPLE

1 cup water
juice of 1 lemon
1 cup sugar
2 slices fresh pineapple cut 1 cm thick

Combine water, lemon juice, sugar
and bring to the boil. Simmer. Cut
pineapple into even pieces. Place in
syrup. Cook until transparent. Leave
to cool. Add extra water if too thick,
or if mixture is reduced too quickly.

RASPBERRY COULIS

1 cup sugar
2 cups water
2 tablespoons Grand Marnier
200 g raspberries

Boil sugar and water until a light
syrup is formed. Add Grand Marnier
and raspberries and simmer. Blend
and strain through a fine sieve.

ASSEMBLY

To assemble, use a hot spoon and
spoon out mousse onto a plate.
Alternate mousse, sable, mousse
(as per photograph). Lastly, place
pineapple on top of sable. Dust with
icing sugar. Add coulis.
Serves 6.

NAUTILUS RESTAURANT,
GULF HARBOUR VILLAGE,
WHANGAPARAOA.

Left: Auckland City's CBD seen from across the inner Waitemata Harbour. The 2000 America's Cup yachting challenge provided the impetus for a building boom on the once-industrial waterfront. Now the gleaming white structures of apartment buildings, bars, restaurants and the Hilton Hotel grace Princes Wharf.

Above: Cafés and bars along Auckland's waterfront. During the summer months Aucklanders and tourists alike flock to these fashionable eateries.

WHITE SAILS AND FOAMING WHITECAPS

Nearly everybody in Auckland turned out to greet the America's Cup champions who brought the Auld Mug to New Zealand in 1996. The Hauraki Gulf is one of the training grounds where New Zealand yachties become expert in the art of sailing and learn respect for the power, surprises and thrills of the ever-changing wind and sea. And after a day's sailing, a relaxing dinner at the yacht club.

LEMON CHICKEN

2 cloves garlic, chopped
¼ teaspoon Chinese Five Spice
¼ cup cider vinegar
¼ cup lemon juice
zest of 1 lemon
¼ cup vegetable oil
1 whole chicken (No. 7)

Place all ingredients in a plastic bag large enough to hold the whole chicken. Place chicken in last. Seal bag and marinate for 24 hours. Remove chicken from bag and place on a wire rack on a tray. Roast at 180°C for 1 hour, basting occasionally with remainder of marinade. Cut and serve.
Serves 4.

NAUTILUS RESTAURANT,
GULF HARBOUR VILLAGE,
WHANGAPARAOA.

CIN CIN
ORIENTAL-STYLE HOCKS

2 bacon or ham hocks
200 ml red wine
3 tablespoons soy sauce
2 each, cinnamon sticks, star anise
1 knob root ginger, sliced
3 cm piece orange peel
2 tablespoons palm sugar

Cover the hocks with water and boil for 30 minutes. Add all remaining ingredients and cook until tender, about 2 hours. Remove the hocks and reduce some of the liquid by three-quarters. Serve with boiled rice which has been moulded onto the serving plate. Spoon the sauce over the hocks. Can be accompanied by rocket leaves.
Serves 2.

CIN CIN ON
QUAY, AUCKLAND.

GULF ISLES

One can fly or float to Waiheke (it is about 35 minutes from Auckland by ferry), and its many beaches, leisurely lifestyle, resident artists, stylish cafés and vineyards have lured many Aucklanders to live there. There are also places to golf, mountain bike, bush walk and kayak. Other Gulf islands are Great Barrier, Little Barrier, Rakino and Kawau. Tiritiri Matangi Island is just off the end of the Whangaparaoa Peninsula and is now a bird refuge. Native bush is being restored, and excursions from Gulf Harbour regularly bring sightseers, who often help with organised plantings.

Matiatia Bay, Waiheke Island. Waiheke is between Ponui Island and the Rangitoto, Motutapu and Rakino cluster of islands. The landward side of Waiheke Island looks across the Tamaki Strait to Maraetai and Beachlands. Its seaward side turns to the Coromandel.

SEARED JOHN DORY ON A WARM SALAD WITH A ROASTED RED CAPSICUM COULIS

ROASTED RED CAPSICUM COULIS

2 cups white wine
¼ cup white wine vinegar
2 bay leaves
6 black peppercorns
6 shallots, peeled, sliced
6 red capsicums, roasted, seeded, peeled
2 cups cream
sea salt to taste

SALAD

16 shallots
¾ cup virgin olive oil
24 French beans, blanched
4 large red capsicums, roasted, seeded,
peeled and cut into strips
20 cherry tomatoes
salt and pepper
¾ cup balsamic vinegar
1 tablespoon clear honey
juice of 2 limes

800 g John Dory fillets

To prepare the coulis, put white wine, white wine vinegar, bay leaves, peppercorns, shallots and capsicums into a heavy-bottomed pot and simmer until liquid is reduced. Then add cream, bring to boil, season with sea salt and blend to a fine red purée. To prepare the salad, sweat shallots off in half the olive oil. Add French beans, roasted capsicums and cherry tomatoes and season with salt and pepper. Add vinegar, honey and lime juice. Tip warm salad into a bowl and toss. Place warm salad in the centres of four hot plates, drizzle capsicum coulis around the outside of salads. To cook the fish, sear fillets in the remaining olive oil and place on top of warm salads.
Serves 4.

KERMADEC RESTAURANT, AUCKLAND.

CHOCOLATE MARQUISE WITH ORANGE COMPOTE & SUMMER BERRIES

CHOCOLATE MARQUISE
325 g dark coverture chocolate
175 g butter
1¼ cups (about 8) egg whites
75 g sugar
100 ml whipped cream

COMPOTE
1 cup sugar
1 litre orange juice
3 tablespoons Grand Marnier
4 oranges, segments and zest

Line 8 plastic rings with silicon paper, reserve. Melt coverture and butter together. Whip egg white and sugar to soft peak and fold into chocolate and whipped cream mixture. Pipe the mix evenly into the plastic rings and refrigerate. To prepare the compote, caramelise the sugar, add the juice and reduce by half. Add the Grand Marnier, zest and orange segments. To assemble, pipe the chocolate across the plates, remove the marquise from the moulds and place in the centre of each plate. Fill one half with the orange compote and garnish with summer berries, tuilles and sugar sparkles. Serves 8.

ESSENCE, HERNE BAY, AUCKLAND.

SESAME TOFU & SOBA STIR-FRY NOODLES

MARINADE

1 ½ cups shoyu
knob of ginger, finely chopped or grated
4 cloves garlic, finely diced
¼ cup water
¼ fresh chilli, finely diced

TOFU STIR FRY

¼ firm block of tofu, sliced
½ cup Arame seaweed
½ packet Soba noodles
sesame oil
mixture of green vegetables, eg julienned celery, cucumber, capsicum, spring onions, courgette, and shredded cabbage
handful of sesame seeds, toasted
juice and zest of ½ lemon

Combine marinade ingredients and cover sliced tofu. Leave for 2-4 hours. Meanwhile cover seaweed with water and soak until soft for 5-10 minutes. Drain. To prepare noodles, cook in boiling water until 'al denté' (soft but firm). Drain and rinse under cold water. Toss a little toasted sesame oil through to prevent sticking. Drain tofu but save marinade. Lightly toss in flour and fry in pan with a little sesame oil until crisp on both sides. Put to one side. Heat wok with 1-2 tablespoons sesame oil, add vegetables, seaweed, sesame seeds and noodles. Add half the marinade and stir-fry for 5-10 minutes. Serve on a bed of salad greens, garnish with sliced fried tofu and black sesame seeds. Add lemon juice and zest for a twist.

ATOMIC CAFÉ, PONSONBY, AUCKLAND.

STEAMED MUSSELS AND RED THAI CURRY SAUCE WITH COCONUT CREAM & CORIANDER

MIREPOIX
1 onion,
1 carrot,
1 celery stick,
1 1/4 leeks, finely diced

RED THAI CURRY SAUCE
1 tablespoon each, chopped garlic,
grated root ginger,
red curry paste
2 teaspoons tomato paste
2 cups fish stock
1 small can peeled tomatoes
1/2 can coconut cream
1 coriander root
sea salt and pepper

STEAMED MUSSELS
1/2 cup olive oil
32 medium mussels, cleaned
1 1/4 cups white wine
chopped coriander to garnish

To make the curry sauce, sweat off mirepoix with garlic and ginger, add curry paste and tomato paste and cook until soft and dry. Add fish stock, tomatoes, coconut cream, coriander and seasoning. Bring to the boil and cook for 20 minutes. Pass through a sieve. To prepare the mussels, heat oil in a heavy-bottomed pan. Add mussels and put lid on pot. As mussels are just opening, add white wine and reduce. Add the curry sauce. Check seasoning and garnish with chopped coriander.

Serves 4.

KERMADEC RESTAURANT,
AUCKLAND.

SECLUSION CLOSE TO THE COSMOPOLITAN

Muriwai is about 40 km from downtown Auckland or less than 20 km from Kumeu. It has an unspoiled beach and boisterous, often dangerous surf, long rambling walks uphill and down dale and a wonderland of craggy cliffs, interesting tidepools and huge boulders carpeted with starfish, barnacles, mussels, and whelks.

Left: Flax plants fringe a lookout point over Muriwai Beach. One of Auckland's better known west coast surf beaches, it is north of Piha on the segment of coast between the entrances to Kaipara Harbour and Manukau Harbour. The iron-sand beach is long and level and bordered by low dunes. The spot is also a favourite of hang-gliding enthusiasts, who launch themselves from the Maori Bay cliffs.

Below: The gannet colony at Muriwai, where the nesting gannets and their chicks can be observed from a distance. This colony is one of the three known mainland nesting sites in New Zealand. The others are at Cape Kidnappers (south part of Hawke's Bay) and Farewell Spit (extreme north of the South Island).

COROMANDEL, BAY OF PLENTY & EAST CAPE

ON THESE PAGES IS A TYPICAL Coromandel Peninsula scene, with gentle sloping farmland, water views and rugged hills. Although the peninsula feels very secluded, it is only about an hour's drive from Auckland, and its attractions (including fishing for trevally, snapper and tarakihi) make it a favourite holiday spot. We began our journey in Thames and, after feasting on flounder in white wine sauce, drove north to the Tapu-Coroglen Road leading to Whitianga. South of Whitianga on the Coromandel east coast, we found superb recipes like upside-down-cake with toffee sauce. The Bay of Plenty was next, with its citrus, kiwifruit and tamarillo orchards. The 200-km-wide bay is rich in New Zealand history, Maori culture, natural resources and good food! In Tauranga we found a deliciously unusual licorice ice cream and discovered that White Island has geological links to Rotorua, the next stop on our itinerary. In Rotorua, showplace of one of the three most well-known geyser groups in the world, we found a sensationally scrumptious version of salmon fillets with mozzarella cheese and capsicum sauce. Then we toured the East Cape, home of rich farmland, remote beaches, mineral hot springs and beach reserves. We discovered many wonderful recipes in this varied and interesting region.

Tapu end of the Coroglen Road on the Coromandel. If you drive north from Thames to Tapu, you can cross the Coromandel Peninsula to Coroglen.

BRIAN BORU FLOUNDER

WHITE WINE SAUCE

½ cup white wine
1 teaspoon lemon juice
½ cup cream
salt and pepper
pinch chicken stock powder
1 teaspoon chopped parsley
1 flounder

Mix together white wine, lemon juice and cream and simmer until slightly reduced. Add seasoning, stock and parsley and reduce further, stirring continually to dissolve the stock powder.

Grill flounder on both sides. Cook until white side turns golden brown. Pour white wine sauce over flounder. Serve with French fries and salad. Serves 1.

BRIAN BORU HOTEL, THAMES

RHUBARB UPSIDE-DOWN CAKE WITH TOFFEE AND COCONUT MILK SAUCE

*400 g rhubarb stems
175 g butter, softened
150 g caster sugar
175 g self-raising flour
½ teaspoon baking powder
1 heaped tablespoon unblanched ground almonds
1 teaspoon ground cinnamon
3 eggs, beaten*

Cut the rhubarb stems into 5 mm pieces and place into the bottom of individual ramekins. Cream butter and sugar until light and pale in colour. Combine flour, baking powder, almonds and cinnamon. Fold into the creamed mixture, alternating with the eggs. The sponge should be fairly soft. Drop spoonfuls over the fruit as carefully as possible, trying not to disturb it. Dip a soup spoon in cold water and smooth the surface of the cake flat. Bake in a moderate oven 180°C for 30-35 minutes. Allow to cool in the moulds for a minute or two then turn out.

WELCOMING WHITIANGA

It is less than a 50 km coastline drive along Highway 25 from Tairua to Whitianga. A very accessible anchorage, Whitianga is a holiday resort with ferry links to Ferry's Landing and Flaxmill Bay. The outdoors minded will be delighted by the swimming at Buffalo Beach, the good scallop hunting, and the places to go fishing and yachting. A visitor can also choose to wind surf, golf, abseil or horse trek as well as try river rafting or rock hounding. There is also a Craft Trail, a Heritage Trail and the Purangi Winery and Craft Gallery. Whitianga is also the base for Air Coromandel.

TOFFEE AND COCONUT MILK SAUCE

250 g unsalted butter
250 g brown sugar
3 tablespoons Butterscotch Schnapps
800 ml coconut milk
200 ml cream

Melt the butter in a saucepan. When boiling, add brown sugar and let the two boil into each other. Add the Butterscotch Schnapps, then add in coconut milk and cream. Bring to the boil, simmer for 5 minutes, strain and pour over the upside-down cakes and serve with homemade vanilla bean ice cream.
Serves about 6.

SHELLS RESTAURANT & BAR, TAIRUA BEACH.

BAKED SUPREME OF SOUTH ISLAND SALMON WRAPPED IN NORI, ON A BED OF GINGER-INFUSED VEGETABLES

VEGETABLES

1 tablespoon diced ginger
5 g dried seaweed
1 tablespoon water
1 each, small carrot and courgette, finely diced
2 tablespoons skinned and diced red capsicum
2 tablespoons sake
salt and freshly ground black pepper
1 tablespoon each fish sauce, rice wine vinegar

SALMON PARCELS

4 x 200 g supremes (fillets) of salmon
salt and pepper
lemon juice
4 sheets nori (dried seaweed)

To marinate the ginger-infused vegetables, blanch the ginger in plenty of boiling water for 15 minutes. Drain well.
Soak the dried seaweed in the water for 1 hour then drain well and chop finely.
Mix all the remaining vegetable garnish ingredients together with seaweed and ginger.
Cover with plastic film and marinate for 24 hours in fridge.
To wrap the salmon parcels, cut salmon fillets in half and season with salt, pepper and lemon juice.
Fold over to create a square.

Brush with a little water to soften, place salmon in centre of each sheet of nori and wrap in a parcel Bake in oven at 180°C for 13 minutes. Place warmed vegetables loosely on centre of plate, slice baked salmon on an angle and place onto vegetables. Serves 6.

PUKA PARK LODGE RESTAURANT, PAUANUI BEACH.

VENISON MEDALLIONS WITH SUNDRIED TOMATO & STRAWBERRY CHUTNEY

200 g Venison Denver leg
1 tablespoon olive oil
¼ cup red wine
50 g sundried tomatoes
6 strawberries
1 tablespoon strawberry conserve
seasoning to taste

Slice venison into medallions across the grain.
Heat a heavy pan with olive oil until very hot. Fry venison for 1-2 minutes each side until cooked rare.
To make the sauce, reduce red wine to half the quantity. Add sliced sundried tomatoes and strawberries and thicken sauce with strawberry conserve. Serve with the venison. Serves 1.

Serve with a bottle of full-bodied red wine (suggestion: Villa Maria Merlot Syrah Cabernet).

KESSALLS RESTAURANT & BAR, PAUANUI.

LICORICE ICE CREAM WITH FRESHLY SQUEEZED ORANGE JUICE

1 litre milk

8 egg yolks

1 ¼ cups caster sugar

1 tablespoon Galliano

2 cups cream

1 kg softened licorice pieces

freshly squeezed orange juice

chocolate-coated dried oranges

Boil the milk. Beat egg yolks and sugar until thick. Add milk, return to a low heat, stirring constantly until thick enough to coat the back of a wooden spoon. Chill until cool, add Galliano, cream and licorice and churn in an ice cream maker or food processor until creamy. Serve in a glass with fresh orange juice and chocolate-coated dried oranges.

SOMERSET COTTAGE, TAURANGA.

SHELTERED ANCHORAGE

The protected Port of Tauranga bustles with commercial activity. The farmlands of Tauranga yield kiwifruit, tamarillo, féijoa and citrus crops, and its offshore waters yield the big game fish that attract sports fishermen to try their luck. The ocean near Mayor and Motiti Islands is especially good for anglers. Other attractions are the city's jazz festival, its many historical monuments and buildings from colonial times and the Tauranga Historic Village, which brings to life New Zealand's colonial era. Walks include Longridge and McLaren Falls Parks, the Puketoki Scenic Reserve, the Katikati Bird Gardens, the Waikareao Estuary and Ohauiti Walkways, and Rerekawau Falls. Many spas and pools can be enjoyed, including the salt water pools at Mt Maunganui, the Maketu, Welcome Bay, and Katikati hot pools and the Plummer's Point Sapphire Hot Springs. A kiwifruit theme park called Kiwi Country specialises in showing the visitor every aspect of kiwifruit production and export.

Right, sunset over Matamata. West of Tauranga, rural Matamata has over 20 thoroughbred studs, many sheep and dairy farms and good access to trout fishing and Kaimai Range walking tracks.

FRESH CHICKEN LIVERS WITH FIG TAPENADE & RASPBERRY VINEGAR

FIG TAPENADE
¼ cup chopped figs
2 tablespoons brandy
¼ cup each water, pitted olives, olive oil
3 anchovy fillets
salt and pepper
1 tablespoon each capers, lemon juice,
balsamic vinegar
1 teaspoon Dijon mustard

POTATO RÖSTI
1 large potato, washed
2 tablespoons oil
extra oil
16 fresh chicken livers
flour
2 tablespoons clarified butter
½ onion, sliced
2 tablespoons each Marsala,
raspberry vinegar
4 teaspoons fig tapenade
4 small potato rösti

To make the fig tapenade, simmer figs, brandy and water for 5 minutes, add remaining ingredients and process until smooth. To make the potato rösti, slice potato into fine julienne and mix with oil. Fry four moulded round shapes in oil. When brown, turn over and fry until crisp. Drain on absorbent paper. To prepare chicken livers, flour livers in a sieve, shake off any excess flour. Melt clarified butter in a frying pan and add livers.

A TAURANGA TREK

Another lovely vacation area is shown above in the photo taken from the top of Mt Maunganui looking out over the coastal town of Mt Maunganui and its ocean surf beaches. Here, holidaymakers will find both hot and saltwater pools plus good swimming and water sports near the steep mountain cone that rises from the beach at one end of the peninsula. From the summit there are splendid views of offshore islands and Tauranga, which is linked to Mt Maunganui by the harbour bridge. Near the mountain are the docks for the Port of Tauranga. The area is also close to Te Puke and is a short drive to Rotorua, famed for its geysers, hot springs, blue-green lakes and other natural wonders.

Cook on high heat until brown on both sides (be careful as they can spit). Add onion, then Marsala. Place onto plate. Return pan to heat, deglaze with raspberry vinegar, then pour around livers. Garnish with potato rösti and fig tapenade. Serves 4.

SOMERSET COTTAGE, TAURANGA.

FILLETS OF SALMON WITH MOZZARELLA, BASIL & CAPSICUM ON A LIME SAUCE

800 g salmon fillet, skinned, filleted and with all bones removed, including pin bones
½ medium-sized red capsicum, thinly sliced and lightly fried in olive oil
4 basil leaves
½ cup mozzarella

POACHING LIQUOR AND SAUCE

½ cup finely diced onion
zest and juice of 4 limes
¾ cup dry white wine
pinch freshly ground black pepper and salt
1 cup cream
50 g butter

To prepare salmon fillets, cut salmon into eight equal squares. Take four squares and place the capsicum, a basil leaf and mozzarella on top of each, then cover with four remaining pieces of salmon. Hold together with a toothpick, then sprinkle with freshly ground black pepper and a pinch of salt. To cook salmon, take a large stainless steel or Teflon-coated frypan (large enough to accommodate the salmon) and place onion, lime zest and dry wine in the pan. Place the salmon fillets in the pan, cover with a lid, and gently steam the fish for about 7-8 minutes or until just cooked. Do not dry the fish. Remove the fish from the pan, place on a dish and cover with foil and keep warm.

To make the sauce, reduce cooking liquor by two-thirds over a high heat. Add cream and lime juice, pinch of black pepper and salt and reduce by half (still on a fierce heat). Remove from the heat and whisk in 50 g of butter. Do not melt the butter first. Season to taste.

To serve the salmon, place on a plate and drizzle the sauce around. Can be served with your favourite salad and vegetables. Complement with small poached potatoes. It is also delightful served on lightly steamed courgettes cut spaghetti style.

Serves 4.

RUMOURS, ROTORUA.

RACK OF LAMB WITH TARRAGON SAUCE & KUMARA CAKE

1 large kumara
4 racks of lamb (French racked, chined and silverskin removed)
½ cup chopped fresh tarragon, mint and parsley
black pepper and salt

SAUCE

1 tablespoon each finely diced onion, dry tarragon, tarragon vinegar
½ cup dry red wine
1 cup demi glaze (packet-made brown sauce will substitute well in a home situation)
25 g butter

Microwave kumará on high until cooked, remove flesh, place through a mincer or food processor and fashion into 4 quite thick cakes. Pan fry in clarified butter and set aside. Coat the lamb racks in the herb mix (outer surface only). Season with black pepper and salt. Heat a thick-bottomed pan, then seal the lamb rack until a nice brown colour is achieved on both sides. Place in a medium oven and cook to the degree you prefer. Do not dry out meat - about 15 minutes should produce a medium-cooked rack. To make the sauce, place onion, tarragon, tarragon vinegar and wine in a small saucepan and reduce by two-thirds. Add in brown sauce, bring to boil.

Remove from heat and whip in the
butter. (Do not heat further). To
serve, pour sauce onto centre of four
plates. Place kumara cake in the
middle of each plate. Cut racks into
individual pieces by slicing between
the bones and lay neatly around the
kumara cake. Serve with your choice
of vegetables.
Serves 4.

RUMOURS, ROTORUA.

*Far left: An impressive carving from
Rotorua. The city and environs have a
wealth of living Maori culture: from ethnic
exhibits and craft studios to the way of life of
Rotorua's Maori residents. Maori dance,
music, weaving, cooking and carving plus
other activities can be enjoyed.*

*Left: Silica formations at Rotorua. Much of
the Rotorua area was reshaped by the violent
1886 explosion of Mt Tarawera, which
destroyed existing formations such as the
often-painted Pink and White Terraces. But
visitors can still see silica terraces, hillocks
and naturally shaped sculpture, much of
which is coloured by the algae that flourish
in the steaming, mineralised waters.*

50

Right: A beach on the East Cape near Gisborne.

Below: A caravan sits in a secluded glen in Tokomaru Bay. Situated about 92 km from Gisborne on East Cape Road (Highway 35), Tokomaru Bay is one of the fine beaches to be seen along the road from Gisborne to Opotiki.

TARANAKI, KING COUNTRY & WAIKATO

FROM THE AIR CAPE EGMONT dominates the Taranaki region. Pictured on these two pages is snow-capped Mount Taranaki, which is situated in the very centre of Cape Egmont and is encircled by lush dairy and sheep pasture. This rich pasturage fostered the establishment of cheesemakers who were first famed for their tangy cheddar cheese. Now local cheesemakers are building on that success by producing many types of cheeses for the domestic market and for export. We began our travels east of Mount Taranaki in the Tongariro National Park area. From there we bring you a very special pumpkin recipe. Then we drove south to Lake Taupo, the largest freshwater lake in the Southern Hemisphere, and sampled a bold onion frittata garnished with black olive pesto. After that we travelled through the lush rolling hillsides of the King Country, which still contains untouched forests and pristine rivers like the Waipa, Mokau and Awakino. (In this book, the King Country encompasses the North Island Central Plateau, Lake Taupo and Waikato.) We ended our pleasant stay in the lovely Waikato environs, where we sampled a scallop platter rich with garlic taste and salmon fillets bathed in a wine, whisky and butter sauce. The tempting dishes from this lush and dramatic region are both unique and memorable.

Right: This August 1995 photo of Mount Ruapehu captures the awe-inspiring billows of ash and steam that poured from its depths, closing ski fields but drawing throngs of volcano watchers. The eruptions caused great hardship to the North Island's most popular winter sports playground, which includes the Whakapapa ski fields, the Chateau, the golf course and the camping areas.

Inset: Mount Ngauruhoe rising above the Rangipo Desert in Tongariro National Park. This spectacular area, which lies between Turangi in the north and Waiouru and Okahune in the south, was given in trust to the Tuwharetoa tribe so that it might be preserved for our generation and future generations to come. Ngauruhoe's base is entwined with its close northern neighbour, Mount Tongariro.

MUMU PUMPKIN

4 miniature pumpkins
2 bananas, sliced
100 g thinly sliced fresh pineapple
2 shallots, finely chopped
orange-scented olive oil
1 clove garlic, peeled and sliced
1 similarly sized piece of ginger root,
peeled and sliced
400 ml coconut cream
salt and pepper

Blanch and peel pumpkins, remove
seeds and fill with banana and
pineapple. Place in casserole dish.
Sweat shallots in a little
orange-scented olive oil, add sliced
garlic and ginger, add coconut cream,
salt and pepper, and simmer for 10
minutes. Strain over pumpkins,
cover and bake until tender.
Remove pumpkins, reduce sauce,
adjust seasoning and consistency
and pour around the pumpkins.
Good served with pork, poultry,
lamb or beef.
Serves 4.

THE RUAPEHU ROOM,
THE GRAND CHATEAU,
TONGARIRO NATIONAL PARK.

58

Waiting for the first visitors... All alone in the dawn, a wooden bench sits before Lake Taupo, the largest freshwater lake in the Southern Hemisphere. Its stillness does not reveal that nearly 2000 years ago a volcanic eruption took place here, with ash and pumice hurled more than 100 km away.

LAKESIDE HOLIDAYS

Lake Taupo graces the centre of the North Island and is on a northeast line from Mount Ruapehu, Ngauruhoe, Tongariro and Pihanga - and is just north of Turangi. The lake is about 619 sq km in area and about 25 km long. The town of Taupo looks southwest over Acacia Bay and across the lake, whose northern rim is bitten out by several other deep coves. The Taupo area is a wonderland for those on a holiday - with thermal baths and pools, jet boating and water skiing and many walks nearby. The Waitahanui River is just one of many good fishing spots where fat and feisty trout can be taken.

FILLED FARMHOUSE LOAVES

There are more varieties of fillings than there are farmhouse loaves. At Replete there is no official recipe for this dish, except it uses the freshest of ingredients and tasty flavour combinations.

1 olive, walnut or rye loaf
spicy mango or your favourite chutney
cottage cheese
Mesclun salad mix
ham or pastrami
alfalfa sprouts

Cut one end off the loaf, being sure not to remove too much. Hollow out the loaf, leaving a thin layer of soft bread under the crust. Keep the scooped-out bread for stuffings, etc. Spread the inside of the cavity with the chutney, then fill the loaf with the variety of fillings starting with the cottage cheese. Pack the fillings in as tightly as you can so they hold their place once the loaf is sliced. Pack in the layer of salad mix, then compress it down with the ham, holding everything in place with your free hand. Fill the remaining cavity with the sprouts. To serve, slice the loaf into thick servings, then carefully place onto a plate. Serve with tossed salad, pasta salad and, if you're really hungry, smoked salmon-filled bagels. Makes one standard loaf.

REPLETE FOOD COMPANY, CAFÉ/DELI & CATERING CONSULTANCY, TAUPO.

ONION FRITTATA WITH BLACK OLIVE PESTO

This dish is very much in keeping with Italian brasserie-style food. It is light, quick, easy to prepare and is based around what is in season. The dish can be increased in size to be a complete entrée or reduced in portion size to become an antipasto.

FRITTATA
7 x no. 6 eggs
½ cup grated fresh Parmesan
freshly-ground black pepper and
Maldon crystal salt
extra-virgin olive oil
1 medium-sized red onion, sliced

BLACK OLIVE PESTO
250 g black olives, in brine (stoned weight)
1 tablespoon capers
1 small clove garlic
zest of ½ lemon
enough extra-virgin olive oil to make a firm paste
freshly ground black pepper and
Maldon crystal salt

TOSSED SALAD
enough Mesclun salad mix for
6 servings (allow approximately
35-40 g per portion)
olive oil
freshly ground black pepper and
Maldon crystal salt

Beat the eggs in a large bowl. Mix in the cheese and season to taste. Heat the frypan over a steady flame with a little olive oil (suggest you use a 25 cm frypan). Add in the sliced onion and cook until tender.

NATIVE PARROTS AND ANCIENT TREES

Not far east of Lake Taupo is the Whirinaki Forest, part of which is rooted in the deep ash and pumice laid down by the Lake Taupo eruption. This forest, known worldwide for its ancient podocarp trees, was declared a DOC conservation park in 1984; thus preserving its rimu, totara, matai, miro and kahikatea from further logging. These coniferous trees are related to the yew family and are home to kakas, large native parrots which love podocarp fruit, honeydew from beech trees, insects from rotting wood and sap both from tawa and the imported pine that grows next to the forest. Sadly, because much of the Whirinaki Forest was so heavily logged, the kakas are under threat because of limited habitat and predators.

Increase the heat and add in the egg mix. Cook until golden on one side. Lift the edges of the frittata as it cooks, then turn and cook until golden on the remaining side. Turn out onto a clean plate and allow to cool completely. Set aside.

To make the pesto, drain and dry the olives and capers. Stone the olives, then place them in a food processor with the capers, garlic and zest. Blend to a medium-fine texture, adding in the olive oil as you go to form a firm paste. Remove from the blender and place in a clean bowl. Season to taste. Set aside.

To serve, cut the frittata into small even wedges and arrange three on each plate. Spoon a little pesto evenly on each one. Very lightly toss the Mesclun in olive oil, then place a portion in the centre of each plate. Grind over plenty of pepper and sprinkle with a few whole Maldon salt crystals. Serve with a dry Italian-style white wine.

Serves 6.

REPLETE CAFÉ/DELI & CATERING CONSULTANCY, TAUPO.

Screened by a green veil of leaves as the sun sets, a homeward-bound yacht catches the late evening breezes on Lake Taupo.

WAITOMO CAVES

Waitomo – The place where the waters of the Waitomo River plunge suddenly into a hillside. The caves are numerous and connected, with most of the tunnels still unexplored. About twelve million years ago, the Waitomo Caves began to form as water dissolved limestone and redeposited it inside the network of caverns. This process creates downward-pointing stalagtites, and upward-pointing stalagmites as well as wrinkles, curls and other fantastic shapes in limestone.

Inside the best known part, Glow-worm Grotto, the larval stage of a gnat spins slender, crystal-clear fishing lines to trap other insects for dinner. The chemical lights in the worms can be flicked on and off as they choose, bathing the fantasia of threads that look like micro-waterfalls hanging hazily in the grotto. A specialist museum at the caves explains in full detail about the geology and history of the area as well as the living ecosystem and the fossils found there.

CANTERBURY TALES

SAUCE
1 nip whisky
1 teaspoon dill
1 tablespoon sparkling wine
25 g butter

SALMON
2 x 100 g fillets salmon, skin on
salt and freshly ground
black pepper to taste
flour
50 g vegetables, julienned and blanched
1 lemon slice and sprig of fresh fennel
to garnish

To make sauce, mix together all ingredients and simmer until blended. Roll salmon in seasoned flour and place on a grill in an oven dish. Oven bake at 200°C until cooked and arrange on a bed of julienned vegetables. Cover with the sauce and garnish with a slice of lemon and some fennel.
Serves 1.

LEFT BANK INTERNATIONAL RESTAURANT & BAR, HAMILTON, WAIKATO.

CHARRED TUNA LOIN WITH WILTED SPINACH AND LIME & GRAPEFRUIT BEURRE BLANC

MIXED TOMATO SALAD

100 g cherry tomatoes
50 g each, sundried tomatoes, shallots, chives
3 cloves garlic
3 tablespoons each, balsamic vinegar, sundried tomato oil

BEURRE BLANC

100 ml each, lime juice, grapefruit juice
100 g shallots
1 teaspoon peppercorns
1 bay leaf
200 g butter

TUNA

160 g tuna steak
salt and pepper
1 teaspoon grated lemon rind
100 g spinach leaves

To make the salad, quarter the tomatoes, chop the sundried tomatoes, shallots, chives and garlic and combine with vinegar and oil. To make the beurre blanc, reduce the liquids and flavourings by half, strain, then slowly add cold butter without boiling the mixture. Sprinkle the tuna with salt, pepper and lemon rind. Chargrill for about 2 minutes each side. Sauté spinach in a saucepan for about 1 minute. Serve the tuna on the spinach topped with the beurre blanc and the tomato salad on the side. Serves 1.

RUSTICI BRASSERIE, HAMILTON, WAIKATO

PICASSO'S SCALLOP PLATTER

1 teaspoon each, chopped root
ginger, crushed garlic, butter
5 scallops
salt and pepper
2 teaspoons each, cheese sauce, raspberry
purée, apricot purée, sesame sauce,
cardamom sauce, blueberry purée*
½ cup boiled rice
15 g julienned vegetables
1 puff pastry leaf
1 fennel sprig
cracked pepper

*Note: You may use a combination
of your favourite sauces.

Sauté ginger and garlic in butter, add scallops and seasoning.

Prepare all sauces separately. Boil the rice, prepare the julienned vegetables and make the leaf with puff pastry. Centre the rice on a small dish and arrange the six sauces around it in equal amounts with colours alternating. Arrange the scallops on the rice and garnish with the vegetables and pastry leaf and top with a sprig of fennel. Add cracked pepper around the plate and serve. Serves 1.

LEFT BANK INTERNATIONAL
RESTAURANT & BAR,
HAMILTON, WAIKATO.

Preceding pages (66 & 67): Sheep graze in a lush and peaceful Waikato setting near Cambridge - about two hours south of Auckland.

Left: The mighty Waikato, slow and serene. Born from Lake Taupo, the Waikato travels north more than 400 km to meet the Tasman Sea south of Manukau Harbour.

WAIRARAPA & HAWKE'S BAY

THIS PLEASANT FARMING REGION is on the road to Cape Palliser. At the extreme southern end of the North Island, Cape Palliser is not far south of Martinborough, where we began our good food search in the Wairarapa. Martinborough, which has gained international status as a fine-wine producer, is situated east of Lake Wairarapa and it shares the related pursuits of farming and market gardening with communities such as Carterton, Greytown and Eketahuna, which perches above the Makakahi River Gorges. In Martinborough we dined on tender beef eye fillet dressed with well-seasoned jus and found a salmon terrine whose taste was spectacular. Then we drove north to fast-growing Masterton, where we found a chewy-good crostata garnished with fresh rosemary. Continuing north to Hawke's Bay, we basked in the sunshine that fosters the region's agricultural success. Abundant grapes, fruits and vegetables feed into local food processing companies, wineries and food exporting companies. Napier and Hastings restaurants contributed excellent recipes, such as a mouth-watering fresh-fruit terrine and a lemon-herbed lamb roulade stuffed with aubergine. One of the brightest stars in the Hawke's Bay area is viniculture, whose success is garnering international respect and financial rewards. You'll love both the wines and the recipes of this region!

TERRINE OF SALMON AND CABBAGE

1 savoy or green cabbage
150 g smoked salmon
450 g fresh salmon
salt and white pepper

Blanch cabbage leaves, refresh in iced water, dry in a tea towel or salad spinner. Line a 650 ml capacity terrine mould with plastic film (oil mould to help plastic film stick). Allow film to overlap for folding over the top. Line mould with cabbage leaves, allowing enough overlap to fold over the top. Line cabbage with smoked salmon, allowing overlap to fold over the top. Layer 3-4 layers of salmon with cabbage, packing well and seasoning well with salt and pepper. Finish by folding the overlapping cabbage and salmon over the top, adding more if necessary. Fold gladwrap over to cover. Cook, covered and well sealed with foil, in a deep waterbath at 180°C for 25-30 minutes. Test with a metal skewer - it should be hot when removed. Remove immediately, press with weights (2 tins of canned food). Cool and refrigerate. To serve, slice and steam or microwave until just warm. Accompany with a soy flavoured Beurre Blanc or a classic Beurre Blanc spiked with a little caviar or lumpfish roe (rinsed and added at the last minute). A soy vinaigrette or mayonnaise is a simpler accompaniment.
Serves 8.

AYLSTONE, PRIVATE LODGINGS, WINE LIBRARY & LARDER, MARTINBOROUGH.

GRILLED BEEF EYE FILLET WITH OVEN ROASTED TOMATOES, WILTED ROCKET, WATERCRESS & BEEF JUS

2 tomatoes
salt and ground black pepper
olive oil
rocket and watercress leaves
melted butter

BEEF JUS

300 ml beef stock
¼ teaspoon tomato paste
¼ cup Winslow Cabernet
Sauvignon/Franc

1 beef eye fillet steak per serve

**Slice tomatoes in half and lightly
season. Drizzle with olive oil and
place on an oven tray cut side up.
Dry slowly in 150°C oven for
approximately 3 hours. Rinse and pat
dry the rocket and watercress leaves.
Toss in a little olive oil and melted
butter. To make the beef jus, heat
stock, tomato paste and wine until
reduced to a quarter of the original
volume. Season and tie to shape a
piece of eye fillet for each serving.
Grill 3 minutes each side or as
required. Assemble on warm plate
with other ingredients.
Serves 1.**

THE MARTINBOROUGH BISTROT,
MARTINBOROUGH HOTEL,
MARTINBOROUGH.

*Left: Seals at part of Cape Palliser's
rugged coastline.*

RED CAPSICUM PESTO TARTLET ON A BED OF MARINATED AUBERGINE SLICES WITH LEMON BASIL DRESSING

Prepare and bake some small tartlet cases from your favourite savoury shortcrust recipe.

AUBERGINE (EGGPLANT)

1 eggplant
salt
basil and mint
1 clove garlic, peeled and sliced
cracked pepper
olive oil

RED CAPSICUM PESTO

4 red capsicums
¼ cup pine nuts
1 clove of garlic, chopped
salt and pepper
a little grated Parmesan cheese
¼ cup olive oil

CUSTARD

2 tablespoons pesto
1 egg
¼ cup cream

DRESSING

handful of lemon basil
1 cup olive oil
2 teaspoons lemon juice
salt and black pepper

To prepare the eggplant, peel, slice and sprinkle with salt. Leave to sweat out the moisture. Rinse and dry. Layer with basil, mint, garlic and cracked pepper. Add olive oil and compress layers to remove air bubbles, make sure it is completely covered. Cover and refrigerate. To prepare the pesto, roast, peel and de-seed capsicum.

CASTLEPOINT AND WINERY CASKS

The photo above shows the lighthouse at Castlepoint, which is on the coast about 68 km due east of Masterton. Castlepoint is the site of an annual horse race on the dunes, and there are many other activities to enjoy

Blend in a food processor with pine nuts, garlic, salt and pepper, Parmesan cheese and drizzle in the olive oil. To prepare the custard, beat pesto with egg and cream. Pour into two tartlet cases. Bake until set in a moderate oven. Multiply the recipe if more tartlets are required. To make the dressing, chop the basil and add to warm olive oil. Leave to infuse. Before serving, whisk in the lemon juice, salt and black pepper. Serve the tartlets with eggplant and dressing. Makes 2 tartlets but enough pesto dressing and eggplant for 6 or more servings.

THE MARTINBOROUGH BISTROT, MARTINBOROUGH HOTEL, MARTINBOROUGH.

as well such as swimming, surf casting, reef fishing and floundering. About 50 km from Masterton is Martinborough, which hosts a yearly wine festival. Visitors can taste wines from local boutique wineries and visit arts and crafts stalls where local artists display their work.

CRISPY COUNTRY CROSTATA

CRUST

1 cup chilled flour
125 g chilled butter
4 tablespoons sour cream
1 tablespoon lemon juice
¼ cup iced water
¼ cup coarse cornmeal

FILLING

2 tablespoons olive oil
750 g gourmet flat mushrooms,
roughly chopped
1 bunch spring onions, chopped
2 cloves garlic, chopped
1 tablespoon fresh rosemary
2 teaspoons lemon thyme
120 g Gladstone Encore Chévre
cheese, crumbled
120 g Kapiti Kikorangi
cheese, crumbled

Combine all ingredients for crust except cornmeal. Mix well. Roll dough on cornmeal to a circle approximately 30 cm in diameter. Place on an oven tray. To make the filling, heat oil and cook mushrooms, onions, garlic and herbs until all liquid evaporates, approximately 8 minutes. Cool and add cheeses. Spread mixture onto pastry, leaving 5 cm border. Pleat border up over filling. Bake at 200°C for 35 minutes until crust is deep golden. Serve hot or at room temperature. Serves 6.

TOADS LANDING, MASTERTON.

MILE-HIGH MARION PIE

CRUST
125 g gingernut biscuits, crushed
50 g butter

FILLING
300 g frozen marionberries
½ cup sugar
2 egg whites
250 ml cream, whipped
fresh berries for garnish

Prepare crust by mixing biscuits and butter together. Press onto base of spring-form tin and bake in oven for 10 minutes. To make filling, beat berries, sugar and egg whites together in bowl of an electric mixer for approximately 15 minutes until sugar has dissolved. Fold in the whipped cream. Pour over biscuit base and freeze. To serve, remove from tin and decorate the top with fresh berries. Serves 6.

TOADS LANDING, MASTERTON.

SCENIC AND AGRICULTURAL

This Wairarapa field south of Masterton soaks up the long summer season. Masterton is the centre of the prosperous Wairarapa, which combines rural beauty, industrial growth and a flourishing art scene. The community, which is approximately 100 km northeast of Wellington, can

be reached via an Upper Hutt to Featherston, Greytown and Carterton route. Masterton hosts the annual Golden Shears competition, has a large Arts Centre and its Queen Elizabeth Park offers boating on the lake, an aquarium and a deer park. Nearby Tararua Forest Park and Honeycomb Rock have walkways, and there is a Wildlife Centre at Mount Bruce.

HAWKE'S BAY FRUIT TERRINE

*a selection of fresh berries -
strawberries, raspberries,
blueberries, about 3 cups
1 cup sparking white wine
2 nips of Blue Curacao
2 nips of Peach Schnapps
(or other fruit liqueur)
100 ml water
200 g caster sugar
5 teaspoons powdered gelatine
3 oranges, peeled and segmented
200 g green grapes, halved*

**Prepare berries by removing
stalks. Place all liquid in a
heavy-bottomed pot, add sugar
and bring to the boil. Simmer
for 2-3 minutes. Dissolve
gelatine powder as per packet
instructions and add to liquid. Allow
to cool slightly. Build up layers of
fruit in the terrine and allow each
layer to set by placing in the freezer
before you put on the next layer.
When the terrine is full, leave to set in
refrigerator for 12-24 hours. To
remove from terrine, run the outside
under hot water and carefully turn out
onto a board or tray so it is easy to
cut. Serve two thin slices per person.
Serves about 6.**

**VIDAL WINERY BRASSERIE,
HASTINGS.**

SEA OF BLOSSOMS

Below, pink-blossomed fruit trees create the exhilaration of springtime in Hastings. Just 20 km southwest of Napier, Hastings lies on the Heretaunga Plains and is known for abundant fruit harvests, food processing and wine making. Areas near the Ngaruroro, Tutaekuri and Tukituki Rivers are especially fertile. Each year Hastings celebrates a Wine Festival, a Blossom Festival and a Highland Games. The region has several lovely parks as well as trout fishing, water rafting, jet boating and horse trekking. Nearby Cape Kidnappers has one of the world's three known mainland gannet colonies.

LEMON-HERBED LAMB ROULADE WITH CHARGRILLED AUBERGINE

4 lamb backstraps

CHERMOULA
2 cloves garlic
½ teaspoon each chilli, cracked pepper,
sumac (lemon spice)
½ cup each coriander leaves, parsley
¼ cup mint
1½ teaspoons preserved lemon (lemon
zest if not available)
¼ cup olive oil

AUBERGINE STUFFING
2 aubergines (eggplants)
1 onion, finely sliced
1 cup breadcrumbs
3 teaspoons chermoula
seasoning

BALSAMIC SYRUP
3 tablespoons balsamic vinegar
100 g sugar

RED WINE REDUCTION
1 onion
6 cloves garlic
1 red capsicum
1 tablespoon olive oil
2 tomatoes, chopped
½ cup balsamic vinegar
2 tablespoons port
750 ml Cabernet Sauvignon wine

CHILLI GARNISH
4 jalapeño chillies
80 g feta cheese
12 rocket leaves

To prepare lamb, beat out the lamb with a meat hammer until flat. To prepare chermoula, finely chop all ingredients, season to taste and add olive oil. To prepare aubergine stuffing, slice aubergines and chargrill until golden and cooked. Once cooled, dice finely. Fry the onion until crisp and golden, toast breadcrumbs and mix all ingredients together, season to taste.

Lay a line of the stuffing along the lamb lengthwise and roll up to enclose the stuffing. Tie lamb with string. Marinate by covering in chermoula mix (best left overnight).

Red wine reduction: sweat onions, garlic and capsicum in olive oil on low heat. Add tomatoes, vinegar, port and wine and reduce by half. Strain through a sieve. Reduce to 1 cup.

To prepare chilli garnish, slice chilli down one side. Scoop out the seeds. Chargrill until skin is slightly blackened. Stuff each chilli with 20 g of feta cheese.

To serve, cook lamb on medium heat for 15-20 minutes. Heat red wine reduction and warm chillies in the oven at the last minute.

Slice each piece of lamb into three. Remove string and stand upright on plate. Cover with heated red wine sauce. Drizzle balsamic syrup around sauce and top lamb with 3 pieces of rocket and the grilled chilli.

Serves 4.

ANATOLES CAFÉ, NAPIER.

PANFRIED BLUE NOSE TOPPED WITH A SMOKED SALMON MOUSSE

300 g smoked salmon
6 tablespoons cream
20 sprigs of dill (keep 8 aside for garnish)
salt and pepper
800 g fresh Blue Nose
lemon pepper
50 g butter
1/2 cup fish stock
1 tablespoon dry white wine
50 g capers
1 lemon
1 tablespoon brown sugar

To make salmon mousse, purée salmon in a food processor. Add three-quarters of the cream and half of the dill (freshly chopped). Season to taste with salt and pepper. Mix to a smooth consistency. Place mixture into a piping bag and keep aside. To prepare fish, pre-heat oven to 200°C. Season the Blue Nose with lemon pepper and salt. Place butter in an ovenproof frying pan and heat until light brown. Quickly sear fish on both sides. Add half the fish stock and top fish with salmon mousse. Place frying pan in oven and bake for 7-10 minutes. Prepare sauce by placing the remainder of the fish stock, wine, capers, chopped dill, juice and zest of 1 lemon and brown sugar in a saucepan. Bring to the boil and season with salt and pepper. Add remainder of cream and reduce to a nice consistency. Spoon sauce onto 4 pre-heated plates. Place fish on top, garnish with fresh dill and salmon slices. Serve immediately. Serves 4.

BAYSWATER ON THE BEACH, NAPIER.

A DECORATIVE FLAIR

A coastal port, Napier was rebuilt in an art-deco style after it was demolished in the 1931 earthquake. The style is nurtured by the city's Art Deco Trust, and there is an Art Deco Walk and Art Deco Weekend, celebrating the city's architectural flavour. In Napier you can find house and wine tours, café crawls and jazz and vintage car festivals. A number of parks and plantings (see pages 84 & 85) add to the atmosphere, including the Norfolk

JOUE DE BOEUF
(BEEF CHEEKS
IN ALE)

1 kg trimmed beef cheeks
salt and pepper
1 medium carrot
1 medium onion
2 cloves garlic
small handful of fresh herbs (bay leaves,
thyme, rosemary, sage)
2 tablespoons tomato paste
300 ml bottle ale or Guinness
300 ml water

Pine-lined Marine Parade, the Botanical Gardens and McLean, Tiffen and Trelernoe Parks. The Kennedy Park Rose Gardens supply a tropical ambience created by double rows of palms planted on each side of Kennedy Road. One of the oldest cities in the region, Napier is also the largest, with an atmosphere reminiscent of a British seaside resort. In the Napier suburb of Ahuriri is the Iron Pot Inlet, once used by early whalers but now an anchorage for small craft. Home of Marineland and the Hawke's Bay Aquarium, Napier also has energetic horticulture and winemaking industries as does Hastings.

Cut meat into large chunks and lightly season.

Pan-fry meat in a heavy pan until brown and sealed on all sides. Remove meat and reserve. Rinse pan. Cut vegetables into bite-size pieces. Place meat back into the pan with vegetables, garlic and herbs and cover with tomato paste, ale (or red wine) and an equal amount of water. Cover and bake in the oven at 180°C for 2½ hours. You may need to add more liquid from time to time.

Remove lid and continue cooking for at least another hour (perhaps as much as two) until the meat is tender and will melt in your mouth. Once cooking is finished there should be enough left to serve your guests!

Serve with creamed potatoes, pasta, rice or polenta.

A crispy salad is also good.

Serves 4.

PIERRE SUR LE QUAI, NAPIER.

Previous pages: Clive Square in Napier. Left: The Rothman's Building, Napier. Described as a jewel of art deco, it was built in 1933.

MANAWATU & WELLINGTON

THE WELLINGTON-MANAWATU REGION takes in the fast-paced capital city of New Zealand and its scenic harbour, pictured on these pages. It also includes the curving Kapiti Coast, the fertile inland valleys of the Manawatu and north as far as Wanganui, the first place we stopped. There we discovered a superb baked cream with the flavours and aromas of fresh pineapple and ginger. We drove south through fertile inland valleys where herds of dairy animals, sheep, lambs and stud sheep were fattening on lush pastures. In Palmerston North, known for Massey University's agricultural research, we indirectly benefited from their work when we dined on tender prime beef fillet garnished with pine-nut pesto and a flavoursome Cumberland sauce. A little way south in Te Horo, we sampled fresh crayfish dressed with a red capsicum mayonnaise, and then travelled to the Kapiti Coast. Nearby the coast the Horowhenua area is sculpted by rivers flowing down from the Tararuas such as the Ohau, the Otaki, the Manawatu and the Waikanae. We stopped awhile in the town of Waikanae to taste a sultry combination of chicken breast, avocado and strawberry sauce. We expected to find many good restaurants to choose from in Wellington, and we weren't disappointed. Included are recipes for a luscious scampi risotto and a sophisticated boudin blanc. You'll love every one!

CHICKEN FILLED WITH OLIVES, CHEESE & SUNDRIED TOMATOES

1 chicken breast
4 olives
50 g cheese
2 sundried tomatoes

**Pre-heat oven to 160°C.
Cut a pocket into the chicken breast,
then fill with the olives, cheese and
sundried tomatoes. Bake in oven for
about 20 minutes, then place on
confit of vegetables.
Serves 1.**

CONFIT OF VEGETABLES
1 each red, yellow and green capsicum
2 onions, chopped
8 cloves garlic, chopped
¾ cup olive oil
salt and pepper

**Cut the vegetables into strips, then
place on oven tray with garlic, onion,
oil, salt and pepper. Cover with foil
and cook in oven at 160°C for
about 20 minutes.**

MICHAEL'S RESTAURANT,
WANGANUI.

PINEAPPLE & GINGER BAKED CREAM

BAKED CREAM

2 cups cream
2 egg yolks
3 whole eggs
150 g sugar
100 g canned pineapple, chopped
60 g crystallised ginger, chopped

Mix all ingredients together, then place into small moulds and bake in a water bath in the oven for about 20-30 minutes at 170°C.
Serves 4-6.

CITRUS SYRUP

2 oranges
2 limes
1 lemon
1 grapefruit
1 cup sugar
1.5 litres water

Cut all the fruit into quarters. Place into a saucepan with sugar and water, bring to the boil, then simmer for about 1-1½ hours or until the liquid reaches syrup thickness.

MICHAEL'S RESTAURANT,
WANGANUI.

BEEF FILLET WITH PESTO & A BEETROOT CUMBERLAND SAUCE

PESTO

1 cup pine nuts
4 cups fresh basil leaves
1 teaspoon sea salt
¼ cup olive oil
3 cloves garlic
1 teaspoon freshly ground black pepper
1½ cups grated Parmesan cheese

BÉARNAISE SAUCE

2 shallots, chopped
6 peppercorns, crushed
1 tablespoon fresh tarragon
1 tablespoon balsamic vinegar
3 egg yolks
200 g butter
salt and pepper
sprig of chervil, chopped

BEETROOT CUMBERLAND SAUCE

2 shallots, chopped
½ cup redcurrant jelly
1 tablespoon lemon juice
2 tablespoons each port, balsamic vinegar
juice of 1 orange
1 large beetroot, grated
¼ cup red wine
1-1½ kg beef fillet

For pesto, pre-heat the oven to 180°C. Place pine nuts on a baking sheet and roast them until golden brown. Set aside until cool. Wash basil leaves, spin dry, then place in a food processor or blender. Add the salt and olive oil. Process for 30 seconds, then add garlic, pine nuts, pepper and Parmesan cheese. Process to a smooth paste, adding a little more oil if necessary. Make a fine but not runny pesto.

Store pesto covered with a little extra oil to prevent the basil from discolouring. The pesto will keep in the refrigerator for 1 week. Makes 2-3 cups. To make the Béarnaise Sauce, make a reduction with the shallots, peppercorns, tarragon and vinegar. Once reduced, pass through a sieve. Whisk the yolks and reduction in a bowl over boiling water until aerated. Gradually whisk in the melted butter and season to taste with salt, pepper and chopped chervil. To make the Beetroot Cumberland Sauce, sweat off shallots, add remainder of ingredients, bring to a simmer and reduce by a quarter. Leave to cool and pass through a sieve.

To prepare the beef, roast the fillet for 15-20 minutes at 190°C. Serve in slices with pesto, Béarnaise and Beetroot Cumberland Sauce. Serves 6.

CAFÉ VAVASSEUR,
PALMERSTON NORTH.

SMOKED SALMON
TIMBALE

250 g light sour cream
250 g light cream cheese
200 g smoked salmon
¼ teaspoon each dill, nutmeg, lemon juice
salt and pepper
1 teaspoon gelatine
Mesclun leaves
herbs
avocado
kumara chips

Mix sour cream and cream cheese
with half the smoked salmon in a
food processor, add seasonings and
gelatine dissolved in a little water.
Place in lined timbale moulds.
When set, place on serving plates
surrounded with mesclun leaves,
garnished with the herbs, other salad
ingredients and kumara chips. Dress
with a light orange vinaigrette.
Serves 6-8.

THE BATHHOUSE CAFÉ & BAR,
PALMERSTON NORTH.

On pages 92 & 93: *The Hay Garden in Palmerston North - just one of the lovely parklike settings in that city. You will also find the International Rose Trial Grounds at Esplanade Gardens; and the Pohangina Domain plus gardens and fountains in the Square. The Square is in the heart of Palmerston North and also includes the Manawatu Art Gallery, the Science Centre and the Manawatu Museum. Massey University is located in Palmerston North, famed for the agricultural research ongoing at AgResearch Grasslands, the Palmerston North Seed Testing Station, the NZ Dairy Research Institute, and the NZ Dairy Board's Awahuri Artificial Breeding Centre. The city has its lighter side as well, with three live theatres contributing to its cultural scene.*

SMOKED SALMON WITH RICOTTA CHEESE & GARLIC CROUTONS

VINAIGRETTE
2 tablespoons honey
½ cup olive oil
¼ cup white wine vinegar

CROUTONS
2 cloves garlic
50 g butter, melted
4 slices white bread
chopped parsley

SALMON
rocket leaves
endive
250 g ricotta cheese
8 large slices smoked salmon
fresh basil to garnish

To make the vinaigrette, combine all ingredients well. To make the croutons, crush garlic and add to butter. Remove crusts from bread and slice diagonally. Brush generously with garlic butter. Bake for 10 minutes at 180°C or until crisp. To assemble, arrange a bed of rocket and endive. Place a spoonful of ricotta in the centre. Arrange croutons, then salmon, then ricotta. Repeat again with remaining ingredients. Drizzle vinaigrette over salmon and croutons and garnish with freshly sliced basil. Serves 4.

CAFÉ VAVASSEUR, PALMERSTON NORTH.

Lush hydrangea and surrounding garden in Palmerston North are framed with exquisite stillness. Such gardens can be found throughout Palmerston North, offering rest for the eye and mind - a truly serene background for family occasions and meals.

POACHED CRAYFISH HALVES WITH ROASTED RED CAPSICUM MAYONNAISE

½ lemon
1 bay leaf
6 peppercorns
sprig of parsley
3 live crayfish
basil, roasted red capsicums, roasted red
capsicum mayonnaise, cherry tomatoes
and limes to garnish

Three-quarters fill a large preserving pan or stock pot with water and bring to the boil. Add lemon, bay leaf, peppercorns and parsley. In another large container or sink, drown the crayfish in cold water. (If they are dead before they go in the boiling water, the legs will stay intact.) Plunge the crayfish head first into the boiling water for 10 minutes. The water must cover the crayfish. Remove crayfish and chill. While crays are still cold, split through the tail and body and clean. To serve, arrange crayfish on a large platter on a bed of basil. Accompany with roasted red capsicum, roasted red capsicum mayonnaise (see facing page), cherry tomatoes and fresh limes. Serve with crusty bread and Chardonnay (Ata Rangi 1994 Craighall Chardonnay is recommended). Serves 6.

ROASTED RED CAPSICUM MAYONNAISE

1 red capsicum
1 clove garlic, peeled
2 egg yolks
salt and pepper
juice of 1 lime
a dash of Tabasco Sauce
1 cup olive oil

Cut red capsicum in half and de-seed. Grill skin side up until skin looks charred and bubbly. Cool, peel and chop. Place red capsicum, garlic, egg yolks, salt, pepper, lime juice, Tabasco and ¼ cup olive oil into food processor bowl with metal blade fitted. Blend until smooth. Pour remaining olive oil very slowly through the feed tube with the food processor running.
Taste for seasoning.

RUTH PRETTY CATERING &
COOKING SCHOOL, TE HORO

CHICKEN BREAST WITH STRAWBERRY SAUCE

CHICKEN
4 skinned and boned
chicken breasts
flour
1 egg, lightly beaten
breadcrumbs
oil or butter
avocado to garnish

STRAWBERRY SAUCE
¼ cup sugar
2 cups water
200 g strawberries
1 tablespoon cornflour

GARNISH
mint leaves
fresh strawberries

Crumb chicken in flour, egg and breadcrumbs. Pan-fry in oil or butter to sear then bake in oven for 15 minutes. Slice and arrange on a sliced avocado. To make sauce, boil sugar in the water, add the strawberries and thicken with cornflour mixed to a paste with a little water. Pour over chicken and garnish with mint and fresh strawberries.
Serves 4.

COUNTRY LIFE RESTAURANT, WAIKANAE.

WONDERFUL WAIKANAE

From picturesque and historic Pukerua Bay, Highway 1 follows the sometimes rocky and spectacular Kapiti Coast to the thriving community of Waikanae. It is favoured by many retired people, some of whom were enticed by hopes of angling for trout in the Waikanae River, said to be

good sport and good eating. The township looks out at Kapiti Island, Waikanae Beach is sandy and lupin covered, and there is also a pine plantation nearby. The area includes a number of enjoyable recreational activities such as walks in the Nga Manu Bird Sanctuary, the Mangaone Walkway or other bush reserves and wetland areas. Visiting the local pottery studio is another pleasant way to spend your time.

Pukerua Bay on the Kapiti Coast, South of Waikanae.

SCAMPI CON RISOTTO ALLO ZAFFERANO E FRITTATA DI SPINACI
(SCAMPI WITH SAFFRON RISOTTO & SPINACH FRITTATA)

12 large simu scampi
salt and pepper
4 tablespoons olive oil
2 teaspoons chopped parsley
4 leaves basil plus 4 double leaves
1 fresh tomato, diced
2 eggs
1/2 cup cream
100 g cooked spinach
200 g rice (Arborio short grain)
3/4 cup fish stock
pinch saffron
4 tablespoons Parmesan cheese
knob butter
1 teaspoon soy sauce

Cut scampi from the back, clean head, season with salt, pepper and oil, and place in a baking dish. Combine parsley, basil, tomato, teaspoon olive oil, salt and pepper and fill scampi heads with mixture. Beat eggs with cream, add chopped spinach, season with salt and pepper. With a medium round pastry cutter form four frittata. Bake approximately 3-5 minutes. Keep warm. Cook rice with fish stock and saffron until soft, about 15 minutes. Add Parmesan cheese and butter. Bake scampi in pre-heated oven at 180°C for about 5 minutes. Place rice on middle of four pre-heated plates, garnish with spinach frittata and arrange three scampi on top. Mix soy sauce with 1 teaspoon olive oil and pour over. Garnish with double basil leaves and serve.

IL CASINO RISTORANTE, WELLINGTON.

CRAB-STUFFED MUSHROOM WITH ROASTED CAPSICUM & BASIL VINAIGRETTE

FILLING

¼ cup each melted butter, Parmesan
cheese, grated cheddar cheese

2 tablespoons sliced spring onions

1 tablespoon chopped parsley

¼ teaspoon cayenne pepper

freshly ground black pepper

¼ cup breadcrumbs

500 g crab meat, picked over for bits
of shell

8 mushroom caps, stems carefully cut off

VINAIGRETTE

½ cup roasted red capsicum

¼ cup fresh basil leaves

2 cloves garlic

salt and freshly ground black pepper

1 tablespoon each lemon juice,
balsamic vinegar

1 cup olive oil

Melt the butter in the microwave. Add
the remaining ingredients, combining
well. Fold in crab meat carefully and
set aside. Mould a portion of the crab
meat mixture onto each mushroom cap.
Bake at 180°C for approximately 12
minutes. To make vinaigrette, blend all
ingredients except oil in a food
processor. Drizzle the oil in a slow
steady stream until the sauce is
combined. To assemble, place two
stuffed mushrooms on top of a crouton
and drizzle with the vinaigrette.
Garnish with a basil leaf.
Makes 4 large entrée or 4 light lunches.

LOGAN BROWN, WELLINGTON.

BOUDIN BLANC:
CHICKEN, SWEETBREADS
& MUSHROOMS

250 g calves' sweetbreads

30 g dried cépe mushrooms

4 tablespoons finely chopped parsley

100 g finely chopped onion

1 tablespoon butter

500 g chicken breast meat, diced

2 teaspoons salt

1 whole egg

2 egg whites

¼ teaspoon each, ground nutmeg, white pepper

500 ml cream

2 metres sausage skins

THE DAY BEFORE
Soak sweetbreads in cold water with 1 tablespoon of salt for 1 hour. Simmer in a court bouillon (stock) for 5-8 minutes, until firm. Drain. While still warm, peel and cut into small pieces. Place in refrigerator.

ON THE DAY
Soak mushrooms in hot water for 1 hour. Drain, dry and finely chop. Mix with the parsley and set aside.

SEASIDE BEAUTY

Above are stylish homes and high-rise apartment buildings on a steep hillside in the Wellington suburb of Oriental Bay. Known for its sunny location and magnificent views over Wellington Harbour, the locale is a popular place for boating and swimming. Its beach is not the natural

Sauté the diced onion in 1 tablespoon of butter until golden. Set aside. Make a purée of the chicken flesh in a food processor, adding the salt, egg, egg white, seasonings and onion as the chicken reduces to a purée. Add the cream last, emulsifying only a little more. Too much speed will cause the cream to curdle. Transfer to a bowl and add the mushrooms, parsley and sweetbreads. Stuff the sausage skins with the mixture. Be careful not to overfill the skins or to leave any air holes. Once the skins are full, twist the sausages into lengths. An easy way is to tie each end with string. Gently poach the sausages at 85°C in a pot of salted water. Do not boil. Allow the sausages to cool then place in refrigerator. Do not keep for more than three days. Serve grilled with pommes purée, creamed spinach and chicken jus.
Serves 8-10.

BOULCOTT STREET BISTRO, WELLINGTON.

Left: A dazzling day of sunshine at Oriental Bay. Its homes and luxury high-rise apartments enjoy stunning bay views as well as proximity to the city centre.

result of tidal action, but has a different history, being composed of ballast conveyed to the Wellington area on sailing vessels. Oriental Parade itself is named for one of the New Zealand Company's sailing ships and is part of Wellington's scenic Marine Drive. This route begins from the Parade, includes Miramar Peninsula, Island Bay, Owhiro Bay and also passes Wellington Airport.

MARLBOROUGH & NELSON

NELSON AND MARLBOROUGH occupy the top of the South Island, which is carved by the beautiful Tasman and Golden Bays. We began our trip in the Picton, Blenheim and Cloudy Bay area, eating at excellent restaurants and enjoying local brews and award-winning wines with our meals. (The photo on this page shows the Brancott Valley vines just south of Woodbourne in the Blenheim region.) We ate scallops in Blenheim that were accented with lime and served on crispy noodles, and in Havelock we just had to taste a thick and creamy mussel chowder. Near Havelock, sea ferries meander through the inlets and sounds of northeast Marlborough, and farther north are the Abel Tasman and Nelson Lakes National Parks, the Heaphy Track and the upwelling Waikoropupu Springs. In the Nelson region we feasted our eyes on the artistry of Nelson potters, who turn local clays into prized ceramics, and we satisfied our chocolate lust with a sensationally-gooey chocolate mud tart. Motueka is one of New Zealand's main fruit-growing areas, and other delicacies such as local free range eggs, smoked salmon and cheeses, as well as trout and seafood are cooked into tempting fare. Every recipe here is more than delicious!

The Marlborough Sounds, wondrous isles and cliffs created by glacial ice gouging deep passages in the land which were later filled by the rising ocean. Blenheim lies south of D'Urville Island, which is part of the ragged eastern border of the Tasman Bay and the western edge of Marlborough Sounds.

CHANNEL CHAMPION

D'Urville Island was named for and by Jules Sebastien Cesar Dumont d'Urville, who explored Tasman Bay during a three-year exploration of New Zealand. One fascinating Maori legend attached to the island refers to Hinepoupou, whose philandering husband abandoned her on Kapiti Island off the coast of the North Island near Wellington. After summoning the assistance of the atua, she survived the mighty Cook Strait and reached the safety of the Brothers on the eastern reaches of Marlborough Sounds. According to the legend, Hinepoupou then made her way from that lonely place of seabirds and tuatara lizards back to her home on D'Urville Island.

ROASTED GLOBE ARTICHOKE WITH SUNDRIED TOMATO PESTO & FRESH PARMESAN

ARTICHOKES

3 globe artichokes

50 g sundried tomato pesto

olive oil

Parmesan cheese, dry and fresh

3 cherry tomatoes

3 cloves garlic

SUNDRIED TOMATO PESTO

1 bunch basil

3 tablespoons toasted pine nuts

2 cloves garlic

2 tablespoons finely grated Parmesan

2 tablespoons sundried tomatoes

3 tablespoons olive oil

To prepare the artichokes, blanch until soft throughout, peel off leaves, cut artichokes in halves, place into a roasting dish and drizzle olive oil over each half.

Season and sprinkle each half with Parmesan cheese, half a cherry tomato and half a clove of garlic. Roast for 15 minutes at 150°C.

To make the tomato pesto, combine all ingredients except the oil in a food processor and work until chopped. With the motor running, add oil in a steady stream to give a smooth pesto.

Garnish with freshly shaved Parmesan.

Serves 3.

HOTEL D'URVILLE,
BLENHEIM.

MARLBOROUGH MUSSEL PASTA IN LEMON & RED WINE SAUCE

1 onion, thinly sliced
1 clove garlic, minced
3 tablespoons oil
850 g can tomatoes,
drained, juice reserved
¼ cup tomato purée
1 lemon, thinly sliced,
pips removed
1 teaspoon dried oregano
1 tablespoon coarsely
chopped fresh basil
½ teaspoon coarsely
ground pepper
¼ teaspoon red
pepper flakes
2 dozen Greenlip mussels,
steamed and removed from shells
1 cup dry red wine
450 g tagliatelle or fettuccine

Sauté onion and garlic in oil. Add all ingredients except mussels, wine and pasta. Simmer for 25 minutes. Add wine, simmer until sauce thickens. Add mussels, whole or quartered depending on personal preference and simmer. Cook pasta in a large saucepan of boiling water. Toss sauce with pasta. If sauce becomes too dry while simmering, reserved cooking liquid from steamed mussels or juice from tomatoes may be added as required. Serves 4.

AN EPICUREAN AFFAIR, BLENHEIM.

EMINENT ESTATES AND BOUTIQUE LABELS

Blenheim can be reached by travelling 29 km south of Picton on Highway 1 or 117 km from Nelson along Highway 6. Both wend their way through the Richmond Range and cross the Wairau River to reach the sunny Wairau Plains, which face Cloudy Bay. Here, leafy vineyards planted in the well-drained local soils have flourished, and Blenheim vintages are becoming known worldwide. Wines from this region have gained international repute over the last few years, especially those made by Cloudy Bay Wineries.

Grapevines at Blenheim. More than 20 prospering wineries have been established in the Blenheim region.

NELSON SCALLOPS WITH A GINGER & LIME CONCASSÉ ON CRISPY NOODLES

SCALLOPS
1 tablespoon olive oil
8–10 large Nelson scallops
1 teaspoon liquid honey
¼ cup white wine
salt and pepper
freshly chopped coriander
juice of ½ lemon

CONCASSÉ
1 small red onion
1 large red tomato
5 mm slice of ginger root
juice and zest of 1 lime
2 tablespoons balsamic vinegar
1 tablespoon olive oil

NOODLES *dry egg noodles*
GARNISH *chives*

To prepare scallops, heat a medium-size heavy frypan. Add olive oil. Once oil begins to spit, add scallops. Gently sear each side, add honey, white wine, seasoning, coriander and lemon juice. Reduce liquid by half. To make the concassé, finely dice the red onion, remove flesh from tomato by cutting into quarters and scooping flesh out. Dice the skin, grate ginger, add zest and lime juice. Bind with balsamic vinegar and oil. Soak the noodles for 10 minutes in warm water until soft, drain and pat dry. Deep-fry for 2 minutes. Arrange noodles in the middle of a plate and place scallops on noodles, spoon on concassé. Garnish with chives. Serves 1-2.

HOTEL D'URVILLE, BLENHEIM.

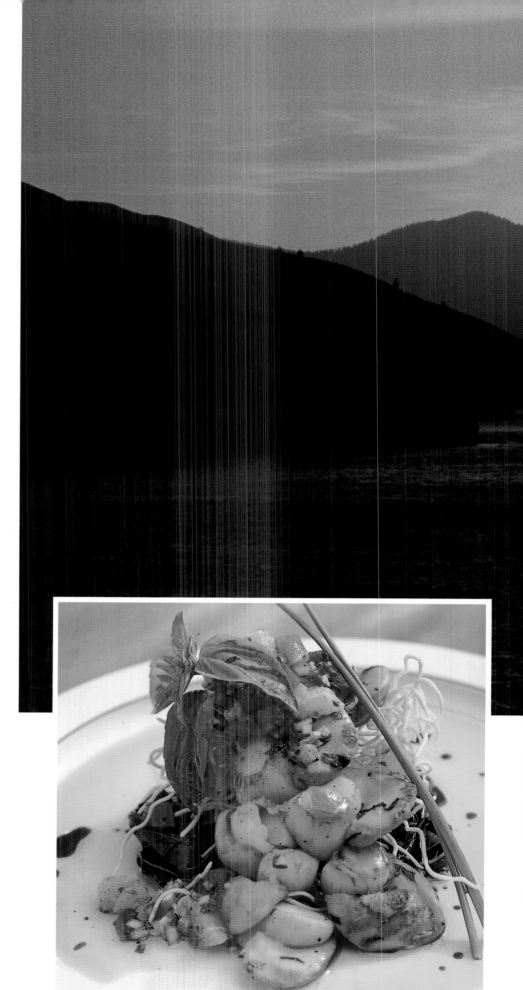

IN THE ARMS OF THE SEA

Highway 6 ripples its way from Nelson to Blenheim, crossing the Pelorus River, the Bryant Range and the wide, straight Wairau River. Roughly two-thirds of the way from Blenheim to Nelson are Havelock and Moenui, nestling in a bay of the Mahau Sound, at the head of the Pelorus Sound. Havelock is a centre for both freshwater and ocean anglers, and scallops are still plentiful. The town came into being after gold was discovered at Wakamarina in 1864, and, when the gold was exhausted, logging sustained the community. Now launches leave from Havelock on both business and pleasure trips. Visitors can enjoy guided sea kayaking trips and walks on the Nydia Track.

Before it vanishes, the sunset light lingers and plays on the waters and cliff faces of the Marlborough Sounds. Greenlip mussels, grown commercially in the Marlborough Sounds, are processed in Havelock. Shucked mussels are marinated or frozen for sale. Premium-grade bivalves are left in the half shell to be quick frozen for export or sale to restaurants.

MUSSEL CHOWDER

1 medium onion, diced
100 g butter
1 nip Galliano
1 teaspoon curry powder
2 teaspoons lemon juice
1 large carrot, diced
1 cup white sauce
seafood stock to taste
350 g mussel meat
extra milk if needed
salt and pepper to taste

WHITE SAUCE
50 g butter
¼ cup flour
1 cup milk

GARNISH
chopped parsley
whipped cream

Sauté onion in butter, add Galliano, curry powder and lemon juice. Steam cook carrots and add to onions. Make up white sauce and add to pot with seafood stock. Dice mussels and add last, adding extra milk if need be. Simmer for 15 minutes and serve, topped with whipped cream and chopped parsley. Serves 4.

THE DARLING DILL CAFÉ,
HAVELOCK.

SALMON CHAR SUI WRAPPED IN SEAWEED & OVEN BAKED

*8 standard-sized sheets of nori (baked
seaweed)*
1 punnet of snowpea sprouts
4 spring onions, cut in half lengthways
1 small carrot, peeled and julienned
*4 sundried tomatoes or 2 normal
tomatoes, de-seeded and cut in strips*
*300-400 g boneless, skinless salmon
fillet, cut in strips*
*1 jar of Lee Kum Kee Char Sui
Marinade (available from most
supermarkets)*

DIPPING SAUCE
100 ml standard Kikkoman Soy Sauce
2 cloves garlic, chopped
1 teaspoon minced fresh ginger
juice of 1 lime
1 tablespoon sweet Thai chilli sauce

ARTISTS' SHOWCASE

The electric flash of sizzling lightning yellow from a gleaming platter.
The exciting roughness of a raku-fired stoneware teapot. The gleam and
shine of a twist of golden metal or the silvery matte of a burnished
bracelet. The rich warmth of handwoven shawls and tasselled wall
hangings. Surely Nelson is one of the most exciting places in New
Zealand for those who love the creative arts. Do you like pots, paintings

Place the nori on a tea towel or a nori mat. Along the bottom one-third place the garnishes, ie snowpea sprouts, spring onions, carrots, salmon and tomatoes.

Drizzle a teaspoon of char sui sauce over top. Using the mat or tea towel roll up to form a large cigar shape or nori roll, seal the leading edge with a little water. Do the same with the other seven nori.

To make the dipping sauce, mix all ingredients together. Divide into 4 little ramekins or other suitable containers.

Heat oven to 180°C. Place the salmon nori rolls on a lightly greased baking tray and bake for 3-4 minutes only.

Slice in half lengthways and arrange attractively on four starter plates. Serve with dipping sauce and other accompaniments of your choice.

Serves 4 as a starter.

BOAT SHED CAFÉ, NELSON.

or pendants? Wood carving or china painting? Weaving, wire sculpture or wool toys? All these and more can be found in the flourishing studios and galleries inside and outside Nelson. And the creative zest doesn't stop here - there are creative adventure tours and innovative breweries, temptingly prepared food at fine establishments plus novel wines and new methods of food processing. The Nelson lifestyle is a happy blend of sunny skies and scenic beauty and, as throughout New Zealand, the friendliness of people who enjoy their way of life.

RAVIOLI OF SCALLOPS WITH CAPER BEURRE BLANC SAUCE

CAPER SAUCE

2 tablespoons capers
2 tablespoons white wine vinegar
½ bay leaf
juice of ½ lemon
150 g unsalted butter
salt and black pepper (to taste)

RAVIOLI

50 g butter
1 cup finely chopped onion
4 cloves garlic, finely chopped
½ large red and yellow capsicum,
chopped
1 tablespoon each chopped basil,
chopped dill
¼ cup chopped parsley
juice and grated zest of 1 lemon
salt and freshly ground
black pepper
32 wonton wrappers
16-32 scallops
(depending on size)

To make the sauce, gently squeeze the juice from the capers into a saucepan. Reserve capers. Add all the remaining ingredients, except the butter and seasoning. Bring to a rapid boil and reduce until only one tablespoon remains. Remove the pan from the heat and whisk in the butter to form an emulsified sauce.

Add the capers and season to taste
with black pepper. Keep warm.
To make the ravioli, melt the butter in
a fairly large skillet. Add the onion,
garlic and capsicum and sweat until
soft, approximately 3 minutes.
Remove from heat and add all the
herbs, lemon juice and zest. Season
to taste with salt and pepper.
Arrange 16 wonton wrappers on a
clean, dry bench and place
1/2 teaspoon of mixture in the
centre of each. Place a scallop or
two (depending on size) on the
mixture, keep the edges clean.
Gently moisten around the edge of
each wrapper with water. This will
allow the top wonton wrapper to
become glued to the bottom one.
Take care not to use too much water
or the wrapper can become soggy.
Meanwhile bring a large pot of salted
water to a rolling boil. Drop one
ravioli at a time into the water, try
not to let the water come off the boil.
Eight at a time will be enough. A little
oil in the water should prevent the
ravioli from sticking together.
Gently simmer for approximately
3 minutes and carefully remove with
a slotted spoon and arrange
decoratively in the centre of four
warmed plates or pasta bowls. Spoon
a little sauce on each ravioli.
Garnish as desired.
Serves 4.

BOAT SHED CAFÉ, NELSON.

PEACE AND QUIET

Pelorus Bridge is 45 minutes east of Nelson and is close to Canvastown, where the closet gold miner can induge a secret whim to pan for gold. There are many walking tracks in the area, pleasant tearooms, untouched native forest and proximity to the Pelorus Sound and launch trips into the Sound. Those seeking the refreshing solitude of casting a lure for wary trout will enjoy themselves here as well as those seeking new sights. Stunning views are all along the scenic Queen Charlotte drive, and from the reserve area walking trails lead to the Maungatapu and Matai Valleys.

The Pelorus Bridge Scenic Reserve has a tranquil atmosphere for outdoor enthusiasts.

GREEN ENCLAVES PRESERVED...

Established as the New Zealand Company's second settlement in 1841, Nelson is now well known for its pleasant climate and attractive lifestyle. One component of this lifestyle is the number of parks and gardens in or nearby Nelson. There is Isel Park with its well established trees, rhododendrons and azaleas and the Botanical Reserves with a tangle of paths up to Botanical Hill and the view of Tasman Bay. There are the Queen's Gardens, Mount Richmond Forest Park, Anzac Park and Rutherford Park, which honours the nuclear physicist Lord Rutherford of

CHOCOLATE MUD TART

2 sheets pre-rolled butter pastry or your favourite pastry base
100 g unsalted butter, chopped
275 g block dark chocolate, chopped
½ cup double cream
½ cup brown sugar
3 eggs
¾ cup ground almonds
fresh summer berries for decoration

Roll out pastry sheets to line the base and sides of a 24 cm diameter loose bottomed flan tin. Refrigerate while preparing the filling. Place butter, chocolate, cream and half the brown sugar in the top part of a double boiler. Allow to melt over simmering water. Stir until cool. Beat the eggs and remaining brown sugar together for 2 minutes until light and frothy. Mix into cooled chocolate mixture, fold through the ground almonds. Pour filling into prepared flan tin and cook at 180°C for 30-40 minutes. Serves 10-12.

KORURANGI CAFÉ, NELSON.

Nelson. In Richmond Forest Park those of active persuasion can stride along the old gold-miners' track, the Waikakaho-Cullen Creek Track or visit Lake Chalice or Mount Richmond. There are walks near Dun Mountain, the Hacket River and Cable Bay, and lovely drives lead to Nelson Haven and the Davis lookout on the Post Hills. The city is also in close proximity to the new Kahurangi National Park and to the Abel Tasman and Nelson Lakes National Parks. In Kahurangi, the second largest National Park in New Zealand, visitors can see Nettlebed and Bulmer, the country's deepest and longest caves. And the renowned Heaphy, Wangapeka and Leslie/Karamea Tracks run through Kahurangi Park.

Central Nelson provides many tree-shaded settings for a pleasant walk or an evening's reverie on a bench by the river.

Following pages show a crescent of beach in Abel Tasman National Park and a Motueka scene with statue.

GOLDEN BAY SCALLOPS SERVED WITH PORT NICHOLSON BEURRE BLANC SAUCE

SHELLS

400 g flaky puff pastry
2 leeks
24 scallops

SAUCE

approx 75 g Port Nicholson cheese
½ cup cream
½ cup good fish stock
1 teaspoon lemon juice
seasoning to taste

**Roll pastry out 5 mm thick.
Prepare four scallop shells from flaky
puff pastry moulded inside
real scallop shells.
Blind bake at 200°C until cooked.
Cut leeks into julienne strips, season
and steam until tender. Steam
scallops for 2 minutes.
To prepare Port Nicholson Beurre
Blanc Sauce, place sauce
ingredients in pan.
Cook on moderate heat until sauce
thickens. Serve immediately over hot
scallops and leeks in pastry shells.
Serves 4 as a starter.**

GOTHIC GOURMET LICENSED
RESTAURANT & TAVERN,
MOTUEKA.

TAME EELS AND RIVERSIDE MEALS

The Tasman coastline is a visual feast of stern headlands and petite beaches of golden sand. Motueka was established on the west side of Tasman Bay just south of the Abel Tasman National Park. Fed by the Arthur and Hope ranges, the Motueka River flows through the town and empties into Tasman Bay. Motueka is full of tourist-oriented activities, including fishing, caving, flights to Abel Tasman, horse trekking, paragliding and skydiving, horticultural and winery tours, sailing, golfing and dining at riverside cafés. Visitors also enjoy the Abel Tasman Coastal Classic fun run, the Salt Water Baths, the January Riwaka Beerfest and the Abel Tasman Seal Swim. On the outskirts of Motueka, hops, tobacco, raspberries and other crops are cultivated, and several tobacco and hop research stations are located nearby. You can handfeed the tame eels and trout on the Anatoki River, or refresh yourself at such places as Ruby Bay Wines, the Redwood Cellars, the Neudorf Vineyards or at one of the many lodges, holiday and leisure parks, hotels and restaurants.

WEST COAST

DAMP BUT DELIGHTFUL, MAJESTIC AND MYSTERIOUS - the West Coast nestles against the western side of the Southern Alps. The Franz Josef Glacier, pictured here, is one of the mighty snowfed rivers of ice moving down from the main divide and the peaks of Mount Cook National Park. Fox Glacier is only 25 kilometres away. We began our tour in Murchison (inland and north of Westport), breakfasted on feather-light pancakes and dined on tender sweet and sour pork fillet in filo baskets. All the way south, we found breathtaking alpine passes, wild rivers, rainforests and estuaries and towns with friendly individualists who love their remote land. The West Coast's Heritage Highways made it simple to discover the great food on offer in Westland such as the Westport seafood medley and the bacon-flavoured loin of boar garnished with salmon cream. There is comfortable accommodation plus lots of local goodies like homemade breads, jams and yoghurt - even farm-fresh goat's milk! Seafood is grand, with salmon and trout plentiful. Venison, duck and whitebait can be sampled as well as New Zealand wines. Do travel here soon to meet the children and grandchildren of goldminers, loggers, coal miners and pioneers and to taste their flavoursome recipes!

SWEET & SOUR PORK BASKETS

SAUCE

1 onion, finely sliced
1 tablespoon oil
1 carrot
½ red capsicum
3 tablespoons cornflour
2 tablespoons soy sauce
¼ cup brown sugar
¼ cup wine vinegar
¾ cup water
2 tablespoons sherry
1 teaspoon chicken stock powder
½ cup pineapple juice
1 cup pineapple pieces

BASKETS

8 sheets filo
butter

PORK

24 slices from a fillet of pork

Sauté onion in oil until clear. Peel and slice carrot and capsicum into matchsticks. Add to onion and stir-fry for 5 minutes. Combine cornflour, soy sauce, sugar, vinegar, water, sherry, chicken stock powder and pineapple juice in a large microwave-proof bowl. Microwave uncovered on high power for 4 minutes, stirring twice. Add onion, carrot and capsicum. Stir well. Add pineapple pieces. Cook on high power for 90 seconds. To make the baskets, take two sheets of filo pastry. Brush one sheet with melted butter and lay on top of other sheet. Fold all four corners to the middle. Place folded edges down into a greased ramekin.

Repeat with remaining filo. Bake 10 minutes at 180°C. Remove filo basket from ramekin.

To prepare pork, cut 6 slices per basket from a fillet of pork. Fry both sides in 1 tablespoon oil on a high heat until pink juices show.

Put 1 tablespoon of sauce in the bottom of the basket, add the pork pieces and cover with hot sauce. Serves 4.

BEECHWOODS, MURCHISON.

PANCAKES BEECHWOODS STYLE

2 tablespoons sugar

1 egg

1 cup milk

1 teaspoon vanilla essence

pinch salt

1 1/2 cups flour

2 teaspoons cream of tartar

1 teaspoon baking soda

1 tablespoon butter

2 tablespoons boiling water

Beat egg with sugar until frothy. Add milk, vanilla essence and salt. Mix in flour, cream of tartar and baking soda, then add butter melted in the boiling water. Pour 1 cup of mix into a well-greased hot frypan. Turn when bubbles appear on the surface.

Serve with slices of fresh fruit, dust with icing sugar and top with whipped cream.

Makes 6-8.

BEECHWOODS, MURCHISON.

SEAFOOD MEDLEY

SAUCE

*2 shallots or ½ onion,
finely diced
¾ cup dry white wine
½ cup cream
150 g unsalted butter, cubed
1 teaspoon lemon juice
salt and pepper*

MEDLEY

*2 or 3 tiger prawns
150 g white fish fillets,
skinned and boned
3 whole mussels
½ crayfish tail
½ cup white wine
½ onion, diced
4 to 6 scallops*

**To make the sauce, simmer onion in a saucepan with wine until liquid has almost evaporated. Add cream and reduce until cream has thickened. Remove from heat, whisk in butter until a creamy sauce is produced. Add lemon juice and seasonings. Peel and de-vein prawns. Cut fish into 3 or 4 bite-size pieces. Remove any debris from mussels and wash. Cut crayfish tail into segments leaving shell on. Steam mussels in white wine and onion until they open. Keep warm. Grill all other fish until just cooked. Arrange on serving plate and pour sauce over, garnish and serve.
Serves 2.**

DIEGO'S RESTAURANT & BAR,
WESTPORT.

Cape Foulwind, near Westport.

TAURANGA BAY
CHILLI MUSSELS

2 large brown onions
1 large carrot
1 stalk celery, diced
1 each, medium red, green capsicum
4 tablespoons olive oil
6 cloves garlic, crushed
1 cup canned whole peeled plum tomatoes
4 sprigs fresh basil
1 tablespoon fresh thyme
1 tablespoon fresh oregano
3 bay leaves
fresh red chilli, finely chopped, to taste
sea salt flakes and freshly ground
black pepper to taste
12 small Greenlip mussels
or mussels in the ½ shell

Finely dice onion, carrot, celery and capsicums. Heat olive oil in heavy-based stock pot then add onion, carrot, celery, capsicums and garlic. Fry gently until ingredients are softened. Do not let them brown. Add tomatoes, herbs and chilli. Add chilli in small amounts until you find the balance that is right for you. Bring to the boil and simmer very slowly for one hour with the lid off. Crush tomatoes with a masher to form a thickish sauce. Add salt and pepper to taste. Pour off amount you need into heavy-based fry pan. Place cleaned mussels into simmering sauce and serve when mussels open. (Discard any that remain closed.) Do not over-cook, or they will be tough. Serve immediately in large wide bowl with slices of French baguette to mop up all the sauce.
Serves 2.

THE BAY HOUSE CAFÉ,
TAURANGA BAY, WESTPORT.

LOIN OF WILD BOAR WRAPPED IN BACON WITH A VENISON SALAMI & SMOKED SALMON CREAM

400 g wild boar or pork loin
4 slices raw back bacon
50 g venison salami
salt and pepper
½ small onion, finely chopped
olive oil
100 ml white wine
50 g smoked salmon, diced
200 ml cream
25 g butter

Cut boar into 4 x 100 g pieces. Remove rind and fat from back bacon. Cut salami into matchstick-sized strips. Season the boar with salt and pepper in a hot pan for a few seconds each side. Wrap the boar in the bacon, holding in place with toothpicks. Place in a hot oven for 10-12 minutes. In the same pan cook the onions without browning in a drop of olive oil. Add the wine and reduce by half. Add the salami, salmon and cream and continue to reduce by a third. Shake in the butter while heating gently but do not allow to boil as the sauce will split. Adjust the seasoning to suit. Place the boar parcels on a warm plate, remove the toothpicks and pour the sauce over. Serves 4.

TRAPPERS RESTAURANT, HOKITIKA.

Punakaiki, or Pancake Rocks, can be found at Dolomite Point, about an hour and a half drive from Hokitika.

Mount Cook, New Zealand's highest peak, towers 3753 metres above sea level. From its summit, a climber can look down on the Tasman, Fox and Franz Joseph Glaciers, the lush green bush of the national park, Lakes Pukaki and Tekapo, the Okarito Lagoon as well as lesser peaks such as Mounts Sefton, Tasman and Malte Brun. From the Mount Cook area, it is about 100 kilometres north to Hokitika. Near the town is an assortment of more than fifteen walkways and tracks, including the Hokitika Heritage Trail. Adventure touring, rural stays and nearly twenty arts and crafts shops also lure many tourists to the area. Hokitika has whitebaiting in season, a gold room, a glassblowing studio and greenstone-working studios as well as scenic drives offering spectacular views of the Southern Alps.

RICH HONEYED FRUIT CAKE

4 cups mixed dried fruit
1 cup whole almonds
½ cup honey
1¼ cups plain flour

Grease deep, 23-cm, round cake tin and line base and sides with baking paper. Combine all ingredients in large bowl, stir until well combined. Spread mixture into prepared tin. Bake in slow oven at 150°C for about 1¼ hours. Cover hot cake tightly with foil. Cool in pan. When cake is cold, drizzle with melted chocolate. Serve thinly sliced.

LAKE PARINGA CAFÉ,
LAKE PARINGA,
SOUTH WESTLAND.

Below: The Lake Paringa Café is now open and welcomes you to try its delicious specialties.

WEST COAST WHITEBAIT OMELET

(A well-seasoned omelet pan is essential for this recipe.)

1 teaspoon butter
¼ onion, finely diced
140 grams whitebait
1 small clove garlic, crushed
3 eggs
salt and pepper
freshly chopped herbs

Melt butter, add onion and sauté until soft and transparent (do not brown). Add whitebait and garlic, toss over gentle heat until cooked, add beaten eggs, salt, pepper and herbs. Cook quickly, moving continuously with a fork until lightly set. Remove from heat. Fold omelet out of pan. Sprinkle with freshly chopped herbs and lemon pepper. Serves 1.

LAKE PARINGA CAFÉ,
LAKE PARINGA.

Left: Driftwood lies scattered in pleasing designs on a wide sandy beach near Haast. In southern Westland, Ship Creek and its walkways near Haast ramble through native Kahikatea forests and beside rugged coastlines.

Top left: Whitebaiters try their luck at a West Coast riverside.

KAIKOURA & CANTERBURY

THE PHOTO ON THESE TWO PAGES LOOKS WEST over the great Canterbury Plains of the South Island. Wide and fertile they stretch from the Southern Alps to the sea. In this part of our tour, we started in Kaikoura, no longer a whaling town but well known for the gentler sport of whale watching. You can also swim with seals or watch dusky dolphins frolic in the shelter of the Kaikoura Range. Eating is a marvellous experience, with recipes like seared crayfish tail heaped with mango and citrus salsa. The Fyffe Gallery is but one of a number of unique resorts: it has an art gallery, a country garden, a large courtyard and a handmade earthblock home with recycled timber and fittings. Next we travelled south to Christchurch, which offers many attractions like terraced houses, Cathedral Square, the casino, Hagley Park, the museum and the Botanical Gardens (recently converted to organic pest control). When we dined in Christchurch, the smoked salmon tartare parcels in sour cream and brandy were too good to resist! Historic Lyttelton was next, with reminders that the first Europeans to arrive in the South Island settled nearby. A harbour town with villas overlooking stunning views, its restaurant menus offered many temptations. Lastly we arrived in Timaru, where we found an appetising turkey salad with a robust honey, orange, mustard and vinegar dressing. We found many outdoor adventures and indoor dining pleasures in Canterbury.

SEARED CRAYFISH TAIL WITH MANGO CITRUS SALSA

SALSA

2 mangoes or 1 x 440 g can
1/2 red onion
1/2 each, green and red capsicum
1 cm piece of ginger, peeled
2 cm piece of cucumber, seeded
1-2 small chillies or to taste
juice of 1/2 lemon and 1/2 lime
1/2 cup fresh orange juice
2 tablespoons chopped coriander

CRAYFISH

1 uncooked crayfish
1 tablespoon olive oil
salt and pepper
assorted baby salad leaves
1 teaspoon sesame oil

To make salsa, peel mangoes and cut flesh from stone in large pieces. If using canned mango, drain and use juice from mango in salsa but only half the amount of orange juice. Dice next seven ingredients and add to reserved juices. Add coriander. Mix all ingredients and stand to develop flavours. Remove tail from body of crayfish by running a small knife up inside the body of the crayfish to where tail joins. Twist and pull firmly to separate. Split the tail with a sharp knife, leaving the tail joined at fin end. Remove vein. To serve, heat olive oil in a heavy pan until almost smoking. Lightly season crayfish tail with salt and pepper; add to pan flesh side down. The tail should curl around and remain joined at fins.

Cook for 30 seconds to 1 minute. Lightly brown the flesh. Remove tail from pan, place on a tray in a hot oven for 3 minutes. While cooking, toss small amounts of salad leaves in bowl with sesame oil to coat. Arrange in centre of a serving plate. Spoon salsa around outside. Place tail on leaves.

Serves 2-4.

GREEN DOLPHIN RESTAURANT & BAR, KAIKOURA.

POULET FACON BASQUAISE

1 kg chicken meat
2 tablespoons pork fat
250 g tomatoes
6 green capsicums
125 g mushrooms
150 g shoulder bacon
salt and freshly ground pepper
2 cups dry white wine

Cut chicken into 8 serving portions. Brown in pork fat and place to one side. Cut the tomatoes and squeeze out the seeds, and cut the capsicums in little pieces, removing the stems, seeds and white ribs. Cut the mushrooms in half and remove the stalks. Cook the vegetables in pork fat over low heat, stirring for 10 minutes or until the vegetables soften and are lightly browned. Cut the shoulder bacon into fine strips and place in the pan with the chicken. Season with salt and pepper and add the wine. Cover and cook over low heat for 40 minutes, stirring occasionally. Transfer the chicken to a shallow dish. Boil the cooking liquid over high heat until thick. Pour over the chicken and serve immediately. Can be decorated with small Spanish hot peppers. Serves 4.

THE OLD CONVENT, KAIKOURA.

ALWAYS CLOSE TO THE SEA

Kaikoura and the surrounding region are fortunate to have bounty from both sea and land. While blessed with the beauty of the Kaikoura Range and a dramatic rocky shoreline, the region also encloses prosperous agricultural land.   In its early days Kaikoura was based on whaling and fishing, and traces of this past lifestyle can still be seen. More recently, Kaikoura entrepreneurs have developed whale, dolphin and bird-watching tours. This emphasis has also led to the participation by New

Zealanders in the collection of information about endangered marine mammal species. It is a great pleasure to take drives along the Kaikoura Peninsula or along the coast road to see the Garden of Memories, the University of Canterbury's field station aquarium, the Kaikoura Lookout or the Takahanga Marae. Other interesting sights include the Kaikoura Coast Track and Fyffe Forest, which contains untouched podocarp forest and many native trees.

Left: Early morning in Kaikoura.
Below: The Crayfish Caravan on the Kaikoura coast offers a 'right-by-the-seaside' location plus temptingly prepared crays fresh from the sea. A pleasant spot to dunk succulent bits in tartare sauce while you have a look around.
Following pages (144 & 145): Framed by the snowy grandeur of the Southern Alps, Christchurch spreads over the Canterbury Plains.

SMOKED SALMON TARTARE PARCELS

360 g smoked salmon
2 small Spanish onions
2 teaspoons sour cream
2 nips brandy
salt, pepper, chopped dill and chives
2 tablespoons white wine vinegar
1 teaspoon each wasabi paste, and
Dijon mustard
pinch salt, pepper, sugar
½ cup walnut oil
Mesclun leaves
dill sprig
cherry tomatoes to garnish
(about 1 dozen)

Put 24 even slices of smoked salmon to the side. Finely chop the rest of the smoked salmon and mix with 1 chopped Spanish onion, sour cream, brandy and seasonings. (Keep the other for onion rings as a garnish.) Make balls from the mixture. Wrap each ball with 2 slices of salmon and tie with chives. Prepare dressing by mixing together vinegar, wasabi paste, mustard and seasoning using a blender. Gradually add walnut oil and adjust seasoning to taste. Arrange Mesclun leaves in the middle of the serving plate. Place salmon parcels around the leaves. Before serving, sprinkle with walnut dressing and garnish with a sprig of dill, onion rings and cherry tomatoes.
Serves 4 as a starter.

MERCHANTS RESTAURANT,
HOTEL GRAND CHANCELLOR,
CHRISTCHURCH.

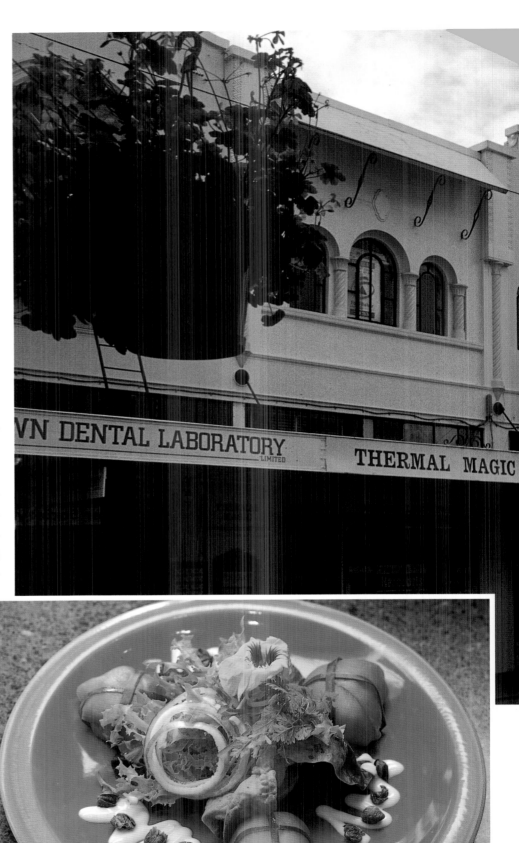

Above: The sunset sky makes an enticing display over Christchurch.

Left: A leisurely way to see the city - just buy a ticket and hop on and off at the tram stops that suit you.

COME TO CHRISTCHURCH

Christchurch - its gardens, its English cosmopolitan air, its university, its theatres and casino, its series of remarkable roadhouses: the Sign of the Kiwi, the Sign of the Bellbird and the Sign of the Takahe - so much to see and enjoy, whether as a tourist or as a resident Cantabrian. For an exhilarating dining experience, ride the Mount Cavendish Gondola up to the summit. There you'll find a restaurant, a multi-media show about the city plus scenic areas where you can ride mountain bikes or paraglide.

GRIMSBY'S STICKY DATE PUDDING

250 g pitted dates, chopped
2 cups boiling water
½ teaspoon baking soda
100 g butter
1 cup sugar
3 eggs, beaten
2 cups flour
2 teaspoons baking powder

SAUCE

1 cup golden syrup
1½ cups sugar
½ teaspoon salt
125 g butter
½ teaspoon vanilla essence
1 cup cream

Soak dates in boiling water and baking soda for half an hour. Cream butter and sugar until fluffy. Add eggs, sifted flour and baking powder. Add dates and liquid. Mix should be wet. Grease a pudding basin, two-thirds fill with mixture and cover with foil. Cook in steamer until firm in centre. Prepare sauce by boiling together all ingredients except vanilla essence and cream. When mixture holds together in a soft ball by testing a sample in cold water, remove from heat and add essence and cream. To serve, flood plate with caramel sauce, spooning some over servings of the warm pudding. Serve with lashings of cream. Serves 6.

GRIMSBY'S RESTAURANT,
CHRISTCHURCH.

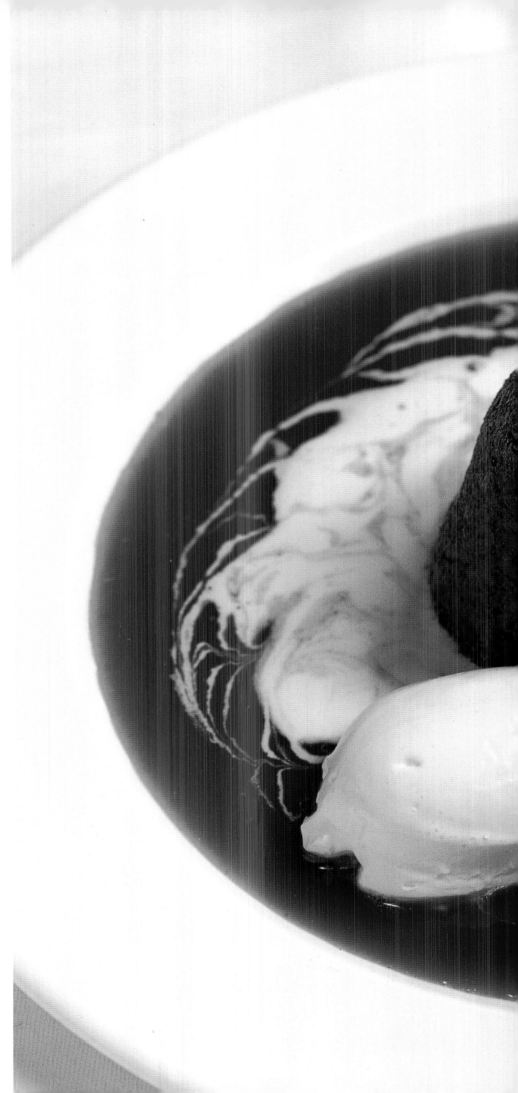

Lyttelton Harbour. Lying south of Christchurch, the area is rich in military lore and history. Launch trips can be taken to Diamond Harbour or to Quail and Ripapa Islands, which have guided walks over the landscape.

THEY LANDED HERE...

Lyttelton is located on the rugged sides of a very old volcanic crater and is named for Lord Lyttelton, a man who was extremely influential in the establishment of the Church of England colony that founded modern day Lyttelton. Its seafaring background and related memorabilia are on display at the Lyttelton Historical Museum. Lyttelton also has three mid-nineteenth century churches (all built of local stone) that contain a number of interesting historical items and original furnishings. Lyttelton and Christchurch are connected by New Zealand's longest road tunnel, nearly 2 km in length.

SALMON STRIPS SAUTÉED RARE IN HOT NOODLES

800 g fresh salmon fillet, bones removed
200 g noodles or linguine
24 x 2 cm square croutons

SAUCE

100 g palm sugar or jaggery
2 tablespoons Thai fish sauce
6 small hot dried red chillies
2 tablespoons lime juice
2 tablespoons grated root ginger
1 cm fresh ginger, peeled and julienned
1/2 cup chopped coriander

Cut salmon in 2 cm strips. Cook the noodles in well salted water until tender. Drain and rinse under cold water. Set aside. Toast croutons in hot oven until crisp and golden. To make the sauce, cook the palm sugar in heavy-based pot with a little water until a light caramel consistency. Carefully add fish sauce, chillies, lime juice and ginger. Remove from heat and cool. Reheat noodles in the caramel sauce over low heat until well coated. Sauté salmon strips (fleshy side first) in a hot pan, with the ginger and coriander. Turn after 20 seconds and sauté skin side down. To serve, in centre of plate twirl sauced noodles, forming a spiral pattern. Place salmon strips over noodles, forming a lattice. Garnish with chopped coriander and the croutons.
Serves 4.

THE LYTTELTON BRASSERIE, LYTTELTON.

GRIMSBY'S CANTERBURY STYLE BOUILLABAISSE

½ onion, finely sliced
¼ leek, finely sliced lengthwise
4 tomatoes, roughly chopped
2 courgettes, finely diced
1 pinch 'Eight Moon' saffron
(from Rangiora)
1 tablespoon crushed garlic
4 cloves star anise
2 tablespoons each olive oil, Pernod
½ cup white wine
4 cups fish stock
50 g each firm white fish, Akaroa
salmon, fresh squid rings, baby octopus,
crayfish medallions
12 each, king prawns, scallops,
oysters and snails
1 sprig fennel or dill
crusty French bread
mayonnaise with a pinch of saffron
and mixed chilli

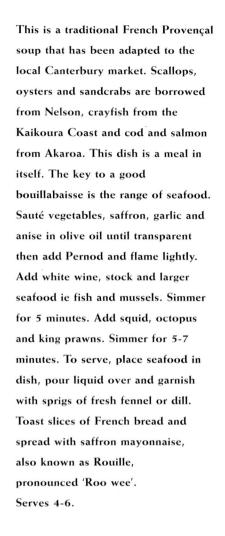

This is a traditional French Provençal soup that has been adapted to the local Canterbury market. Scallops, oysters and sandcrabs are borrowed from Nelson, crayfish from the Kaikoura Coast and cod and salmon from Akaroa. This dish is a meal in itself. The key to a good bouillabaisse is the range of seafood. Sauté vegetables, saffron, garlic and anise in olive oil until transparent then add Pernod and flame lightly. Add white wine, stock and larger seafood ie fish and mussels. Simmer for 5 minutes. Add squid, octopus and king prawns. Simmer for 5-7 minutes. To serve, place seafood in dish, pour liquid over and garnish with sprigs of fresh fennel or dill. Toast slices of French bread and spread with saffron mayonnaise, also known as Rouille, pronounced 'Roo wee'.
Serves 4-6.

GRIMSBY'S RESTAURANT, CHRISTCHURCH.

Above: Akaroa. This charming colonial-style town is situated on the east side of Akaroa Harbour on Banks Peninula.

Left: A dramatic view of Banks Peninsula, with Lyttelton Harbour in the foreground.

NICE FOR A SUMMER HOLIDAY

Timaru is bounded by Patiti Point to the south and the Washdyke Lagoon to the north. The town curves around the beaches of Caroline Bay, which are sought by summer holidaymakers who flock each year to swim and sunbathe or attend the three-week summer carnival there. Caroline Bay also includes parks and gardens to enjoy as well as the relocated wooden lighthouse which was built in 1877. Timaru also has a botanical garden, a large art gallery and the South Canterbury Museum, which contains a number of displays and collections relating to local European and Maori history. Temuka is not far from Timaru - just a few kilometres north where the Opihi River flows into the sea. In Temuka sportsmen can easily find pleasant tree-shaded river banks where salmon and trout can be caught - later to be fried, baked or grilled as the main course of a delicious gourmet meal.

Old shed on a paddock near Timaru.

TURKEY SUMMER SALAD

1 small turkey breast

1 cinnamon quill

6 whole peppercorns

2 oranges

2 bay leaves

2 whole cloves

1 bunch young spinach

1 sprig fresh coriander

1 red onion

1 orange

DRESSING

½ cup olive oil

juice of ½ orange

1 tablespoon wholegrain mustard

4 tablespoons cider vinegar

freshly ground black pepper and salt

1 teaspoon Manuka honey

Place turkey breast and next five ingredients into a saucepan and add enough cold water to cover turkey breast. Gently poach until turkey is cooked, approximately 30-40 minutes. Cool turkey in cooking liquid. Remove turkey and slice very thinly and place on a plate. Wash spinach and coriander, removing any coarse spinach stems. Slice onion finely and segment the orange. Arrange ingredients on turkey slices. Make dressing by combining all ingredients. Drizzle on and around turkey and salad. Arrange some coriander sprigs and orange peel knots around salad for decoration. Serves 4.

GINGER & GARLIC LICENSED RESTAURANT, TIMARU.

CENTRAL OTAGO & FIORDLAND

THERE ARE ENOUGH HOLIDAY DESTINATIONS in Central Otago and Fiordland for even the most enthusiastic jetsetter. Sweeping harbours, endless rugged mountains, coastal bays and lakes - all offer their unique beauty. One famous scene is shown here: the splendour of Mitre Peak reflected in the Milford Sound. For this part of our journey, we started near the Haast Pass and drove east to Lake Wanaka to sample food from Wanaka's superb restaurants. We tried tender rack of lamb garnished with couscous and savoured a most glamourous Grand Marnier cheesecake drizzled with creamy white and dark chocolate. Next, we visited Arrowtown and then Queenstown, where you can re-explore the historic gold fields, ride a gondola ferry to the restaurant high on Bob's Peak or jetboat down the Shotover River. The prime slopes near Queenstown draw winter sports lovers to the snow for breathtaking skiing and all the fun a resort can offer. From Queenstown we bring you medallion of wild boar with chicken breast and Applewood Cheddar. After that, it was on to Clyde, where we found a moist, incredibly good carrot cake topped with orangy cream-cheese icing.

WHITE CHOCOLATE & GRAND MARNIER CHEESECAKE

CRUST
1 cup biscuit crumbs
200 g butter, melted
1 teaspoon finely grated lemon zest

CHEESECAKE
160 g white chocolate
¾ cup white sugar
750 g cream cheese
2 large eggs
1 teaspoon finely grated lemon zest
1½ tablespoons lemon juice
2 teaspoons vanilla essence
1 tablespoon Grand Marnier
4 large egg whites

To make the crust, first pre-heat oven to 180°C. Combine all crust ingredients and press into a 20-22 cm cake tin lined with baking paper and sides brushed with butter. Bake for 5 minutes until lightly browned. To make filling, melt chocolate slowly over double boiler, stirring occasionally to avoid over-cooking. Place half the sugar, cream cheese, eggs and lemon zest in mixer on high

AIRSHOWS & ADVENTURING

Above is Lake Wanaka, which borders Haast Pass. This lovely lake near the Harris Mountains is fed by the Matukituki River. The township of Wanaka looks north up the lake, which is bordered by willows and poplars whose rustling leaves exhibit a golden beauty in the autumn season. The Mount Aspiring National Park Headquarters is located in Wanaka. From there visitors are guided to the best places for their particular pursuits. Skiers find their way to the Treble Cone and Mount

Cardrona skifields and anglers to the many rivers in the locale. There is also a nordic ski area at Waiorau as well as opportunities for heli-skiing and ice skating. Walkers have too many choices to mention them all: from trips to lakeshores such as the walk to Lake Hawea to those with a lofty viewpoint, such as the track up to Mount Roy. Mountaineers and rock climbers find exhilarating climbs in the alpine areas. The Wanaka environs are heaven for the adventurous, with every sort of mountaineering available; with rafting, canoeing, gliding and paragliding; plus hunting and fishing excursions as well as horse trekking and scenic flights. Wanaka also hosts the yearly Warbirds over Wanaka Airshow, attended by aviation history buffs from all over the world.

speed for 5-6 minutes until light and fluffy. Add lemon juice, vanilla essence, Grand Marnier and continue beating. Transfer mix to another bowl and fold in white chocolate. In a clean bowl, beat egg whites to soft peaks and add remaining sugar. Beat until all sugar is dissolved. Fold egg white mixture into cream cheese mixture and turn out into pie crust. Smooth over top and bake. Bake for 10 minutes at 180°C then 50-55 minutes at 110°C.

WHITE CHOCOLATE SAUCE

80 g white chocolate melts
1/4 cup cream
boiling water to mix

Melt chocolate in double boiler over medium heat, add cream and warm over low heat. Mix well so all the chocolate is dissolved. Add boiling water and mix to a smooth sauce.

DARK CHOCOLATE SAUCE

80 g dark cooking chocolate
boiling water

Melt chocolate in double boiler over medium heat and gradually stir in boiling water until smooth.
Leave cake in tin until cold and refrigerate overnight. Cut into slices and drizzle with white and dark chocolate sauces. Add whipped cream and fruit.
Chocolate sauces can be left in refrigerator and warmed to soften again when required.
Serves 6-8.

CAPRICCIO RESTAURANT,
WANAKA.

FRENCH RACK OF LAMB WITH FRENCH BEANS, COUSCOUS & RED CAPSICUM AIOLI

HERB CRUST
5 slices white toast bread
4 tablespoons chopped parsley
1 teaspoon chopped rosemary
2 teaspoons chopped garlic
1 tablespoon whole grain mustard
salt and pepper
200 g butter, melted

LAMB
4 x 250 g French lamb racks
salt and pepper

AIOLI
1 large red capsicum
oil
1/2 cup each yoghurt, sour cream
1 teaspoon each finely chopped garlic,
mint

COUSCOUS
120 g couscous
knob of butter

2 cups reduced lamb or beef stock (jus)
120 g French beans, blanched
sprig of mint to garnish

To make herb crust, place bread in food processor on high until bread is crumbed. Add parsley, rosemary, garlic, mustard, and salt and pepper. Slowly pour in the butter. To prepare lamb, seal off racks by quickly cooking all sides for a few seconds and lightly season meat with salt and pepper. Place herb crust mixture on top of meat to form a thin crust and bake in oven for 15-20 minutes at 190°C.

To make the red capsicum aioli, brush capsicum with oil and bake in a medium oven until covered in blisters. Quickly drop into cold water and then peel the skin away, removing core and seeds from the centre. Place into food processor until smooth. Add yoghurt, sour cream, chopped garlic and mint. To prepare the couscous, lightly steam couscous, adding a knob of butter and season with salt and pepper. Place 4 large mounds of couscous on a baking tray and flatten slightly. Top with the aioli and bake for 5 minutes until just starting to brown.

Heat lamb jus and add blanched beans into jus.

To assemble, place beans and jus in centre of plates and place couscous on plate with metal slice. Place lamb racks (which have been rested for a few minutes after removing from oven) on plate and garnish with a sprig of mint.

Serves 4.

CAPRICCIO RESTAURANT, WANAKA.

WHERE THE RIVER MEETS THE SEA

Cold smoked salmon and eel with
asparagus and tartare sauce
3 asparagus spears
3 pieces smoked salmon
3 slices smoked eel

Cook asparagus on high power in
microwave until just tender for about
1 minute. Put smoked salmon on
board, place smoked eel on top of
salmon, and roll around each
asparagus spear. Cut in half and
arrange around a bowl of
tartare sauce.

TARTARE SAUCE
3 tablespoons mayonnaise
1 tablespoon each, chopped gherkins,
chopped olives,
chopped chives

Mix all ingredients together.
Serves 1.

RIPPLES RESTAURANT, WANAKA.

RACK OF LAMB WITH MINTED PEA PÂTÉ ON A ROSEMARY JUS

MINTED PEA PÂTÉ
500 g minted peas, cooked
1 teaspoon crushed garlic
salt and pepper
1 teaspoon lemon juice

LAMB
4 racks of lamb
1 tablespoon olive oil
2 cups red wine
freshly ground black pepper and salt
chopped rosemary
fresh mint
sprig of rosemary

To make pâté, place all ingredients in food processor and blend until puréed.

Season lamb racks and seal in hot pan with olive oil. Cover rib bones in foil to prevent charring. Place in moderate oven for approximately 15 minutes. Remove racks from pan. Deglaze pan with red wine. Add pepper, salt and chopped rosemary and reduce by half.

To serve, place minted pea pâté in centre of plate. Arrange lamb rack around pâté.

Pour rosemary jus over rack.

Garnish with fresh mint and a sprig of rosemary.

Serves 4.

THE STABLES RESTAURANT & WINE BAR, ARROWTOWN.

SWISS CHOCOLATE DACQUOISE ON A FLOWING SEA OF RASPBERRY & CHOCOLATE

MERINGUES

4 egg whites

³/₄ cup sugar

CHOCOLATE MOUSSE

325 g dark chocolate

1 cup cream

1 teaspoon powdered gelatine

2 tablespoons water

2 eggs, separated

¹/₄ cup Grand Marnier

1¹/₄ cups cream, lightly whipped

RASPBERRY COULIS

250 g raspberries

³/₄ cup icing sugar

CHOCOLATE SAUCE

1¹/₄ cups water

¹/₂ cup sugar

250 g dark chocolate, chopped

1 tablespoon brandy

GARNISH

3 strawberries

cocoa powder

sprigs of mint

flowers

To make meringues, place egg whites in mixer and whip until peaks form. Gradually add sugar until well blended. Place meringue mixture in piping bag and pipe 5 cm rounds onto a greased oven tray. This should yield 12 individual meringues. Place in oven for 2 hours at 90-100°C. To make the chocolate mousse, melt chocolate and 1 cup cream in a double pan, whisking constantly. Dissolve gelatine in water. Add egg yolks, liqueur and dissolved gelatine.

FIND THE PAST - TODAY!

Follow Highway 6 northeast out of Queenstown, and you will soon find Arrowtown, which is pleasantly situated on the Arrow River. Gold from the river built the town and gold still hides under the Arrow's flowing waters - enough to keep weekend prospectors busy fishing sparkling flakes from the last swirl of sand in their gold pans.

The Millbrook Resort and Country Club just outside Arrowtown. This stunning resort area includes large homes that overlook the third fairway of the Millbrook International Golf Course.

Fold in lightly whipped cream. Then fold in lightly whipped egg white. Refrigerate for 4 hours. To make raspberry coulis, blend ingredients together and pass through sieve to remove seeds.

To make chocolate sauce, place water and sugar in a pan and bring to boil. Remove from heat. Add chopped chocolate and whisk until melted. Add brandy and whisk until blended. Refrigerate for 1 hour.

To assemble dacquoise, cover half a large plate with raspberry coulis and the other half with chocolate sauce. Place meringue in centre. Pipe with mousse. Place a second meringue on top and repeat. Then place a third meringue on top. Garnish with strawberries and dust with cocoa powder, then top with a sprig of mint and a flower.

Serves 4.

THE STABLES RESTAURANT & WINE BAR, ARROWTOWN.

Arrowtown has preserved the charm of its historic past while offering up-to-date amenities and amusements for the ever-growing numbers of tourists who visit here each year to see Miner's Monument, the Lakes District Centennial Museum, Tobin's Track or to wander through Macetown, 15km upriver. Now a quiet ghost town, Macetown once bustled with miners manning the machines that crushed gold-bearing quartz rock to extract its ore.

MEDALLION OF
WILD BOAR

¼ chicken breast, chopped
1 clove garlic, crushed
2 leaves green sage
15 g Applewood Cheddar
4 cups plain flour
8 egg yolks
3 whole eggs
1 tablespoon salt
1 tablespoon oil
50 g medallion of wild boar
1 teaspoon apricot mustard
*2 shallots, diced (or red onion if shallots
unavailable)*
1 teaspoon chopped pistachios
2 teaspoons redcurrant jelly
2 tablespoons orange juice
2 teaspoons pickled ginger juice
1 teaspoon fresh lime juice
white wine
paprika to garnish
herb garnish

**Season chicken with garlic, green
sage, Applewood Cheddar. To make
pasta, place flour, egg yolks, salt and
oil in food processor and blend.
Immediately wrap in plastic film as
discolouration will occur within 20
minutes. Put in refrigerator to rest.
Roll out pasta, working quickly to
prevent the pasta from drying out.
Roll through each setting on pasta
machine until the lowest setting is
achieved and the pasta becomes
transparent. Cover with a damp cloth
immediately. Cut rounds of pasta.
Place cheddar mixture into centre of
rounds and fold into crescent shape.**

Smear top of boar medallion with apricot mustard, shallots, pistachios. Seal on the bottom of meat only and place on finely cut root vegetables. Spread with butter and place in oven. When cooked rare, rest for 2 minutes. Reduce redcurrant jelly and orange juice by half. Season with lime and ginger juice. Correct consistency with white wine. Blanch pasta and then pan fry and dust with paprika.

Serves 1

CLANCY'S RESTAURANT, LAKELAND HOTEL, QUEENSTOWN.

Breathtaking aerial view of the approach to Queenstown, Lake Wakatipu and the Remarkables.

SEARGRILLED SALMON ESCALOPE

*700 g boneless salmon escalope
with skin on
1/4 cup each flour, olive oil,
chopped fresh herbs
8 shallots, chopped
2 cloves garlic, finely chopped
1 cup balsamic vinegar
1 cup red wine
2 tablespoons sugar
80 g smoked crayfish medallions
1 1/2 cups mashed potato
2 teaspoons chopped fresh tarragon
1/2 cup Beurre Blanc
salt and pepper*

Heat chargrill or grill to high.
Lightly flour salmon before dredging
through olive oil and fresh herbs.
Grill for 30 seconds skin side up.
Place in pre-heated 180°C oven for 4
minutes then rest in warm place.
Dry roast shallots and garlic in hot
pan, add balsamic vinegar, red
wine, sugar and reduce until a
syrup is formed.
Combine crayfish with mashed
potato, seasonings, add
tarragon and warm through.
Spoon onto a plate drizzled
with Beurre Blanc and
balsamic reduction.
Garnish with mizuna or
rocket greens.
Use a fish slice to separate
skin from salmon, place salmon
on top of mash and use crisp
skin as a garnish.
Serves 4.

BOARDWALK SEAFOOD
RESTAURANT, QUEENSTOWN.

*Above: Jet boating in Queenstown - only
one of many sports to enjoy here.
Queenstown also offers scenic walks, boat
tours of Lake Wakatipu and round trips to
Arrowtown in four-wheel drive vehicles.*

*Left: Reminiscent of Mexico or the North
American southwest - an adobe house built
in Queenstown.*

A RESORT OF DISTINCTION

Queenstown: truly a unique resort community of distinction with its
awe-inspiring lakeside setting and mountains sternly guarding every
direction. The Coronet Peak ski field to the north and the Remarkables
ski fields east of Queenstown are recreation areas enhanced with full
facilities for the enjoyment of sportspeople. Lifts, restaurants, ski
instruction, and - for the over-the-top adventurous - wilderness skiing
accessible by helicopter. This holiday town has other attractions too,
such as the Queenstown Underwater World, the Skyline Gondola and
Restaurant, the Queenstown Motor Museum, historic Eichardt's Hotel,
Winkys Goldfield Museum and the Kiwi and Birdlife Park.

CARROT CAKE

3 eggs

1 cup each brown sugar,

raw sugar

¾ cup oil

2 teaspoons vanilla essence

2 cups wholemeal flour

½ teaspoon salt

2 teaspoons each baking soda,

ground cinnamon

1 teaspoon ground nutmeg

¼ cup milk

3 cups grated carrot

1 cup desiccated coconut

½ cup chopped walnuts

225 g tin crushed pineapple, drained

ICING (optional)

50 g butter

1 teaspoon grated orange rind

¼ cup cream cheese

½ teaspoon vanilla

1 cup icing sugar

1-2 tablespoons orange juice

Beat eggs, add sugars, oil and vanilla
and beat well. Mix together flour,
salt, baking soda, spices and fold into
egg mixture. Add milk, carrot,
coconut, walnuts and pineapple. Stir
gently but thoroughly. Put in greased
and floured 23-cm, round tin. Bake at
180°C for approximately 1½ hours.
Leave in the tin for awhile before
turning out. To prepare the icing,
cream together butter and cream
cheese, add vanilla, orange rind and
icing sugar. Stir in enough orange
juice to make it smooth and creamy.
Spread over top and sides of cake.

OLIVERS RESTAURANT AND
LODGE, CLYDE,
CENTRAL OTAGO.

It's easy to see why Olivers Restaurant has won national acclaim. Built in 1874 of stone quarried from the Cromwell Gorge, its atmosphere is unhurried and traditional. It's a place to relax and enjoy fabulous cuisine like the luscious carrot cake pictured here, and to look around and appreciate the added enhancements like beautifully presented jars of homemade fruit and jam.

Left: Lake Te Anau, a gateway to Fiordland.

Below: A long lingering look down a curve of the Doubtful Sound. One of the deep, glacier-carved channels cutting into Fiordland National Park, the sound is not completely cut off for those who would like to experience its spectacular reaches. Launch trips cruise this steep-sided inlet, and a road from Deep Cove links the Doubtful Sound with Lake Manapouri.

OTAGO & SOUTHLAND

OTAGO AND SOUTHLAND are east of Mt Aspiring National Park and south of the Canterbury Plains. Oamaru, known for splendid stone architecture, is north of Dunedin, a city made prosperous by the Otago gold boom. We began this trek in Oamaru, where we struck a rich lode of tangy chicken heaped with berry-fruit sauce and stuffed with local Brie cheese and Otago apricots! Just as lucky in Dunedin, we found a dark chocolate pudding with rich-as-can-be banana caramel sauce and a super-good sourdough recipe that makes a loaf so delicious it will vanish before it has cooled. As we travelled in Otago and Southland, we found the seafood fresh and tasty – the heart of many good meals. Bluff, the southernmost town in the South Island, has its oyster season. And what a season! People wait all year to taste them. We found an Invercargill restaurant that uses Bluff oysters to perfection in a grilled-oyster salad with balsamic dressing. The Southern Scenic Route and the beautiful Catlins Forest are not far from here, and a Catlins scene appears on these two pages. We never went hungry with mouth-watering meat, poultry and seafood wherever we went. Add local produce, freshly baked breads, scones and shortbreads – a wonderful variety of tastes to savour!

Below: Oamaru, centre of a lush sheep-farming area, is renowned for its striking stone architecture.

BREAST OF CHICKEN FILLED WITH APRICOT & BRIE CHEESE, SERVED WITH A TANGY BERRY FRUIT SAUCE

TANGY BERRY FRUIT SAUCE
100 g each raspberries, blackberries, boysenberries
1 cup caster sugar
1¼ cups Madeira Port

1 chicken supreme
1 apricot, pitted
Brie cheese, two slices

Cook berries, sugar and port together and strain. Fill chicken with apricot and Brie cheese. Seal in a hot frypan with a little oil. Bake in oven for 12-15 minutes at 190°C. Place a little sauce on garnished plate, slice chicken in three, place on top of sauce, trickle more sauce on top of chicken. Serve with fresh side salad.

LAST POST RESTAURANT,
OAMARU, SOUTHLAND.

CADBURY'S CHOCOLATE PUDDING WITH BANANA & CARAMEL SAUCE

PUDDING

100 g each butter, sugar
2 eggs
100 g flour
2 tablespoons Cadbury's Cocoa Powder
1 teaspoon baking powder
50 g Cadbury's Chocolate Buttons

CARAMEL & BANANA SAUCE

200 g caster sugar
200 g cream
1 banana

Mix butter and sugar, add the eggs, gradually mix in the flour, cocoa, baking powder and chocolate buttons. Place 3 tablespoons of the mixture into a buttered and floured ramekin. Cook in the microwave for 1 minute or until set, but not too firm. Repeat with remaining mixture. Note: Microwaves vary in power so experiment with your own to find the right time for your appliance.
To make the sauce, caramelise sugar, then gradually add warm cream to avoid overflowing.
Add sliced banana.
Serves 4-6.

NINETY FIVE, DUNEDIN.

JUTLAND CHICKEN

4 boneless chicken breasts

FILLING

500 g ham ends
1/2 cup dried apricots
2 medium onions
100 g cream cheese
large splash of green ginger wine
seasoning to taste
4 slices mozzarella cheese
oil
handful of seeds - eg sesame or
poppy seeds

SAUCE

500 ml apricot pulp
1 tablespoon brown sugar
rum to taste

Make a pocket in each chicken breast. Blend all filling ingredients except mozzarella, oil and seeds in food processor. Consistency needs to be stiff. Place a spoonful of filling into each chicken breast. Place a slice of mozzarella on top. Fold flap of each breast back over the top. Oil a pan or baking dish and put breasts in dish. Allow plenty of space between each breast. Brush breasts with oil and sprinkle with seeds. Bake at 220-250°C for about 20-25 minutes or until cooked. To make the sauce, heat pulp and brown sugar until sugar is dissolved. Add rum to taste. Place cooked breast on plate and pour sauce over and around it. Serves 4.

PALMS CAFÉ, DUNEDIN.

Right: A view over the city of Dunedin.

MIXED GRAIN SOURDOUGH

THE DAY BEFORE BAKING

Feed the sourdough starter:
Add 200 g wholemeal flour
and 2 cups lukewarm filtered water
to 500 ml sourdough starter*
(* a wholemeal and water ferment).
Allow to ferment overnight in a
covered, but ventilated glass
container, at room temperature.
Soak together in 250 ml filtered
water: 4 tablespoons each
kibbled wheat, coarse cornmeal,
rolled oats, linseed.

THE DAY OF CREATION

Reserve 2 cups of starter for next
day's baking. To the remaining 700
ml of starter, whisk in 100 ml of
lukewarm filtered water, add soaked
grain, 1 teaspoon of sea salt and
750 g of wholemeal flour.
Knead to form a dough, correcting
consistency with additional water or
flour. Knead for 10 minutes, until
dough is smooth and springs back
when indented.

Lightly oil with cold-pressed canola oil, mist with water and prove until a third risen, (up to 1 ½ hours depending on how active the starter is), then rest for 10 minutes at room temperature. Shape into 2 loaves. Prove loaves until they 'bloom' up in tins, 1½ hours. Bake for 1 hour in a medium/hot oven until bottom of loaf is golden. Good eating!

If you have difficulty in obtaining the starter, Tangenté can supply.

Makes 2 loaves.

TANGENTÉ BAKERY & CAFÉ, DUNEDIN.

Left: Larnach Castle, one of Dunedin's most well known examples of Scottish architecture. Built in 1871, it is furnished with Venetian glass and early New Zealand furniture and its impressive entry stairs have stone lions. Larnach Castle also has a hanging staircase, battlements 300 metres above the sea and extensive grounds.

Dunedin has over twenty buildings of great historic importance and is known for fine Victorian architecture and well-appointed gardens.

PARSLEY & PINE NUT PESTO

250 g bunch of parsley
50 g Parmesan cheese, grated
50 g lightly toasted pine nuts
½ teaspoon sea salt
3 tablespoons cold-pressed canola oil
1 tablespoon crushed garlic

Remove the parsley tops from any stalks. Place all ingredients into food processor and blend to a smooth paste. Correct consistency with oil and taste for salt. Use on pasta, breads or in dressings. Makes about ¾ cup.

TANGENTÉ BAKERY & CAFÉ, DUNEDIN.

CHARMS OF THE CATLINS

The Catlins district is about 100 kilometres southwest of Dunedin and is just south of Balclutha. The town of Owaka is considered its centre, and the Owaka reserves are prized for their rugged beaches, native bush, waterfalls and sea caves. One interesting sight is Curio Bay, which is a fossilised forest floor, and another is Catlins Lake, which is actually a tidal river about 8 kilometres upstream from the sea. The lake is stocked with sea-run trout at certain times and is also a favourite of boaties, yachties and duckshooters. Nearby the lake are Cathedral Caves. Well worth a visit, the caves are only accessible during the two hours around low tide.

Left: The photo left shows a many-tiered waterfall in the Catlins Forest Park area. The park has many walkways and a variety of waterfalls to view, including Barr, Wilkes, Purakaunui and Matai Falls.

PALMS-STYLE FISH OMELET

oil
400 g fish fillets
flour
4 eggs
1 tablespoon grated cheese
2 teaspoons assorted seeds (eg pumpkin, poppy, sesame)
2 teaspoons Parmesan cheese

Heat medium omelet pan and oil base and sides well. Dust fillets in flour. Beat eggs until thick. Place fillets in egg mix and spread in pan. It is best to have fillets contact bottom of the pan or the top layers will be slow to cook. Pour remaining mix over and around. Sprinkle top with cheese, seeds, and Parmesan. Bake in oven at 200-250°C until set and golden brown, about 10-12 minutes. To remove from pan run a flexible slice all around and under to free sticky bits. Take pan to a warm plate. Tilt over plate and slide omelet onto plate with the aid of the slice. Serves 2.

For more servings, increase ingredients proportionally and use a bigger pan. The bigger the omelet, the more difficult it is to remove in one piece.

PALMS CAFÉ, DUNEDIN.

Right: A striking example of the architecture for which Invercargill is famous.

MUTTONBIRD IN TARRAGON & FENNEL SAUCE

4 muttonbirds
1 small onion, sliced
½ teaspoon crushed garlic
1 tablespoon oil
½ cup dry white wine
4 stalks fresh tarragon
2 teaspoons fennel seeds
200 ml cream

Simmer muttonbirds on low heat for 2-3 hours. Discard fat, remove legs and breast meat. Sauté onion and garlic in oil. Add wine to pan with tarragon and fennel seeds and reduce by half. Remove tarragon and add cream, muttonbird breast and legs. Simmer to reduce to good consistency. Excellent served with a kumara and pickled ginger salad. Serves 2-4.

GERRARDS RESTAURANT,
INVERCARGILL, SOUTHLAND.

GRILLED BLUFF OYSTER SALAD

3-4 bluff oysters
2 slices each roasted green and red capsicums
1 slice mozzarella cheese
salad greens, including purple basil if available
2 marinated Kalamata olives

DRESSING
1 tablespoon balsamic vinegar
¼ cup virgin olive oil
½ small clove garlic, crushed
1 tablespoon capers

Wrap oysters in capsicum with a small slice of mozzarella. Grill for about 3-4 minutes, until oysters are warm and cheese is melted. To make the dressing, slowly pour oil over vinegar and garlic in food processor. Pulse in capers when dressing is desired consistency. Place oysters on top of salad and drizzle over dressing. Add olives. Serve with freshly ground pepper. Serves 1.

GERRARDS RESTAURANT,
INVERCARGILL,
SOUTHLAND.

SUCCULENT SOUTHERN SEAFOOD

Just 27 kilometres south of Invercargill, the major port of Bluff faces Foveaux Strait and Stewart Island. Bluff is home to the Foveaux Strait oyster, known as Tio para by the Maori, and more commonly called the Bluff oyster. Bluff holds its Oyster Festival in April, about a month after the

oyster season begins. The Paua House with its display of beautiful greeny blue shells is a reminder of other succulent seafood available here. After a walk up Bluff Hill to view Tiwai Point, the Awarua Lagoon, the Foveaux Strait, Toetoes Bay, Dog Island and Ruapuke Island, what could be better than looking forward to a meal of paua fritters, grilled oysters, sautéed muttonbird, savoury lobster, salmon fillets or perfectly prepared mussels?

Bluff is a fishing town, and the photo above shows fishing boats at rest in the harbour, awaiting the next voyage out to sea.

WEIGHTS AND MEASURES

The recipes in this book are adapted from original recipes. They have been tested by the chefs who created them and by appreciative diners who enjoyed them. For best results when you prepare the recipes, use standard metric measures (250 ml cup, 15 ml tablespoon and 5 ml teaspoon) unless otherwise stated. *

Follow recipe instructions carefully, use level measurements and follow the specified cooking times. (The oven-temperature table below is a guide only. For best accuracy, refer to your own cooker instruction book.)

* In NZ, USA and UK, 1 tablespoon = 15 ml.
  In Australia 1 tablespoon = 20 ml.

OVEN SETTING EQUIVALENTS (TO NEAREST 10°C)

Description	Fahrenheit	Celsius	Gas regulo No
Very cool	225 - 275	110 - 140	1/4 - 1
Cool	300 - 325	150 - 160	2 - 3
Moderate	350 - 375	180 - 190	4 - 5
Hot	400 - 450	200 - 230	6 - 8
Very hot	475 - 500	250 - 260	9 - 10

Grams to Ounces: These are converted to the nearest round number.

GRAMS	OUNCES	GRAMS	OUNCES	GRAMS	OUNCES
25	= 1	175	= 6	325	= 11
50	= 2	200	= 7	350	= 12
75	= 3	225	= 8	375	= 13
100	= 3.5	250	= 9	400	= 14
125	= 4	275	= 10	425	= 15
150	= 5	300	= 10.5	450	= 16

1 kilogram = 1000 grams = 2 lb 4 oz

SHORT GLOSSARY

The following is a short glossary of some cooking terms used in this book.

BÉARNAISE SAUCE: A French classic. Vinegar, wine, tarragon and shallots are reduced together and then finished with egg yolks and butter. For meat, fish, eggs and vegetables.

COMPOTE: Fresh or dried fruit cooked in syrup. Sometimes flavoured with liquor or spices.

COULIS: Thick purée or sauce. Can be made from a variety of ingredients.

COUSCOUS: Cooked granular semolina or steamed cracked wheat. Can also refer to a Middle Eastern dish that combines semolina or cracked wheat with lamb, chickpeas and vegetables.

COVERTURE CHOCOLATE: Professional-quality coating chocolate. Has a high gloss and forms a thinner coating than ordinary confectionery coatings.

CUMBERLAND SAUCE: Of English origin. Traditionally contains redcurrant jelly, port, orange and lemon zests, mustard and other seasonings. Used for poultry and game.

DACQUOISE: Round, sometimes nut-flavoured meringues which are stacked and filled with whipped cream or buttercream. Can be served chilled with fruit.

DEGLAZE: To add stock or liquor to a frypan after food and excess fat are removed so that browned bits can be loosened and then mixed with other ingredients to make a sauce base.

MESCLUN: Also called salad mix. A potpourri of tender salad greens.

MIREPOIX: A mix of diced vegetables and herbs sautéed in butter. Can be a seasoning or a bed on which foods are braised.

RISOTTO: Italian dish made by adding hot stock to rice as it cooks. Liquid is added just when rice has absorbed all the original liquid. Makes creamy rice with grains that remain separate.

RÖSTI: Swiss term meaning golden crisp.

ROULADE: A thin meat slice rolled around a bread, vegetable, cheese or meat filling.

TAPENADE: A thick paste of capers, anchovies, black olives, olive oil, lemon juice, seasonings and occasionally tuna. From Provence.

WHITE CHOCOLATE: Mixture of sugar, cocoa butter, milk solids, lecithin and vanilla without chocolate liquor.

ZEST: The coloured part of fresh citrus peel. Contains the aromatic oils that lend flavour to food.

Note: The recipes in this book are original creations. In some cases the classic methods have been changed to suit the chef's style.

PHOTOGRAPHIC & ILLUSTRATION CREDITS

All photographs by Ian Baker except;

John Cobb/Penguin: 12-13, 14-15, 55 (insert). 108-109, 122-123 (insert), 124-125, 132-133, 152-153, 156-157, 158-159, 169, 172-173, 174-175, 182, 184, 188-189, 190-191, 194-195.

Fiordland Travel: 173.

Gareth Eyres: 22-23

Bob McCree: 23 (insert)

Doc Ross: 167.

Tourism Taranaki: 52-53.

Tourism Waikato: 62-63.

Pauline Whimp: 11 (map).

Tranz/Joan Willis: 34-35, 36-37, 50-51, 66-67.

Visual Impact: 24-25, 26-27, 74-75, 80-81, 106-107, 138-139, 144-145, 166-167, 180-181.

RESTAURANT GUIDE

NORTHLAND & AUCKLAND

ATOMIC CAFÉ, 121 Ponsonby Road, Ponsonby, Auckland, ph 09 376 4954
BISTRO 40, 40 Marsden Road, Paihia, Bay of Islands, ph 09 402 7444
CIN CIN ON QUAY, 99 Quay Street, Auckland, ph 09 307 6966
ESSENCE, 70-72 Jervois Road, Herne Bay, Auckland, ph 09 376 2049
GERHARD'S RESTAURANT & BAR, 572 Great North Road, Grey Lynn, Auckland, ph 09 320 1705
KERMADEC RESTAURANT, Level 1, cnr Lower Hobson & Quay Streets, Auckland, ph 09 309 0412
NAUTILUS RESTAURANT, Gulf Harbour Village, Whangaparaoa, Auckland, ph 09 424 3549
STANMORE COTTAGE RESTAURANT, 201 Brightside Road, Stanmore Bay, Whangaparaoa, Auckland, ph 09 424 7074

COROMANDEL, BAY OF PLENTY & EAST CAPE

BRIAN BORU HOTEL, 200 Richmond Street, Thames, ph 07 868 6523
KESSALLS RESTAURANT & BAR, Shop 3, The Village Centre, Jubilee Drive, Pauanui, ph 07 864 8825
PUKA PARK LODGE RESTAURANT, Mount Avenue, Pauanui Beach, ph 07 864 8088
RUMOURS RESTAURANT, 81 Pukuatua Street, Rotorua, ph 07 347 7277
SHELLS RESTAURANT & BAR, 119 Pepe Road, Tairua Beach, ph 07 864 7540
SOMERSET COTTAGE, 30 Bethlehem Road, Bethlehem, Tauranga, ph 07 576 6889

TARANAKI, KING COUNTRY & WAIKATO

LEFT BANK INTERNATIONAL RESTAURANT & BAR, Marlborough Place, Hamilton, ph 07 839 3354
REPLETE CAFÉ/DELI & CATERING CONSULTANCY, 45 Heu Heu Street, Taupo, ph 07 378 0606
THE RUAPEHU ROOM, The Grant Chateau, Mt Ruapehu, Tongariro National Park, ph 07 892 3809
RUSTICI BRASSERIE, 312 Victoria Street, Riverbank Mall, Hamilton, ph 07 839 1111

WAIRARAPA & HAWKE'S BAY

ANATOLES CAFÉ, 12 Browning Street, Napier, ph 06 835 7800
AYLSTONE, Private Lodgings, Wine Library & Larder, Huangarua Road, Martinborough, ph 06 306 9505
BAYSWATER ON THE BEACH, 5 Harding Road, Ahuriri, Napier, ph 06 835 8517
THE MARTINBOROUGH BISTROT, Martinborough Hotel, The Square, Martinborough, ph 06 306 9350
PIERRE SUR LE QUAI, 62 West Quay, Ahuriri, Napier, ph 06 834 0189
TOADS LANDING, Windover Gardens, Homebush, Masterton, ph 06 377 3793
VIDAL WINERY BRASSERIE, 913 Aubyns Street East, Hastings, ph 06 876 8105

MANAWATU & WELLINGTON

THE BATHHOUSE CAFÉ & BAR, 161 Broadway Avenue, Palmerston North, ph 06 355 0051
BOULCOTT STREET BISTRO, Plimmer House, 99 Boulcott Street, Wellington, ph 04 499 4199
CAFÉ VAVASSEUR, 201 Broadway Avenue, Palmerston North, ph 06 359 3167
COUNTRY LIFE RESTAURANT, Main Road, Waikanae, ph 04 293 6353
IL CASINO RISTORANTE, 108-112 Tory Street, Wellington, ph 04 385 7496
LOGAN BROWN, 192 Cuba Street, Wellington, ph 04 801 5114
MICHAEL'S RESTAURANT, 281 Wickstead Street, Wanganui, ph 06 345 2690
RUTH PRETTY CATERING & COOKING SCHOOL, 41 School Road, Te Horo, ph 06 364 3161

MARLBOROUGH & NELSON
An Epicurean Affair, Stone Aerie Estate, Dog Point Road, Blenheim, ph 03 572 9639
Boat Shed Café, 350 Wakefield Quay, Nelson, ph 03 546 9783
Gothic Gourmet Licensed Restaurant & Tavern, 208 High Street, Motueka, ph 03 528 6699
Hotel d'Urville, 52 Queen Street, Blenheim, ph 03 577 9945
Jester House Café, Coastal Highway, Tasman, ph 03 526 6742
Korurangi Café, Korurangi Farm, Lansdowne Road, Richmond, Nelson, ph 03 544 6500
The Darling Dill Café, cnr Main Road & Neil Street, Havelock, Marlborough, ph 03 574 2844

WEST COAST
The Bay House Café, Beach Road, Tauranga Bay, Cape Foulwind, Westport, ph 03 789 7133
Beechwoods, State Highway 6, Murchison, ph 03 523 9993
Diego's Restaurant & Bar, 18 Wakefield Street, Westport, ph 03 789 7640
Lake Paringa Café, Main Road, State Highway 6, Lake Paringa, South Westland, ph 03 751 0110
Trapper's Restaurant, 79 Revell Street, Hokitika, ph 03 755 5133

KAIKOURA & CANTERBURY
Ginger & Garlic Licensed Restaurant, 335 Stafford Street, Timaru, ph 03 688 3981
Green Dolphin Restaurant & Bar, 12 Avoca Street, Kaikoura, ph 03 319 6666
Grimsby's Restaurant, Cranmer Court, cnr Kilmore & Montreal Streets, Christchurch, ph 03 379 2999
The Lyttelton Brasserie, 3 Norwich Quay, Lyttelton, ph 03 328 8841
Merchants Restaurant, Hotel Grand Chancellor, 161 Cashel Street, Christchurch, ph 03 377 7457
The Old Convent, Mill Road, Kaikoura, ph 03 319 6603

CENTRAL OTAGO & FIORDLAND
Boardwalk Seafood Restaurant, Steamer Wharf, Queenstown, ph 03 442 5630
Capriccio Restaurant, 123 Ardmore Street, Wanaka, ph 03 443 7085
Clancy's Restaurant, Lakeland Hotel, 14-18 Lake Esplanade, Queenstown, ph 03 442 7600
Olivers Restaurant & Lodge, 34 Sunderland Street, Clyde, ph 03 449 2860
Ripples Restaurant, Pembroke Mall, Wanaka, ph 03 443 7413
The Stables Restaurant & Wine Bar, 22 Buckingham Street, Arrowtown, ph 03 442 1818

SOUTHLAND & OTAGO
Gerrards Restaurant, 3 Leven Street, Invercargill, ph 03 218 3406
Last Post Restaurant, 12 Thames Street, Oamaru, ph 03 434 8080
Ninety Five, 95 Filleul Street, Dunedin, ph 03 471 9265
Palms Café, 18 Queens Garden, Dunedin, ph 03 477 6534
Tangenté Bakery & Café, 111 Upper Moray Place, Dunedin, ph 03 477 0232

INDEX

A

Aioli, red capsicum, for French rack of lamb 160

Apricot & ham filling for Jutland chicken 180

Apricot sauce for Jutland chicken 180

Artichoke, roasted globe, with pesto 109

Aubergine, baked, with venison sausage & roe 14

Aubergine stuffing, for lamb roulade 83

B

Baked cream, pineapple & ginger 91

Baked Supreme of South Island Salmon 40

Balsamic syrup, for lemon-herbed lamb roulade 82

Balsamic dressing for oyster salad 190

Banana & caramel sauce for chocolate pudding 179

Basque-style chicken 142

Béarnaise sauce, for beef fillet 93

Beef, grilled beef eye fillet with beef jus 73

Beef, jus, for grilled beef eye fillet 73

Beef Cheeks in Ale 86

Beef Fillet with Pesto & Cumberland Sauce 92

Beurre blanc, for charred tuna loin 67

Beurre blanc, for ravioli of scallops 118

Beurre blanc, for salmon escalope 168

Beurre blanc sauce, for Golden Bay scallops 122

Biscuit crust, for Grand Marnier cheesecake 158

Blue Nose, with smoked salmon mousse 85

Boar, loin wrapped in bacon 130

Boar, medallion of 166

Boudin Blanc: Chicken & Mushrooms 104

Bouillabaisse, Grimsby's Canterbury-style 152

Bread, filled farmhouse loaves 58

Bread, crispy country crostata 76

Bread, mixed grain sourdough 182

Breast of Chicken with Apricot & Brie 177

Brian Boru Flounder 37

Butter cream sauce 148

C

Cabbage, and salmon terrine 72

Cadbury's Chocolate Pudding 179

Cake, carrot 170

Cake, kumara, for rack of lamb 48

Cake, rhubarb upside-down 38

Candied pineapple, for pineapple sable 21

Canterbury Tales 64

Capsicum, aioli for French rack of lamb 160

Capsicum, mayonnaise, for crayfish 99

Capsicum, red, for pesto tartlet 74

Caramel & banana sauce for chocolate pudding 179

Carrot Cake 170

Chargrilled Venison Sausage & Peppered Roe 14

Charred Tuna Loin with Lime Beurre Blanc 67

Cheesecake, white chocolate & Grand Marnier 158

Chermoula, for lemon-herbed lamb roulade 83

Chicken, Basque style 142

Chicken, boudin blanc 104

Chicken Breast with Strawberry Sauce 100

Chicken, breast, filled with apricot & Brie 177

Chicken, breast, with olives & cheese 90

Chicken, breasts, Jutland 180

Chicken Filled with Olives, Cheese & Tomatoes 90

Chicken, fresh livers with tapenade 44

Chicken, lemon 25

Chicken supreme 177

Chilli garnish, for lemon-herbed lamb roulade 83

Chocolate dacquoise 164

Chocolate, dark couverture, for chocolate marquise 30

Chocolate, white, & Grand Marnier cheesecake 158

Chocolate Marquise with Orange Compote 30

Chocolate mousse, for dacquoise 164

Chocolate mousse, for pineapple sable 20

Chocolate Mud Tart 120

Chocolate pudding 179

Chocolate sauce, for Swiss chocolate dacquoise 165

Chowder, mussel 114

Chutney, sundried tomato and strawberry 41

Cin Cin Oriental-style Hocks 26

Citrus syrup, for pineapple & ginger baked cream 91

Compote, orange, for chocolate marquise 30

Concassé, ginger & lime, for Nelson scallops 112

Concassé, of red onion, ginger and tomato 112

Confit, of vegetables, for chicken 90

Coulis, capsicum, for John Dory 28

Coulis, raspberry 165

Coulis, raspberry, for pineapple sable 21

Couscous, with French rack of lamb 160

Crab-Stuffed Mushroom with Capsicum 103

Crayfish, halves with capsicum mayonnaise 98

Crayfish medallions, for salmon escalope 168

Crayfish, seared tail with mango citrus salsa 140

Cream cheese & orange icing, for carrot cake 171

Crispy Country Crostata 76

Crust, biscuit, for cheesecake 158

Crust, for crispy country crostata 76

Crust, for marion pie 78

Cumberland sauce, beetroot, for beef 93

D

Dacquoise, Swiss chocolate 164

Dark chocolate sauce, for cheesecake 159

Dark couverture chocolate, for chocolate marquise 30

Date pudding, Grimsby's 148

Denver leg, venison medallions 41

Dressing, for grilled oyster salad 190

Dressing, honey, for turkey salad 154

Dressing, lemon basil, for pesto tartlet 74

Dressing, vinaigrette, for smoked salmon 96

Dressing, for warm salad of seared game fish

E

Eel, smoked 162

Eggs, onion frittata with black olive pesto 60

Eggs, whitebait omelet 136

Eggs, Palms-style fish omelet 186

F

Filled Farmhouse Loaves 58

Fillet, grilled beef eye, with beef jus 73

Fillet, pork, for sweet & sour pork baskets 126

Fillets, salmon, sautéed rare in hot noodles 151

Fillets of Salmon with Mozzarella 46

Filling, cheese & mushroom, for crostata 76

Filling, crab, for stuffed mushroom 103

Filling, ham & apricot for Jutland chicken 180

Filo pastry, for sweet & sour pork baskets 126

Fish

  Brian Boru flounder 37

  Canterbury-style bouillabaisse 152

  fillets of salmon 46

  Palms-style fish omelet 186

  panfried Blue Nose 85

  salmon, baked supreme of South Island 40

  salmon, baked with wine sauce 64

  salmon and cabbage terrine 72

  salmon char sui 116

  salmon strips sautéed rare in hot noodles 151

  seared game with quail eggs and potato 17

  seargrilled salmon escalope 168

  smoked salmon tartare parcels 146

  smoked salmon timbale 94

  smoked salmon with ricotta cheese 96

  tuna, charred loin of 67

  West Coast whitebait omelet 136

French Rack of Lamb with Couscous & Aioli 160